ATLANTIC AND TRANSATLANTIC:

SKETCHES AFLOAT AND ASHORE.

BY CAPTAIN MACKINNON, R.N.

AUTHOR OF "STEAM WARFARE IN THE PARANA."

NEW YORK:

HARPER & BROTHERS, PUBLISHERS,

329 & 331 PEARL STREET,

FRANKLIN SQUARE.

1852.

INTRODUCTION.

ENGLISHMEN usually flatter themselves with a notion that they look upon all foreign countries without prejudice; and they believe they are thoroughly conversant with the peculiarities of every nation on the face of the globe.

No doubt, a large portion of them have a general insight into the habits of the nations of Europe, and a cursory knowledge of Oriental countries; but of many other portions of the world they are profoundly ignorant. This defect is very strongly marked in the upper classes of English society, particularly with regard to the United States of America. The educated American, on the other hand, which includes nearly the whole native-born population, is a strong contrast to the Englishman. Many Americans are fully acquainted with England, in the most extended acceptation of the term.

Such were my impressions, when I determined to visit the great American Republic; and I may truly assert, that, after a sojourn among our transatlantic brethren of fourteen months, I am more than ever confirmed in my opinion. Not a year passes, but numerous active, ambitious, and intelligent young Americans cross the Atlantic, and traverse England from end to end. No novelty, no ingenious or useful invention, escapes their shrewd observation. The knowledge thus acquired is speedily acted upon, and brought into profitable use, throughout the length and breadth of the vast and fertile regions of the United States. It frequently happens that, in a few months, the English invention returns to us with material improvements before it is generally known and adopted in England. As this policy is totally neglected by the English, the result must be obvious to the most careless and indifferent. That is to say, Brother Jonathan is rapidly going ahead, and leaving England behind in all useful and scientific pursuits—an effect not to be wondered at, as he has the advantage of the experience of both countries.

The civility of Americans is very striking to a stranger, especially to Englishmen, as it is exactly the reverse of their expectations. Very few indeed, who for the first time visit the States, do not, in ignorance of the people, think they will have to encounter republican bluntness or rudeness. But, on the contrary, Americans are courteous and obliging to all. It can not be denied, however, that they have some of the prominent faults of the Saxon race; of which inordinate self-esteem can not escape observation. This characteristic fault, which they partake with the English, is in a great measure hidden among us at home by a reserve, growing out of the insuperable barriers of social distinctions, and is only offensively shown forth on occasions favorable to its development. In America, on the other hand, it is "let out" at every opportunity in private intercourse; and the glorification of the "Stars and Stripes" is a necessary ingredient at all public meetings, if the orator intends to succeed.

Little is known in America of English gentlemen. This is easily accounted for, as it is a rare thing for an Englishman of independent fortune, to visit the States. Brummagem gentlemen, therefore, frequently pass as the genuine article to the great depreciation of the class in the Yankee mind. Let it not be supposed that all Americans are unprejudiced about Englishmen. It can not be denied, that among our transatlantic brethren, a very few may be found who look upon an Englishman with blind and stupid dislike. For the credit of the intelligence of America, however, we should say not one-tenth part so many as are to be found in England who blindly under-rate the Americans.

I have endeavored, in the following pages, to give a few slight sketchy details, about the United States, and Brother Jonathan, as he is at present. I say *at present*, for the improvement is so general and so rapid, both in people and country, that a very short time may render these pages an unfaithful index of the giant Republic. I must acknowledge, that I look back at my sojourn in the States with great satisfaction; and am sure that I shall not lose a single friend among the many I was fortunate enough to acquire in America, because I speak exactly as I conscientiously believe. My endeavor has been to write an honest book, without prejudice for or against either country.

Of the " Miscellaneous Narratives," the second appeared in " The United Service Magazine," the others in " The New Monthly."

In publishing the present work, I have been encouraged by the approbation of my friend, Charles Ollier, whose literary opinion not only admits of no dispute, but whose assistance and advice have often contributed to success.

LYMINGTON, *May*, 1852.

TOUR IN AMERICA.

CHAPTER I.

NEW YORK.

The "Empire City:" its Population, Site, present Prosperity, and former Disasters—Overthrow of the United States Bank—Influx of precious Metals—England and America—Health of Americans—Disregard of Prudence in Sanatory Matters—An enchanting Procession—"Just over the Furnace"—Energy and Strength of American Workmen—Singular Taste for living in Basement Floors—Premature Decay—Quick Perception of Americans; Anecdote—Extreme Sensitiveness to Foreign Opinion—Physical Decadence of the Saxon race in America—American Servants—Unfounded Notion of "Republican Rudeness"—Erroneous Demeanor of Englishmen in America—New York Hotels—Dinners and Balls in private Houses—American Matrons—Zinc Paint—Political Prospects of America—Letter from a distinguished English Gentleman.

New York, or, as the Americans who dwell in it love to say, "The Empire City," can not fail to excite the interest and wonder of a stranger. If we glance from the commencement of this century to the present time, we can not help being amazed at its rapid progress. Its population was estimated in November, 1850, at 725,000 souls, exhibiting a rate of increase equal to 100 per cent every sixteen years. Should this proceed in the same ratio, the inhabitants of New York will, in twenty-five years, be equal to the present population of London, namely, two millions. At the end, therefore, of the present century, it is not too much to say that New York will be as large as any city on the face of the earth! A recent Scotch author having surveyed the enormous metropolis of Great Britain, and estimated its population, happily called it "the London *nation*." The time may soon arrive when the term "nation" may, with equal felicity, be applied to New York.

It is impossible for the imagination of man to conceive a finer site than is possessed by "The Empire City." A tongue of land, jutting forth into deep water, and protected by the curved point and islands which form New York Bay, present altogether such facilities for commercial purposes as the world can not rival. Added to this, the magnificent Hudson gives access to regions more magnificent still; and pours, in a ceaseless stream, the countless wealth of the most fertile portions of the earth into the bosom of the city.

The wonderful prosperity of New York, and the violent fluctuations in the value of real estate, deserve some notice. Prices at the present time, are somewhat higher than those which existed in 1836, the period of the former great crisis. There are a few situations, however, in the lower part of the city which have fallen in value much beneath the rates of those days. The property in the upper part, taken as a whole, is considerably higher than in 1836. In certain situations, especially on the Fifth Avenue and its vicinity, as also on the borders of both rivers, the prices are sometimes even 300 per cent higher. The basis, however, on which the present prices stand, is essentially different from the former period. In 1835 and 1836, a spirit of blind speculation, amounting to mania, seized upon the inhabitants, and lasted some years, until disasters, which ought to have been foreseen, burst the speculative bubble with a fearful explosion.

The first mischance was the fire in 1835, by which the city

sustained a loss of at least twenty million dollars (four millions sterling). The consequences were scarcely felt at the time; but were soon fully developed by the contest between the government and the United States Bank. The overthrow of the latter came with crushing effect upon the public, and, like the Philistine temple of old, shaken down by Samson, fell

"With burst of thunder
Upon the heads of all beneath."

In 1837, occurred the severe commercial crisis in England; and its consequences extended to the most remote parts of the Union. The city of New York was the first victim, sustaining a loss of more than fifty millions of dollars (ten millions sterling). This was caused entirely by the financial calamity in England, and the complete prostration of credit among the State Banks and individuals of high financial position in the South and West

Alarmed and crippled by these successive disasters, it is not to be wondered at that those who had capital were anxious to nurse it. An unprecedented accumulation of deposits consequently took place in the private banks. At this time, money could scarcely be obtained at any price, or on any description of security. The panic continued until 1844, when a reaction took place, which has steadily progressed until the present moment.

In the interval between 1844 and 1851, the population has doubled itself; and the circulating medium has more than doubled itself. The influx, likewise, of precious metals proceeded so rapidly as to set at defiance the quackery of political financiers. Commerce was enormously and profitably extended; so much so, that, with ordinary care and prudence, no serious or permanent interruptions may be anticipated. Still it can not be denied that the great and sudden rise in stock and shares, shows somewhat of the speculative mania of England in 1846.

The United States Bank, which once controlled the mercantile transactions of the country, is, as already stated, defunct; and the banking system of the States is thrown open to a fair and healthy competition, founded on actual, and not imaginary resources. The position of the United States of America is such as to render her a very valuable friend, or a dangerous enemy, as the case may be. Any hazard of collision between England and the United States is, however, not worth a thought. The good sense of the community in both countries is combined to put down agitators, who wickedly and selfishly try to create "political capital" by heart-burnings and dissensions between two great people, who, above all others in the world, are united by every tie that binds nation to nation. Long may this continue!

No stranger landing in New York, can fail to be painfully struck by the pale, wan, slight, and delicate appearance of both men and women. After residing some time in the country, and acquiring a knowledge of their habits, instead of being surprised that so many of them die prematurely, one is astonished that they manage to live as long as they do, or look so well.

In a lecture recently delivered in New York by Dr. Fitch, it is mentioned, as a striking fact, that in the States only four out of every hundred individuals live to the age of sixty. In England, however, he asserts that seven out of every hundred attain that age. Still, though the climate in the latter country is warmer, and more temperate, it is much damper, and has all those atmospherical and other conditions which contribute to produce an immense amount of consumption. The people are so confined and closely packed—millions live so poorly, and in such miserable habitations—that a far greater tendency to the above disease exists in England than in America. Why then should a greater mortality prevail in the United States? The reason is to be found in the different habits of the people. In England, the experience of the old is reverently regarded, and taken as a guide; while in America, experience is but little estimated, and the young consider themselves more knowing than their fathers. The result is, that they often find a fool for a teacher, and die prematurely for their presumption.

The average of human life in the city of New York, reaches only to twenty-five years; some years it runs up to thirty.

A few instances which have come under my own knowledge, show such utter disregard of common prudence and common sense, in reference to health, that I can not avoid mentioning them, in the hope that my friends in America may read and profit by these home-truths. A beautiful and intelligent, but rather faded American lady of twenty-six years of age, was complaining bitterly of the infirm health of herself and her little son, about nine years old. In the course of a long conversation, it transpired that she rarely went out of doors, never solely for exercise. Her rooms in winter were not suffered to be at a lower temperature than 70°, and they were often above 90°. She was in the habit of eating a hearty meat breakfast; meat again for luncheon; and a third time at dinner. If by any chance she took a walk, either during wet weather or dry, she had nothing to protect her feet but light and thin shoes, such as an Englishwoman would be considered almost insane to appear abroad in. Who can wonder at her delicate health or faded beauty?

"But your little boy," said I, "what sort of a life does he lead to make him so tender?"

"I fear to let him out at all," she replied, "he is so delicate; and his appetite is quite gone."

"Do you, then," pursued I, "keep him all day in this stifling stove heat?"

"What else can I do?" she ejaculated with a sigh.

As I had previously seen this young urchin play a tolerable knife-and-fork when his mother was absent, I determined to watch him narrowly, and examine his diet. I had not long to wait; for on the succeeding day, I peeped into the room where luncheon was prepared, and perceived the "tender chicken" regale himself with the following danties, after he had first looked carefully round to see that the coast was clear. Taking up a small pitcher, he poured some molasses into a plate, then cut a large slice of butter, and mixed it well with the molasses.

"You nasty little beast!" exclaimed I to myself; "that is a capital receipt for bile, indigestion, and other complaints of the stomach."

Seizing a spoon with one hand, he looked about the table with an anxious eye. Suddenly he pounced upon some pickles, and having amalgamated them with the other ingredients, he commenced eating this hideous mess. I was quite overcome with anger and nausea, and rushed out of the room to inform his mother. To my intense astonishment she was not at all surprised, but appeared to consider the exploit as a matter of course.

This is, perhaps, an exaggerated example of the great error in diet prevalent at New York. It can not, however, be denied —indeed the citizens themselves admit it—that life in this city is materially shortened by too full a diet, especially of animal food, and the neglect of fresh air and exercise.

Another practice fruitful of disease and death, is the habit all classes have of wearing the same amount of clothing in every season of the year. They make no allowance for the weather; and, wet or dry, wear the thinnest and lightest covering for the feet. It is difficult to purchase in New York a pair of thick English shooting-shoes.

I was enjoying a cigar one Sunday forenoon in the smoking-room of the Union Hotel, of which more anon. A close and distinct view was afforded of the crossing at the head of Broadway, and I beheld a stream of people proceeding through Union-square to Calvary Church, to hear the celebrated Dr. Hawks. My attention was first attracted by the beauty and elegant proportions of the ladies, and the costly dresses they wore. It is impossible for a man (women would be "at home in it") to describe the exquisite texture of these garments, which were extremely long, and trailing on the ground. Onward swept the enchanting procession. Not one lady attempted to raise the folds of her drapery from mother earth; but, regardless of mud and wet, they all tripped daintily along, with their little (almost shoeless) feet sullied with liquid mud. I could not help "moralizing on this spectacle:" sad it was to reflect that, in all human probability, many of these lovely and fragile hot-house plants were sowing the seeds of fatal maladies. Thick shoes and English habits, would fortify them against the consequences of exposure to a sudden shower. But to sit in church all bemired and bedraggled, betokens a recklessness of health perfectly astounding.

The following evening, several of these ladies attended the Opera. Again they were arrayed with admirable taste and lavish cost. I was sitting with a party of three, who, complaining of the heat, wished the box-door to be opened. As soon as the performance was over, they did not hesitate to go bareheaded into the open air, although the thermometer was about zero. Their extremities were almost completely exposed during their walk home over frozen snow, having carelessly dispensed with their carriages. How is it possible to expect health and strength, when such liberties are taken with the constitution?

On one occasion, during an evening visit to a celebrated literary character, the present writer ("albeit unused to the swooning mood") being seized with sudden faintness, was supported into the open air. On his recovery and return, he was coolly informed that he was the third visitor that day who had suffered in the same manner.

"How unfortunate!" exclaimed the host; "how unfortunate! You all took the same position just over the furnace."

The furnace! Only imagine the effect of this infernal blast

upon the human system! By such constant "demi-baking," the New York ladies become, when within doors, painfully susceptible of the slightest breath of air. Their nerves are gradually affected, and the brightness of heaven is offensive. This feeling causes them to shut out light as well as air, and makes a large number of gorgeous drawing-rooms, dark and dismal traps to break the shins of unwary visitors.

There can be little doubt that the climate of the States, from its exceeding dryness, has a tendency to emaciate the human frame. I do not believe, however, that it is prejudicial to health and longevity: indeed, all the people whose employment is in the open air are remarkably wiry, healthy, and strong. Close and suffocating rooms, want of exercise and air, and the heating nature of the diet—these are the influences which cause early loss of teeth, dyspepsia, wan looks, and all the concomitants of an enfeebled frame. I am grieved to say that this appears to be the case with a large majority of the population of New York.

The extraordinary energy and strength of the workmen must not be overlooked. It is an ascertained fact that, in ship-building, the men average nearly twice the quantity of work per diem as in England. Carpenters, painters, and all other operatives, toil in like proportion. The price of labor, therefore, although nominally much more than that in England, is in reality less for the amount of work done.

It is difficult to account for the fancy which many persons have for living in basement floors. The upper apartments, decked with the utmost splendor, are deserted, unless on state occasions, for the dismal, gloomy, and cave-like ground-floor. If Americans could be persuaded that these apartments in England are generally used for kitchens, it would have a tendency to break this uncomfortable habit.

Robert Knox, the able author of "The Races of Man," asserts, that "Under the influence of climate, the Saxon decays in

Northern America and in Australia, and rears his offspring with difficulty; he is transplanted from the soil in which he could physically thrive. Were the supplies from Europe not incessant, he could not stand his ground in these new continents. A *real, native, permanent* American is a dream which can never be realized."

The above is quoted from memory.

There may be some foundation for these remarks; but I imagine that the "forcing-pit, hot-bed" life led in America, is the chief cause of premature decay. Little doubt, however, can be entertained that any native of the United States, whose blood for three generations has not been refreshed from Europe, and whose immediate ancestors have lived in cities, bears unfailing signs of the Saxon or Celtic American. Firstly, the early loss of the subcutaneous adipose cushion; secondly, the decay of the second teeth before they are fully grown; thirdly, the premature appearance of age; and, lastly, the small number of the progeny, and the few even of these reared to maturity. Perhaps, however, as the corporeal degenerates, the mental may increase in strength and activity. Waller, the poet, writing of the infirmity of age, says, very finely,

> "The soul, with nobler resolutions decked,
> The body stooping, does herself erect."

And it might easily be imagined that this spiritual influence would enable the spare and attenuated Yankee ax-man to get through a large amount of physical labor. "Will you tell me, Master Shallow," asks Sir John Falstaff, derisively, "how to choose a man? Care I for the limb, the thews, the stature, bulk, and big assemblance of a man! Give me the *spirit*, Master Shallow." Place an American ax-man alongside the most Herculean and practiced English woodman, and it would be seen that the Yankee would do double the work, with less labor and greater ease. This also may be the reason why American artificers are the quickest and most skillful in the world. So alert are their perceptions, that they are impatient of verbose commentaries. Many Europeans consider this impatience to be inattention and rudeness. I have often heard complaints of this nature from prosy Britishers; such as, "Why, sir, I was giving that damned Yankee important information; and the rude fellow would not attend to me, but bolted." Most likely the Yankee had anticipated the whole matter, and had levanted to take immediate measures to put the ideas thus suggested into practice.

I have seen extraordinary business-proceedings of this rapid and summary nature. For instance: I was acquainted (at an hotel) with an agreeable and gentlemanly American, who had just discovered on his property huge beds of coal, of which the seams are forty feet thick. He was then occupied in forming a company to work them, and eventually succeeded. At the hotel he chanced to fall in with another gentleman, who had invented a steam-boiler of great merit. In five minutes, they understood each other's projects perfectly, and had exchanged shares in their respective concerns. Just as these preliminaries were arranged, a third individual joined them; and after a few words of explanation, understood the whole thing. Pulling out his pocket-book, he spoke as follows:

"I'm off to England to-morrow, I guess. I will take out a patent for the steam-boiler in London, and pay all expenses, if you will give me a right to half the profits there."

"Done, done!" all round; and the business was settled.

These parties had never met before, and were utterly ignorant of each other's existence!

Truth compels me to acknowledge, that the mind of Americans is the keenest and most adaptable in the world. They acquire information of any kind so rapidly, and have such ready dexterity in mechanical employments, that the very slightest efforts put them on a par with Europeans of far greater experience. They do not, however, possess much of the English "stability of character." The consequence is easily foreseen: they have the faults of quick and ardent temperament, and are satisfied to rely upon their almost intuitive perceptions; rarely making themselves, by careful study, thoroughly masters of a subject. Generally speaking, they have a wonderful stock of miscellaneous information; but it is mostly of a superficial character. Not one American out of a hundred applies his mind to sift thoroughly any abstruse subject. If such a man appears on the stage of life, he is sure to take a powerful and original position in any undertaking with which he chooses to grapple.

The chief reason of the extreme sensitiveness of the Americans to foreign opinion, particularly that of England, arises from an instinctive dread of the decadence of their race on the continent of America, which will likewise satisfactorily explain the intolerable aversion Americans express, and no doubt entertain, for the negro blood. How can they possibly feel otherwise, when one great physiological fact is constantly pressing on them; namely, that the Celt and the Saxon breeds are undeniably, however slightly, depreciating, while the negro flourishes as in an indigenous soil? I do not adopt Knox's opinions entirely. I do not think the American continent so unfavorable to the Celt and Saxon as he infers; but imagine the mischief may be attributed, in a great measure, to the insane physical education of the young, as hinted at in these pages; and the extreme neglect, or, rather, I should say, contempt of the adult, for all the common-sense precautions for health, often successfully and systematically carried out in the mother couutry. As a singular corroboration of my opinion on the erroneous physical education of the young, I will mention a sign that is patent to all, if they will only use their powers of observation. I allude to the deep red color of the children's gums. Nine-tenths of the juvenile Americans appear to have a chronic inflammation of the gums. I had abundant opportunities of observing this fact, as I was living while in America with a large family of English children. The difference in the color of their gums, as compared with American children, was quite remarkable. A pale blue, with a slight tinge of red, denoted health and coolness of blood in the English infant; while the inflamed appearance of the American child's gums as surely indicated the hot-bed, forcing nature of its *physique*, arising chiefly from too much flesh food. There can be no doubt that this heated state of the stomach drives the system to early maturity, and as a necessary consequence, to early decay. It is very difficult to account for so erroneous and fatal a mode of life among a people so remarkable for keenness of perception, and for so large a share of common sense. They are well aware of these facts; and therefore evince great irritation and impatience when strangers allude to them. The general answer to questions on this subject is given in a petulant and evasive manner. "Oh, our teeth will last quite long enough; we don't want to live too long." Now I can not help thinking that such hasty answers are thoughtless and shallow, particularly as the evil, in my opinion, can be almost entirely removed.

It is common to hear bitter complaints of the badness of servants in America This is quite a fallacy as regards wealthy people, who can procure excellent servants if they choose to pay for them. The usual number of domestics in New York houses is far less than in England. They are expected to do much more for the same wages, and are naturally dissatisfied. Let the American gentry follow the English custom of engaging particular servants for particular duties, and the evil they complain of will speedily diminish, particularly if they hire a sufficient number of servants to make the work tolerably easy.

It is hardly possible for an Englishman (who has only *read* of the States) to arrive in any one of them for the first time without some little apprehension of the supposed "Republican rudeness" of the citizens. The moment, however, he lands, this apprehension leaves him. He feels at once, almost by intuition, that he is among as civil people as any in existence. This, of course, only if he keeps a civil tongue, and does not offend their prejudices, which are not more marked in the States than in other nations.

An American citizen will listen to any argument with attention and courtesy, as long as he believes you to be sincere, and not actuated by the depreciating spirit unhappily so common with Englishmen when traveling in the United States. Although our transatlantic brethren are intensely national, I have always found them just and fair to those who meet them on the same terms. I have heard abuse of England, certainly; but it was always excited by the vulgar remarks of ill-informed Englishmen. The exaggeration which many travelers attribute to the American character, is the result of a lively and ardent imagination on the part of the people. This they will readily admit, if urged with gentleness and moderation; and I have frequently, by good-natured banter, made individuals correct with a smile, exaggerated statements in which they had previously indulged.

Few, if any, English authors have given a just estimate of an Englishman's chances in American society. The Americans are warrantably proud of their country, and feel a just resentment against prejudiced foreign authors who, laying stress upon minor points of etiquette and good-breeding (such as eating with a knife, chewing tobacco, and so forth), have carefully kept silent respecting their admirable schools and local institutions; their plain common-sense arrangements; their freedom from humbug and from absurd restrictions. This feeling makes Americans cautious in their first intercourse with a stranger, particularly if he be an Englishman. They are too proud to make the first advances; and a reserved Englishman, with the best letters of introduction, will find himself in an awkward position if he adhere strictly to European etiquette. But if he have the sense to break the ice of formality, and is truly a gentleman, I promise him great success in American society. No people on earth are keener, or quicker, or better judges of a gentleman, than Americans.

I fell in with a reserved but most worthy English gentleman, who had been some months in the States. He complained bitterly that, although be had brought excellent letters of introduction, they had been of no avail after the first formal civility. "I never," said he, "met with so haughty and precise a set. They don't appear to care a farthing about me."

"And whose fault," I asked, "is that?"

"Why theirs, of course," replied he.

"Your manner," I rejoined, "does not convince them that you are anxious to cultivate their acquaintance. You must alter it, and be more cordial. You will then succeed."

My prognostications were verified by the result; and my friend soon making a large and pleasant circle of acquaintance, speedily altered his opinion of American society.

The Hotels in New York are a remarkable feature, and excite the astonishment of a wanderer from Europe by their enormous size. Many of these huge establishments are capable of affording accommodation for six hundred persons. During the year 1850, most of them (and "their name is legion") were crammed to suffocation, their proprietors realizing large fortunes. This overflow of business has caused some of them to increase their charges, and treat their customers with indifference. A gentleman from Europe having taken up his abode at one of these large houses, was rather alarmed at the prices, and after two days' experience, addressed the clerk as follows:

"Sir, I shall remain in New York for several months; and, I think you might make some reduction in your charges."

The clerk continued writing without looking up; and, after a pause, replied: "Not a cent, Sir. Not a cent."

My friend, somewhat disgusted, left the hotel immediately.

Another gentleman who went incautiously to a large Broadway establishment, without making a bargain, found that his week's bill amounted to 180 dollars; equal to £37. A member of Congress informed me that on his way to Washington he stopped three hours in bed at the Astor House, and was charged for his brief nap one and three-quarter dollars (nearly eight shillings). Thus it appears that the citizens are victimized equally with strangers.

The cookery is admirable in these hotels, which are far more comfortable and better conducted than in Europe: it is, however, desirable for a stranger to live at the public table. Here he will be struck by the absence of conversation. The solemnity is contagious. A very distinguished Englishman lived for six weeks at the New York Hotel; and, although two hundred persons sat down to dinner daily, not a single word was addressed to him during the whole time!

The Union Place Hotel, although comparatively small, is one of the most comfortable I was ever in. As the statistics may be amusing, I venture to put them on paper. The house has a hundred and sixty rooms, and can accommodate two hundred persons. The charge for board and lodging for one person, is 2½ dollars, or 10*s.* 10*d.* per day. Families, however, can be accommodated with private rooms at any price up to 300 dollars a week. Ten cooks are employed, and, as may be seen by the bill of fare, good ones too. Sixty men as waiters, fire-makers, boots, lamp-cleaners, &c. Cost of provisions: 50 dollars daily, equal to £10. 8*s.* Rent per annum: 12,000 dollars, or £2250. Gas: 2000 dollars, or £420. Croton water: 200 dollars or £40. Cannel and anthracite coal: 3000 dollars, or £600. Total expense of this establishment: 200 dollars, or £40 a day. The situation of this hotel is admirable. Warm baths are attached to every suite of apartments.

Although on a small scale, this is undoubtedly the most comfortable hotel in New York. The Irving House is three times larger, and of course accommodates three times as many persons. Such a constant crowd and bustle can not, however, be agreeable to strangers. It is much the same with the other large establishments.

As a specimen of the viands, I give the "bills of fare" of both hotels; assuring my readers that the cookery is remarkably good in each.

BILLS OF FARE

Irving House, Oct. 29, 1850.

Mutton soup

Baked black-fish, champagne sauce.

Boiled: ham; bacon; tongue; smoked jowl; mutton, caper sauce; chickens; corned beef.

Roast: beef; veal; pork; chickens; lamb; geese, apple sauce; ham, champagne sauce.

ENTREES.

Filets of beef, champagne sauce; chicken pies; pork chops; weak-fish; fricandeau; roast robins; calves' head; lambs' fries; rissolles of chicken; maccaroni à l'Italienne; ducks braisés with olives; chicken salad.

Game: roast wild ducks, cranberry sauce.

Pastry: farina pudding; quince pies; apple pies; Italian cream; almond cake; Condé.

Dessert: Brazil-nuts, apples, filberts, raisins, Madeira-nuts, hickory-nuts, grapes, almonds.

Thirteen kinds of vegetables.

Union Place Hotel, Jan. 9, 1851.

Soup, Julienne; fish, smelts; boiled chicken, celery sauce; corned beef and cabbage.

HOT DISHES.	COLD DISHES.
Oyster pie.	Ham.
Baked maccaroni.	Pressed corned beef.

ENTREES.

Grouse piqués, sauce Madère; pigeons à la Flamande; cotelettes d veau panée à l'Anglaise; laperaux sautés aux fines herbes; canards domestiques aux olives; pieds de veau en marinade; canards sauvages rotis, sauce au vin d'Oporto; poulets sauté à la Marengo; tête de veau en tortue; blanquette de veau au céleri; fillet de mouton piqué à la puré de navets.

Roast: beef; mutton, cranberry sauce; goose, apple sauce; turkey; veal; capon.

Game: wild turkey.

Pastry: whortleberry pie, mince pie, gelée au Xeres, sago pudding, cranberry puffs, jelly cakes, ice cream.

Dessert: apples, Brazil nuts, almonds, oranges, raisins, filberts, pecan nuts, figs.

Ten kinds of vegetables.

There is no city in the world where household furniture is so gorgeous and highly decorated as in New York. The Americans, however, do not understand society so well as it is understood in Europe. The grand dinners in private houses are truly magnificent, and are generally supplied by contract. No doubt this system saves trouble and annoyance in the household, but it is extremely expensive. As a general rule, the hospitality of the table is less practiced than in England; none but the wealthy being able to entertain their guests in what is considered the proper style. Moreover, they do not understand the art of making a dinner-party pleasant, chatty, and agreeable. The lady of the house generally goes in after her husband, leaving the company to follow as they best can. This certainly is not as attentive as if the lady came in last, according to English custom. After the cloth is removed, cigars are lighted, and the wine is passed round, as in England.

Nothing can exceed the delicacy of the wine and viands

B

Madeira, of enormous value, that has been ten, twenty, and even fifty years in bottle, is introduced; but this wine, although keenly relished in America, rarely suits the palate of a newly-arrived Britisher. When a dinner-party is given, no pains or expense is spared to make it perfect; and it is no more than justice to the entertainments of New York to assert, that they are superior in wines, viands, lighting, and general splendor, to those either of Paris or London.

At a grand ball, given in one of the best arranged and most tasteful houses in America, one dish at the supper-table cost forty-two dollars, equal to £8 12*s.* As every other arrangement for six hundred guests was on a similar scale, it is easy to imagine the enormous expense. Should any of my readers be curious to know the composition of so costly a dish, I am able to acquaint them that it was compounded of English pheasants, doctored up with truffles and other dainties. As the expenses of this ball alone would have amply supplied a dozen in Europe, to the great gain of society, so lavish an outlay of money prevents numerous parties of the same nature. Americans dislike to be outdone in any way; and this creates an ostentatious feeling, which materially affects the sociality of New York. At the above-mentioned ball, there was a show of diamonds that it would be difficult to match in England, except upon a state occasion.

There are two things to be seen in New York so pre-eminently exquisite that no Englishman ought to pass through the country without witnessing them. Let him, then, get admission to one of the "Upper Ten's" balls. Let him, as soon as supper is announced, hie to the supper-room, and there feast his eyes until they wink again upon the beautiful American girls. The exertion of dancing has created on their cheeks a gentle bloom, heightened into the most animated loveliness by a bumper of champagne. When his eyes ache with enjoyment, let him attack the next relay of roasted "canvas-backs,"* and fill his mouth and feast his eyes alternately. This is true epicurism, which a man can never forget, and of which he is not likely to grow tired.

Two anomalies in American society struck me forcibly; and I do not think I am betraying the kindness and hospitality with which I was treated in naming them. In the first place, ladies are seldom invited to a great dinner-party; the lady of the house, therefore, is frequently the only female present. Sitting at the head of the table, she is solely occupied in attending to her guests. The gentlemen, talking loudly and earnestly, appear almost to forget there is a lady present. The lady herself is in a false position, and clogs, though not quite prevents the usual hilarity of a bachelor-party. I have mentioned this matter to several American ladies, and they fully agree with me. I venture to "guess" that this inconvenient custom will soon cease.

Secondly, I have been much surprised, at the magnificent and luxurious fêtes, to perceive that elegant and beautiful married women—who, in Paris or London, would be the centre of attraction to all the talent and *esprit* of society—are left alone, and comparatively unnoticed. These charming American matrons do not hold their proper place in society. They allow themselves to be pushed aside by boys and girls, and become mere lookers-on. The latitude allowed to "children let loose" is a bane to American society; and I fully believe that the greater proportion of thinking people in America agree with me. I have witnessed painful scenes, enacted by young American boy-men, at the close of grand entertainments in New York. I will not, however, annoy my kind American friends, by publishing that of which I am quite sure the actors are heartily ashamed.

* A delicious duck, so called, peculiar to the United States.

Every lady in New York receives calls on a certain day in each week. From an early period she is dressed *en bal costume*, and devotes the whole day to entertain any friend who chooses to call. This is a sensible custom, and enables strangers, if they choose, speedily to become personally acquainted with society.

The American people do not give their attention and devote their energies exclusively to politics, commerce, and speculative enterprise in the rapid formation of new cities; but are anxious to rival the old countries in domestic elegance, and other refinements of social life. Among many instances of their ingenuity they have invented a new kind of paint, produced by a certain admixture of zinc, which, in its application to doors and shutters, covers them as with a surface of white porcelain—hard, polished, and apparently durable as marble. The lustre and whiteness of this pigment imparts a grace to the interior of fashionable houses in New York, which would be vainly sought in the best mansions of England.

Respectable Englishmen are extremely rare in New York; and I fear some of my countrymen have not left a very good impression. Very many pay flying visits, and are famous for the "mighty haste" with which they rush "helter skelter" through the country. Living at private tables, and aloof from the inhabitants, how can they form a just opinion? A few well educated and gentleman-like Englishmen, without prejudice, temporarily residing here, would correct many erroneous impressions. They would enjoy the trip much more, and learn and see much more than could be afforded by a tour in Italy or the East, except classic remains. The East, for the most part, is a world defunct: the West is a world to come. It is high time that the young men of England should know and understand the practical working of the institutions of this great country. It is high time that the willful blindness and ignorance of those who ought to know, and who really do know better, should be dispelled.

In twenty-five years from this time, as before asserted, the population of New York will be equal to that of London at this period. In twenty-five years from the present time the United States will have a population of above fifty millions. Not, be it noted, a population like that of Europe—namely, one-third absolute idlers and drones, and another third starving by ill-paid labor—but a population the whole of which are working as if their lives depended on their exertions. With such intense action, such marvelous energy and enterprise, such powerful means of combination, if actuated by any strong excitement, they will become morally and physically irresistible. It behoves all intelligent lovers of their country to be prepared for the grand result to which every American confidently looks forward; a result that must follow sooner or later from the enormously increasing wealth and power of the great Republic. I allude to the modification of the old forms of government, and an amelioration of the social evils of Europe.

No person who calmly watches the working and progress of this wonderful country, can avoid the conviction that the above result is only a question of time. Let, then, the intelligence of the old world be prepared to meet that which no earthly power can fend off. The extreme desire of every American to preserve the Federal Union is a remarkable fact. It is one of the strongest points in their nationality, and renders, for some time to come, the maintenance of the present form of government more certain than that of any government on the surface of the globe.

An English literary gentleman, whose works are known and respected wherever civilization extends, has given the following opinion upon the United States of America, in a letter to one of his friends in London, dated "New Haven, Connecticut, 27th of

October, 1850." I agree so cordially with the spirit evinced in this passage, that I can not help transcribing it.

"This is a very wonderful country; and no Englishman that I know of has done justice to it; nor, indeed, do the Americans do justice to it themselves. We all think that, in point of polish, and the accumulation of conveniences, and even of the conventionalities which grow gradually upon old lands, this country, only two centuries and a half old, ought to be on a par with others where civilization has been going on with a steady progress for more than treble that period; and we are disappointed when we find any small particular deficient. We go to see a new building and are surprised that we do not find Westminster Abbey. Then we abuse it, not for what it is, but for what it *is not*. But, my dear O——, in passing through this land, one sees no poverty, no squalid wretchedness, no hovels with windows stopped with rags and old hats. Great good-humor, too is visible every where among the people: each man seems to feel that by industry he can get on as well as another; and each is willing to help another. There is little of that jealous rivalry, none of that irritable envy that we see in older lands, where we are all struggling for a portion of that bread which is not sufficient for the whole. There is undoubtedly an eager craving for money. It is not only the whole land that is making its way upward, but every individual in it. Each man is encouraged by a probable hope of fortune, and each man seeks it with eagerness; but every one holds out his hand to the one lower than himself on the ladder, and tries to help him up too. The carping at small faults and petty annoyances which many of our countrymen have displayed, and the overlooking great advantages, and even great virtues, shows no philosophical spirit. The things I mention are on the surface—open to every eye: no poverty, except among Irish immigrants; general good-humor and good-will; a wide diffusion of education; a certainty of industry producing competence, and of industry and talent acquiring fortune. One great advantage of this country is, that here circumstances are comparatively powerless; that they can not exercise such an influence upon a man's fate as in Europe; that it is more in his own hands. Doubtless there is much that I object to; doubtless there is much which may and will be improved; but, depend upon it, this is a great and extraordinary country; and England must not sit still contented, if she would not be pushed from her stool."

CHAPTER II.

BROOKLYN DOCK-YARD.

Huge Dry Dock—Men-of-war—Improvements in Gunnery, as carried out in Her Hajesty's Ship "Excellent," immediately known in America—The "Saranac" and "San Jacinto"—Promotion in the United States Navy—Discouraging Prospects—Resignations of American Naval Officers—Abolition of corporal Punishment in the U. S. Navy—Its Effects—High Character of American Naval Officers—Amazing Progress of the United States—Grain-elevator—Ferry-boats from New York to Brooklyn, &c., contrasted with the Steam Ferry from Portsmouth to Gosport—A Launch of three huge Vessels in one Day from Webb's Ship-building Yard—The Clipper-fever—Mr. Steers the Ship-builder—Qualities of Clipper-ships—Vessels built by Messrs. Inman, of Lymington, Hants—American naval Architecture and Rigging—Comparative Performances of the four great Steam-ship lines between New York and Europe.

THE United States Navy-yard at Brooklyn, a suburb of New York, is the second in importance in the country. It is situated on Long Island, opposite New York, and at present occupies about fifty acres of land. Like all things in this wonderful nation, both public and private, it is in a state of rapid improvement, and contains perhaps the finest dry dock in the world. This beautiful work has just been completed, in the face of extraordinary difficulty; the foundation having to be secured in a shifting quicksand. The dimensions are, length three hundred and sixteen feet; breadth one hundred and three feet. To clear the water from this vast basin, a huge engine is in preparation (since completed), and is calculated to draw off the water in three hours.

Several fine specimens of men-of-war are lying here; and one is on the stocks—the "Sabrina," forty-four. This vessel, from some unexplained circumstances, has been twenty-seven years building, without any immediate chance of completion.

A magnificent corvette, the "Germantown," rated as twenty, but carrying twenty-four guns, deserves some description. She carries eighteen thirty-two pound guns of forty-seven cwt.; and four sixty-three cwt. eight-inch guns. As all the recent improvements in gunnery carried out in the "Excellent" at Portsmouth, are immediately known at Washington, she has the advantage of them, with such improvements as the 'cute Yankee mind might suggest. For example, the gun-locks are simpler and more perfect than those used in the English service. We are informed, upon unquestionable authority, that no new implement of war is elaborated in England without being immediately known to the authorities in the United States; and we are told that the commission of naval officers, now sitting at Washington to re-organize the naval ordnance and gunnery exercise, are assisted materially by the experience of men educated in Her Majesty's ship "Excellent."

"It all leaks out, I guess," were the words used by one of the most intelligent officers in the American navy; and there can not be any doubt about it.

The sisters, "Saranac" and "San Jacinto," are models of architectural beauty. The "San Jacinto" is intended for a screw, and the "Saranac" for a paddle-wheel steamer. These beautiful vessels are one thousand five hundred tons each, two hundred and thirty-three feet over all, thirty-eight feet beam, and seven hundred and twenty horse-power.

The armament intended for the "San Jacinto," rated in the navy list as carrying six guns, will enable her to cope with almost any vessel afloat. She is to carry sixteen broadside eight-inch guns, fifty-seven cwt. each, and two pivot guns weighing one hundred and seven cwt., forward and aft, of the same calibre as the broadside guns; and the vessel is fitted in such a manner that both pivot guns can be used at either extremity. The crew of both steamers is composed of two hundred and fifty men; and four hundred tons of coal can be stowed under hatches. At full power, they use about twenty-five tons a day; but, by cutting off the steam and working by expansion, they can go ten knots, and carry fuel for thirty days; or expending fuel at the rate of about fourteen tons a day. The usual speed of the paddle-wheel steamer, "Saranac," is from twelve to fourteen knots. As the engines are not yet fitted to the "San Jacinto," the speed can only be a matter of guess. The American officers, however, are very sanguine as to her performance, and expect great speed. Each vessel carries her guns twelve feet above the deep load mark, namely, seventeen feet.

At present, the "Saranac" mounts only six guns; but in case of active service has room for six more. Since her experimental cruise, she has been fitted with a light "hurricane-deck" between the paddle-boxes, of which the American naval officers approve extremely. On the top of this deck are stowed the hammocks on shelves alongside the paddle-boxes. This expedient obviates the necessity of hammock-nettings, and permits a light movable rail to surround the side.

There are not at present any means of raising the screw in the "San Jacinto;" but no doubt this will soon be obviated.

The promotion in the United States navy being strictly by seniority, it can not be denied that, as a body, the officers have greater experience in naval affairs than those of the same grade in the English service. It is equally clear, however, that some change must take place, as the lists are getting so crowded, that promotion halts lamentably. Of the sixty-eight captains, the senior has been fifty-two years in the service; the junior thirty-nine.

Commanders, ninety-seven in number; the senior thirty-nine years; junior, thirty-two years.

The following extract from the Navy Register of the United States, will afford some interesting information.

"The number of lieutenants allowed by law is three hundred and twenty-seven. Of these, one quarter are on shore-duty connected with the dock-yards, shipping-rendezvous, &c. Three-eighths afloat on foreign stations; and about the same number on leave or waiting orders in consequence of sickness or other causes. Tho number of masters in the line of promotion is but eleven; one-fifth the number necessary to afford one to each vessel in commission. In consequence of the small number of lieutenants, junior officers are frequently called upon to perform their duties.

"In the Mexican war, a midshipman performed the duties of executive officer of a sloop of war—the number of lieutenants being insufficient to answer the exigencies of a sickly climate. The number of passed midshipmen is two hundred and thirty-three; the average number of promotions to the rank of lieutenant has been during the last nine years, twelve and a half per year. These gentlemen have rather discouraging prospects; the seniors being in their fourteenth or fifteenth year of service. By way of illustration, let us take those standing about the middle of the list, and who entered the service in 1841. We find they can not be lieutenants for nine years to come; while those at the bottom of the list are unable to get promotion under nineteen years. Most of these latter gentlemen have already served ten years, and their age is probably about twenty-six; consequently, under the most favorable circumstances they must be (seniors) thirty-five, and (juniors) forty-five, before they are lieutenants; the last year serving as masters. In the mean time, their situation is a trying one, neither their duties or position being defined. They are subject to many vexations and annoyances, as their grade is not settled by law or regulation. This condition is calculated to cause discouragement to the most sanguine temperament, and to destroy all zeal in the duties of a profession to which they have devoted the best years of their lives.

"The average number of promotions, during the last nine years, to the rank of commander, have been only five per year. As the majority entered at fourteen years of age, the officers of this rank must be from forty five to fifty-three years. As there are ninety-eight on this list, the juniors can hardly expect further promotion.

"If we take the liberal allowance of fifty per cent for casualties in the lieutenants' list, the past mid. may, at the age of eighty-one, have command of a brig or corvette.

"The youngest lieutenants of the present day are older men than most of the captains in the war of 1812. Decatur, when he re-took the Philadelphia, was but twenty-five; and when the 'Macedonian' was captured, but thirty-three. McDonough, at the time of the victory of Lake Champlain, but twenty-eight. Perry, at that on Lake Erie, twenty-eight. Lawrence, when he took the 'Reindeer,' was but thirty-three; and the same year he fell, in command of the 'Chesapeake.' Can there be a doubt that the 'boy officers' of the war of 1812, were quite as efficient as the old men of the present day?

"Some measures of reform are imperatively called for to revive the drooping *esprit-de-corps*, and to place in responsible situations men who are in possession of every faculty in full vigor.

"We shall not then see, among other anomalies, gray-headed young gentlemen, who say, 'To be good for any thing, we should have been promoted years ago.'"

From the above data, it is clear that, unless some comprehensive system of retirement is established, very few of the lieutenants can hope to gain a step. This slow promotion is not the only disadvantage against which the United States Navy has to contend. Let a man be ever so active and distinguished—even let him make the most gallant and successful capture against any odds—he can not get promotion.

The chances in private life of acquiring wealth and position in society are so great, that it is wonderful how the country can command such able and gifted men as the majority of the United States officers undeniably are. There is no doubt that the army and navy are not only considered to be, but are, the aristocracy of the country. Still, the devotion to those services is a heavy price for an untangible advantage.

From June the 1st, 1849, to the end of the year, the following resignations took place in the United States navy: six lieutenants, one assistant surgeon, seven passed midshipmen, thirteen midshipmen, two boatswains, one gunner, one carpenter, one sailmaker, eight engineers, one navy-agent, one timber-agent. Total, forty-two officers. And these resignations, be it remembered, took place with an amount of pay considerably more than in the English service.

The recent order to abolish corporal punishment in the United States navy, without providing any substitute for the purposes of correction, is almost universally looked upon by the officers with dismay. It is not too much to anticipate some frightful disaster—some horrible massacre—rendering a second "Somers" example necessary. As a slight specimen of the effect already produced, it may be well to allude to what happened to a large frigate, the "Constitution," which, on arriving in New York Bay, was immediately deserted by a hundred and sixty of her crew. As these men had upward of three years' pay due, which could not be withheld, and knew that no adequate punishment could be inflicted in the few days that would terminate their period of service, they became quite indifferent to discipline. The outcry against corporal punishment, is mainly upheld by persons utterly unacquainted with the hard necessities of discipline. Truth was distorted to prejudice the public against bodily punishment; and the number of lashes inflicted on one of the crew of a frigate was multiplied by nine (the number of tails to the cat), to excite public execration against it: unhappily, with too much success.

The officers of the American navy, therefore, have a very difficult game to play. They are expected to keep their splendid ships in order, without adequate means of coercing the crews.

It is not too much to say that, as a body of men, the officers of the United States navy are second to none; indeed, it would be extremely difficult to find so large a proportion of educated, enlightened, and well-informed individuals in any service. The manners and customs in their ships are precisely the same as in English men-of-war; and their kindness and cordiality to Englishmen, particularly naval officers, is extremely pleasant. Long may this continue! And may it be reciprocated between the two nations.

Among the numerous officers of the United States navy, with whom I was fortunate enough to become acquainted, was one so remarkable for intellect and manly candor, that it was impossible not to like him. Two days before my departure, he was suddenly called to his last home. As sepulture is immediate in America, the funeral ceremony took place the following day, and I was invited. My last act in the States was accordingly one of mourning. It was, indeed, a touching spectacle, and gave rise to grave and solemn reflections as I marched up the aisle of Calvary Church in company with a crowd of American naval officers.

An unprejudiced mind can not avoid being struck with amazement at the progress of the United States. Whichever way the eye is cast it is met with unmistakable signs of rapid progress and improvement. Magnificent houses rise as if by magic; mammoth ocean-steamers are completed with astonishing celerity; their sharp entrance through the water giving convincing testimony of their prodigious speed. River-boats, nearly four hundred feet long, appear to glide like meteors on the surface of the Hudson and East river. Place one of these on end alongside St. Paul's Cathedral, and its foremost extremity would nearly reach the noted ball and cross! The first object of interest was a large ship, which was being loaded with wheat for Europe. To accelerate the introduction of the cargo, a grain-elevator was employed. This novel machine pumped the grain from barges, or canal-boats on one side, in a continuous stream into the ship's hold at the rate of two thousand bushels per hour. It was not only passed into the vessel at this prodigious rate, but likewise accurately measured in the operation. American naval officers have taken a hint from this ingenious labor-saving contrivance, and successfully adapted it to the purpose of supplying powder with great speed and regularity to the batteries of large ships; thereby saving numerous hands that could be better employed in the other parts of the vessel.

What are those huge castles rushing madly across the East river? I see at one time five steam ferry-boats wafting carriages and passengers from New York to Brooklyn, Williamsburg, &c. Let us cross in the "Montauk" from Fulton ferry and survey the freight. There are fourteen carriages; and the passengers are countless, at least six hundred. Heavens, what a pace she rushes over! her powerful engines vibrate to one's very marrow. Onward she darts at headlong speed, until, apparently in perilous proximity to her wharf, a frightful collision appears inevitable. The impatient Yankees, heaven help them! crowd, and press, and struggle to get to the extreme edge of the vessel, and be the first to jump ashore. On the wharf is a dense crowd more impatient, if possible, to jump aboard. Forward dashes the vessel, while the uninitiated quake with apprehension at the horrid crash which seems inevitable.

A loud "twang" is suddenly heard, and then a bell. The powerful engine is quickly reversed, and the way of the vessel so instantaneously stopped, that the dense mass of passengers insensibly lean forward from the sudden check. Before she is secured, an avalanche of jumpers have crossed one another, penetrating with a rush the crowd of passengers on board, and the expectant passengers on the wharf.

Accidents frequently happen, and lives are sometimes lost; but certainly no blame attaches to the boats, as they are handled in the most careful and masterly style.

The "Montauk," "Manhattan," and "Bedford," are the vessels now working on the Fulton ferry. They are admirably fitted with light, airy, and warm rooms for passengers, each passenger having a partitioned seat. A large cabin is set apart for ladies, another for gentlemen, who smoke there if they please. The fare, one cent (a halfpenny). I have been told that these boats cost about 30,000 dollars; equal, in round figures, to £6,000. In economy, beauty, commodiousness, and speed, they form a striking contrast to the steam-ferry from Portsmouth to Gosport; as it has been stated that the latter cost £20,000, or 100,000 dollars.

The author strongly advises persons in Europe, who have any intention of projecting steam-ferries, to take a leaf out of the Yankee book. As an example: if the Portsmouth ferry had been conducted on the same principles as the Fulton ferry, a very large profit would have ensued, instead of the concern being overwhelmed in debt; and the inhabitants of Portsmouth and Gosport would have had something to be proud of, in lieu of a miserable and clumsy abortion.

Let us now take an example of Yankee *go-aheadism*. We will depart from the Union Place Hotel, and march down Seventh-street. Long before we arrive at the East River, we perceive tall and tapering spars, extending far above the houses.

Streamers and flags are abundant; but above all, and eclipsing all, are numerous magnificent "star-spangled banners."

A launch is about to take place.

Open your ears, O ye John Bulls! Listen to the truth from a brother Bull. "Read, mark, learn, and inwardly digest."

We are now in Webb's ship-building yard. Look around—five huge vessels are on the stocks; three are to be launched at high-water. Let us examine them.

First, the "Isaac Bell," of 1708 tons, is intended for a Havre liner. She is built for running, and, with a fair wind, will out-sail any man-of-war afloat.

Second, a steamer, the "Illinois," of 2500 tons. So sharp is she from the cutwater, that it involuntarily suggests the same painful idea to the mind as on first beholding Langham Church steeple, in Portland Place, London. Her midship section is perfectly flat, which causes an unsightly protuberance amidships, that offends the eye when looking along the bottom. Like most of Brother Jonathan's sea-steamers, she does not come up to John Bull's idea of sufficient strength of construction; still, every fair and unprejudiced Britisher must allow that, for models, the Yankees, as they express it, "whip the world." They do not, however, build their sea-steamers strong enough. The reason is obvious: hitherto their experience has been mainly with river-boats; and although they have some of the finest-looking craft of this denomination ever seen, many of them are utterly unsafe and unsound. The lighter a river steamer is built, the faster she will go; the less water she will draw; and it is a notorious saying, in reference to certain boats on the Mississippi, "the engines are intended to wear out three hulls, if the vessel don't blow up."

This impeachment of American judgment will not last long. Brother Jonathan has received a warning which he is not the man to neglect; and we may confidently look forward to his producing sea-steamers as stable and fast as, if not faster than, any that can elsewhere be built.

Go ahead, brother—go ahead! You are the greatest benefactor your old mother ever had. The venerable lady begins to discover that "she doesn't know you're out."

Third, the "Gazelle," a gigantic yacht, of 1500 tons. She is nearly as sharp as any yacht in England; slightly fuller in the midship section. Her model is perfectly beautiful.

Here is a launch indeed; and by *one* builder!

At a quarter before twelve o'clock, January 21, 1851, the dogs-shores of the mammoth steamer, "Illinois," were knocked away. In a few seconds, she glided majestically into the East River (properly Long Island Sound), amidst the exultant shouts of many thousands. After a short interval, the "Isaac Bell" followed her example; and, lastly, the enormous yacht, "Gazelle," was sent gliding beautifully into her element. Never, probably, has such a launch happened in one day; most certainly not from the yard of one constructor.

Read the tonnage again, John Bull; and mind, it is no fable. Five thousand seven hundred and eight tons were launched from one builder, and within thirty minutes!

Since the above was written, the clipper fever in the United States is quite over; and well it may be. If we only take the result of two years' trial of perhaps the most successful clipper in the States (the "N. B. Palmer"), we shall have most lamentable results.

This magnificent clipper earned an immense freight between New York and California. She then proceeded to China, and was chartered to London and back for £6 10*s*. a ton. These voyages will take about twenty months or two years. The owners do not expect to net more than 25,000 dollars (£5000). This will not by any means pay for wear and tear.

I was much struck at perceiving two vessels lying side by side at a wharf. They were both ready to discharge cargoes of teas from China. One was a clipper, and had been a considerable time in the port; the other was a round-bottomed, old-fashioned Boston vessel. Although the clipper had distanced the Boston craft eighteen days, the latter began to discharge her cargo first. Moreover, the Boston vessel carried a cargo three times greater, in proportion to her tonnage, than the clipper, at about one third the expense. I venture to predict that few clippers will be built for the future, unless any great improvement in build and speed be discovered, which is likely to take place in consequence of the great success of the "America" yacht.

Mr. Steers, the intelligent builder of the latter vessel, is about laying down a clipper of 2000 tons. The estimated size is as follows: length 233ft., breadth 48ft., and she is to draw, when deep, 20ft. Mr. Steers is very sanguine that he will produce a faster vessel than has yet plowed the seas. He expects that, if allowed to "pick his time" within six months, the new clipper will achieve a speed of eighteen miles an hour. From what I have seen of this model, I am inclined to agree with his sanguine expectations. This vessel will stow as much as, or more than any clipper proper afloat, and will, no doubt, be as superior to them all in sailing as the "America" yacht was to the English yachts, which, by the way, are the prototypes of the Yankee clipper-ships. If such turns out to be the case (of which I have little doubt), the first of these clippers will, I hope, make a better thing of it than the "N. B. Palmer."

The ship yards in New York show a striking contrast to the activity prevalent in them a year ago. They are now comparatively deserted. I have been informed by a large ship-owner that timber is 30 per cent cheaper, and wages materially lower than a year ago. In fact, the market for the sharp and expensive "clipper proper" is overstocked; and it is the opinion of experienced men in the States, that, unless some new and powerful impulse is given to trade, two thirds of the clippers will lose money.

The clipper-ships, although certainly the finest class of vessels afloat are very uneasy in a sea. They are likewise said to strain violently, and from this cause make water, and damage their cargo. If a class of clipper-vessels, such as Mr. Steers proposes, is built, they will be as much superior in sailing as easy in their motion, and will thus secure so great an advantage that they must completely distance the old clippers in all respects. The yacht "America" is superior on these points, as well as in every respect, to the English yachts, which are excessively uneasy in a sea, and draw an inconvenient draft of water. The great merit of Mr. Steers, as the builder of the 'America,' is, in his having invented a perfectly original model, as new in America as in Europe. In some of the long conversations I have had with him, he informed me that this idea, so successfully carried out in the "America's" model, struck him when a boy of eight years old. He was looking on at the moulding of a vessel by his father (an Englishman), when suddenly it occurred to him that a great improvement might be made in the construction; and the *modus operandi* speedily took possession of his mind.

The first vessels he constructed on the full extent of his improved lines were the pilot boats, "Moses Grinnell" and "Mary Taylor," and it is my deliberate opinion that the "Cornelia" yacht, or either of these vessels, though under a hundred tons, are more than a match for any yacht in England

Mr. Steers thinks that a shallow vessel, with a sliding keel, can be built to out-sail any vessel even on his improved model. This is likely to be tested next summer in England, as a sloop, the "Silvia," built by Steers on this construction, is preparing to try her speed at Cowes next season. I carefully noted this craft when on the stocks alongside the "America," and I believe that no vessel in England has the ghost of a chance against her. Next year will, however, decide the question.

England is not likely to remain long behind Brother Jonathan in yachting, as the following list of vessels, building at the justly celebrated Messrs. Inman, of Lymington, will plainly prove.

First, the "Alarm" is lengthened twenty feet, with the American, or wave-line bow. She will be schooner-rigged, and of the burden of 240 tons.

Second, two schooners, about 75 tons each.

Third, a very beautiful schooner of 150 tons. The Messrs. Inman have taken time by the forelock, and are more open-minded than the builders of this country usually are. I have carefully examined these vessels, and plainly perceive evidence of great genius and artistic skill. They will be formidable rivals to any yachts that Brother Jonathan may in future send over the Atlantic.

American naval architecture is, without doubt, very admirable, whether we take the sailing qualities of their vessels, or their symmetry of form. I spent some days at Baltimore, carefully examining the different varieties of clippers. On one occasion, I observed a group of these fine models surrounding an English coaster. The contrast in proportion was most marked. The hideous English coaster, surrounded thus, was like "a young donkey grazing amidst a herd of gazelles."

The English ship-builders have a great deal to learn from Brother Jonathan, not only in the fashion of build, but likewise in the "fitting and rigging." The modern-built American vessels are infinitely better fitted and ventilated than any British ships which have come under my notice. The Americans speak very highly of some ships constructed by Green and Wigram, which I have not had an opportunity of examining.

An American London liner is sailed with half the number of men required by an English ship of the same size; and yet the work is got through as well and as expeditiously. The various mechanical contrivances to save labor might be beneficially copied by English ships. For example, "gipsies," or small windlasses, and the large "gipsy," or chain-lifter. This very useful mechanical help enables three men to manage, and easily haul on deck, a huge chain-cable of the largest size.

The system of lower-rigging, likewise, I think a great improvement. When an American ship is first rigged, the lower rigging is much larger and stronger than is usual in England. It is, however, intended and expected to last without lifting, as long as the ship retains a first class letter on the commercial list. This saves time and labor, and is found to succeed admirably.

The following is a condensed report of the performances of the four great steamship lines between New York and Europe. In comparing the average trips of the two main lines, namely, Collins and Cunard, it will be seen that the latter are ahead of their opponents on the eastern passages by about two hours; but the former (Collins) more than make it up on the western passages, their trips having been accomplished in fifteen hours less than their competitors. The eastern passages of the Havre line to Cowes average rather more than a day longer than the Liverpool lines. They are also on the western passages twenty-three hours longer than the Collins line; but only eight hours behind the Cunarders.

The trips of the Bremen steamers, both east and west, have been rather longer, having made only one trip in twelve days during the whole year.

	Hours.	Min.	Sec.
Collins line (eastern passages). Total time of twenty-four passages....................................	267	6	30
	Days.	Hours.	Min.
Average time each passage................................	11	3	16

	Hours.	Min.	Sec.
Western passages. Total time of twenty-five passages.	288	17	55
	Days.	Hours.	Min.
Average time each passage........................	11	13	12
	Hours.	Min.	Sec.
CUNARD line (eastern passages). Total time of twenty-one passages...............................	243	8	15
	Days.	Hours.	Min.
Average time each passage.......................	11	1	26
	Hours.	Min.	Sec.
Western passages. Total time of twenty-three passages....................................	279	23	10
	Days.	Min.	Sec
Average time of each passage.....................	12	5	1
	Hours.	Min.	Sec.
HAVRE line (eastern passages). Total time of eleven passages..	135	8	30
	Days.	Hours.	Min.
Average time each passage.......................	12	7	18
	Hours.	Min.	Sec.
Western passages. Total time of eleven passages.....	137	14	25
	Days.	Hours.	Min.
Average time each passage.......................	12	12	13
	Hours.	Min.	Sec.
BREMEN line (eastern passages). Total time of ten passages....................................	144	19	0
	Days.	Hours.	Min.
Average time each passage.......................	14	11	38
	Hours.	Min.	Sec.
Western passages. Total time of ten passages.......	146	17	30
	Days.	Hours.	Min.
Average time each passage.......................	14	16	10

The following table shows at once the average time of each line for the year.

EASTERN PASSAGES TO EUROPE.	Days.	Hours.	Min.	WESTERN PASSAGES TO NEW YORK.	Days.	Hours.	Min.
Collins line	11	3	16	Collins line	11	13	12
Cunard line	11	1	28	Cunard line	12	4	8
Havre line	12	7	19	Havre line	12	12	13
Bremen line.....	14	11	30	Bremen line.....	14	16	10

To this we will add the average passage of sailing-ships between Liverpool and New York. Bearing in mind that from the wonderful improvement in marine architecture (wholly due to "Brother Jonathan"), the passages both ways are gradually shortening, as the model of hull improves, and the education and science of the officers increases.

	Days.	Hours.		Days.	Hours.
Eastern passages (average of all)....	32	12	Western passages (average of all)..	22	12

CHAPTER III.

PHILADELPHIA.

Uninteresting Road—Immense Orchards of standard Peach-trees—Lank and meagre Woods—Philadelphia—The Water-works—Fairmount—A Boarding-house for Pigs—Overland Transport of large Boats, with their Freights, in Sections—School System of Philadelphia—Enormous Consumption of Paper by ten Newspapers in the United States—The Dockyard in Philadelphia—The Sectional Dock—Journey to Baltimore—Railroad Carriages—Ingenious Scheme of General Green.

THE journey by rail from New York toward Washington is flat, and destitute of any feature of interest, except the immense orchards of standard peach-trees, which are pruned and kept in excellent order. The trees are generally renewed every five years, as the fruit is supposed to degenerate after that age.

Occasionally, lank and meagre woods are passed, forming a strong contrast to the clear and well arranged peach-trees, and having beneath them a growth of underwood, principally composed of rhododendrons, which, however, are far inferior, in size of leaves and luxuriance, to their congeners in England; probably from want of care and cultivation.

Philadelphia, although abounding in beautiful buildings, does not "show forth" to much advantage; a defect mainly attributable to its site, which is nearly flat. The population of this city, in 1840, numbered 300,000, and has increased in ten years to 412,000, an increase chiefly attributable to the demand for hands in the manufacturing establishments, as the foreign trade of Philadelphia has fallen off.

The water-works, which give an ample supply to the town, are formed by a dam on the river Schuylkill, which raises the river fifteen feet. A portion of the stream thus confined, is allowed to escape on several powerful water-wheels, which revolving rapidly, pump up the needful supply into an immense elevated reservoir. The simplicity and great power of this contrivance is obvious to the slowest comprehension. From Fairmount, a very fine prospect is revealed to the gazer's eye. I was wrapped in a mantle of pleasant ideas, on beholding this fair and beautiful scenery, when my brown study was abruptly disturbed by my companion—one of the kindly Yankees I had the good fortune to convert into friends during my sojourn in the States.

"Do you see that large, many-storied house?" inquired he.

"Yes," I replied. "Who could help taking notice of so huge a pile of building?"

"Well," continued he, "there is a story attached to that house, which gives a good example of Yankee 'cuteness.'

"Let me hear it, by all means," returned I.

Seating himself on a large stone, he related the following story, which I give verbatim.

"Some years ago, a 'cute Yankee rented that house, and set up a distillery. After a year or two he became dissatisfied with his profits, which did not exceed *ten per cent.* This he regarded as a very poor return, hardly worth consideration. So many others were engaged in the same trade, and so much competition existed, that he clearly perceived his gains were more likely to diminish than to increase.

"After considerable reflection, he determined to lower the price of his whisky, and set up 'a pigs' boarding-house!' Accordingly, he commenced advertising to take pigs in at a certain price. As his terms were considerably less than the swine cost their owners, he was speedily overrun with *boarders.* The immense quantity of grains produced by his increase of business, consequent on his reduction of the price of whisky, enabled him to make his *boarding-house* a mine of wealth.

"His arrangements were capital. Squeakers, he placed in the garret; porkers, next floor; and so on downward, until his premises round the base of the house were swarming with magnificent grunters.

"Money came in apace; and fame soon followed. In a few years he had amassed a considerable sum, and his business had increased so much, that he had several acres of pig-styes, filled with fat and contented grunters. Alas, for all porcine greatness! The horrible odor of his boarders became unbearable. The neighbors grumbled; then loudly complained; and lastly, flew into violent rage. Our enterprising pig-boarder was indicted for a nuisance. His enemies prevailed, and this unique and luxurious establishment was broken up forever.

"He had, however, cleared a large fortune."

My friend having finished his narrative, we returned on foot toward the city. On passing down Broad-street, my attention was attracted by the figure of a man smoking his pipe, and apparently looking out of the stern windows of a decked vessel.

"Hallo!" exclaimed I, "what can that craft be doing on land? Why, her stern is toward the wharf."

On approaching nearer, I perceived that it was the stern section of a canal-boat. Three other sections were also there, all mounted on trucks, ready to start, per rail, on their journey, to Pittsburg. The vessel was one hundred feet long, and nine wide, divided into four nearly equal sections; the bow and stern being slightly longer than the midship section, in consequence of the fineness of run. These divided compartments are loaded with emigrants and with goods manufactured in Philadelphia, the latter of which are forwarded, without breaking bulk, three hundred and sixty miles. The first hundred miles, they are conveyed by rail through Lancaster to the Susquehanna; thence to a spur of the Alleghanies. An inclined plane now takes hold of the sections separately, with all their freight, and transports them over a considerable elevation, the greatest height of which is fifteen hundred feet. Then, crossing the mountain-range, they are launched peaceably into a canal, and again united; and after being tracked or towed another hundred miles, are safely deposited in the town of Pittsburg.

Here is another specimen of the "go-ahead" system of Brother Jonathan. These full-freighted vessels are transported several hundred miles overland, including two ranges of mountains.

There are numerous objects besides the above, of great interest in Philadelphia; but, as neither time nor space is afforded to chronicle one-tenth of them, I must unwillingly pass them over.

One of the most remarkable and admirable objects, is the school-system of Philadelphia, which is deservedly considered among the best in the world. The number and designation of the several establishments are as follows: one high school, one normal school, fifty-three grammar schools, twenty-nine secondary, one hundred and thirty primary, and forty unclassified. Total, two hundred and fifty. In these, there are 45,383 students. And be it remembered that, with moderate abilities and perseverance, any student can gain access to the high school, where the system of education is above all praise, and very far superior to any college of which I have ever heard.

By the polite attention of Professor Hart, I was enabled to examine thoroughly the different classes. I can not sufficiently express my admiration of the proficiency of the pupils, particularly in the classes of anatomy and physiology under Professor McMurtrie, every student in which appeared to be thoroughly conversant with the structure of the human frame. All that choose can enjoy gratuitously the advantage of this or any other class.

The High School has eleven professors, of whom Mr. Hart is the head. These gentlemen give instructions in every branch of education, embracing languages and spherical trigonometry. I was much edified to hear boys, of thirteen years old, answering questions with ease, that few grown persons under the old system of education would understand, or even dream of understanding.

To what an elevating effect must this admirable system of education lead! Here are 45,383 young persons (upward of nine per cent. of the population of Philadelphia, namely, 415,000) receiving a first-rate education. As a still stronger proof of the advantages thus derived, it may be mentioned that five daily and five weekly journals in the United States consume alone nearly as much paper as all the journals in Great Britain put together, according to the American report, which asserts that all the paper used by the public prints in England amounts to 175,000 reams per annum. In the United States, the "New York Herald," "Tribune," and "Sun;" the "Philadelphia Sun," and "Baltimore Sun," and five weekly papers, use 136,000 reams. There are at present in the United States 2500 newspapers, and they are increasing at the rate of 60 or 70 per annum.

It is impossible for a seaman to leave any maritime city without a glance at its naval establishments. The United States Dock-yard in Philadelphia is of minor importance, as compared with those of New York or Boston. It covers a surface of thirty-two acres, and has a frontage of a few hundred yards on the Delaware River.

The only object of interest herein is the sectional dock. This vast fabric (one hundred yards long, and fifty wide) is divided into several sections, each of which is of eight hundred tons burthen. The whole is of enormous size; certainly the largest in the world, being nearly eight thousand tons capacity. It is calculated that the largest ship ever built can be raised with ease. In spite of the stupendous character and magnificent proportions of this gigantic work, I can not congratulate Uncle Sam upon its utility or economy. There is quite sufficient depth of water to construct a stone dry-dock, and it is calculated that the expense would be little, if any, more than that of the sectional dock. When the enormous cost necessary to keep this huge wooden structure in repair is considered, I think Uncle Sam will have to pay very dear for his whistle. It is not too much to assert that, in ten years, the present dock will require repairs, more than equivalent to the first outlay; whereas, a substantial stone structure would last for years, without any renewed outlay whatever.

The journey to Baltimore is extremely "jolty," and, compared to the English railways, very slow. The carriages, constructed to hold about seventy passengers each, are very comfortable, and not more expensive than a first class carriage in England, which holds only eighteen. I therefore strongly recommend them to the directors of English railways, as being not only more economical, but infinitely more convenient and safe; the conductor or guard being able to communicate with the engine-driver, if necessary.

Apropos of railways; the following remarks and ingenious scheme of a Yankee (General Duff Green) may be interesting to the English reader. The portion referring to the post-office is well worthy of note.

"It is estimated," says the General, "that nearly ten thousand miles of railroad are now in operation in the United States, and that there soon will be at least twenty thousand miles. The capital invested is more than six hundred millions of dollars (roughly, a hundred and twenty millions sterling.) It is proposed that the post-office department should make contracts with railroad companies for the perpetual use of their roads, and that, instead of being paid, as now, on contracts for a term of years, the railroad companies shall receive an amount of 5 per cent. bonds, chargeable on the revenues of the department; the interest of which would be equal to the service rendered. Thus, we now pay three hundred dollars per mile, per annum, for carrying the mail on first-class railroads, which is 6 per cent. on five thousand dollars, and which, at five per cent., would reduce the charge on the department to two hundred and fifty dollars per mile per annum, leaving fifty dollars per mile per annum as a sinking fund to pay off the principal, which it would do in less than thirty-three years.

The effect of this would be, to give the use of the railroads for ever, free of all charge, and consequently to save to the department twenty millions of dollars (four million sterling) in thirty-four years."

CHAPTER IV.

BALTIMORE.

The far-famed Baltimore Clippers—Gigantic Strides of Baltimore in Population, Wealth, Luxury, and Refinement—A freehold House possessed by almost every Family—Situation of the City—The fashionable Quarter—Beauty of Baltimore—Ship-building and domestic Architecture—Society in this City, and the happy Appearance of the Negroes—The Federal Hill—Oyster-boats and other Vessels of Burden—TheBrig-of-war 'Lawrence'—Cheapness of Ship-building in Baltimore—Cotton-duck Sails—Hospitality.

No person of any reflection, brought up to sea-life, can avoid being extremely interested on approaching the town of Baltimore.

It has been my lot, in various parts of the world, to fall in with the far-famed clippers of this town. Whether in calms or storms; under close-reefed sails, or with all the snow-white "cotton-duck" canvas, courting the breeze, these vessels can not fail to fascinate every beholder. Such graceful and elegant proportions have an exceeding charm for the true nautical eye.

Baltimore is a type of the great sea-board American cities; that is to say, it is advancing with gigantic strides in population, wealth, luxury, and refinement. Ten years ago, the number of its inhabitants was 120,000. Now, the population has increased to 170,000. Although Maryland is a slave state, the working classes are famous for their high moral standard, mainly attributable to the fact that each family, almost without exception, possesses a neat and comfortable freehold-house of its own.

The city itself, one hundred and eighty miles from the sea, is situated on undulating ground, on a branch of the Patapsco, a river which ramifies suddenly into several "*cul-de-sacs,*" thus giving an immense water-frontage to this inland sea-port. Taking advantage of the chances thus offered to them by the bountiful hand of Providence, the Marylanders have raised one of the most elegant and well arranged cities, perhaps, in the New World.

The fashionable quarter, situated around the fine monument to Washington, is probably as striking to the eye, for its architecture, as any quarter of any city in existence. The plentiful supply of marble in the immediate neighborhood, adds not a little to the general effect.

In every direction, large blocks of new buildings are in progress; giving ample proof that the good people of Baltimore are moving onward with rapid strides. It is impossible for any one but a sailor to appreciate the exceeding beauty of their ship-building. It is therefore truly gratifying to perceive that the same faculty which produces the vessels, is extended to the architecture of their houses. This is clearly indicated, not only in the mansion of the wealthy merchant, but likewise the dwelling of the humble artisan.

The society of Baltimore has all the hospitality of New York. A stranger can not divest himself of the idea that a greater degree of refinement exists in Baltimore, in all classes, than in most other cities in the Union. The happy, careless air of the negroes is likewise remarkable. It is extremely difficult for an Englishman, to "realize" that he is in a Slave State. As to the fanciful pictures which an imaginative mind is apt to draw of the misery and degradation of slavery, I can only refer them to the happy, good-natured, and "devil-may-care" appearance of the slaves themselves.

Opposite the centre of the town, across a portion of the harbor, stands the Federal Hill, on the side of which is a singular geological formation, presenting a miniature representation of Alum Bay in the Isle of Wight. The beautiful white sand, for which the latter is famous, juts out of the earth in exactly the same position, close to the water.

The Pongees, or oyster-boats, and the Chesapeake Bay coast-vessels, are the most elegant and yacht-like merchant-craft in the world. They are from sixty tons downward; and can be built and fitted for sea under forty dollars, or eight pounds a ton.

It is remarkable that the vessels intended for the lowest and most degraded offices (such as carrying manure, oysters, and wood) are of elegant and symmetrical proportions. An English schooner from Bideford, was lying among some of the worst Baltimore coasters. She looked like a hog amid a herd of antelopes.

The true Baltimore clipper, the ideal of perfection thirty years ago, is now quite out of date. All the Baltimore ship-builders have been gradually modifying their forms, but still retaining their graceful appearance.

In the Washington navy-yard, there is a model of a large brig of war, the "Lawrence," of about four hundred tons, built on the old Baltimore-clipper principle. Being found to be a failure, she was consequently sold out of the American navy. With a slight difference in the shape of the forefoot and length of bow, she is nearly the same as the yacht-schooner "America." Although a complete failure as a man-of-war, she proved herself a remarkably fast sailer.

A merchant-vessel, on the clipper principle can be turned out by a Baltimore builder for from £10 to £12 a ton, complete in all her fittings. This is much cheaper than in England; which appears unaccountable, as the wages of artificers, as well as most articles of ship-fittings are much more expensive in America, wood being the only exception.

"Cotton-duck" sails are almost exclusively used by American vessels under 300 tons. No doubt can be entertained that for fore-and-aft vessels, this material is infinitely better than the canvas generally used. I do not hesitate to assert that it is particularly adapted for yachts; and that it will give a vessel an immense advantage in sailing, particularly in light winds. This "cotton-duck" is well worthy the attention of the yachtsmen in England. Indeed, for all pleasure-vessels it is far better, being whiter, cleaner-looking, much lighter, and easier handled. Above all, "cotton-duck" would cost only two-thirds of the present high charges for yacht canvas.

Adieu to thee, Baltimore! Famous for thy beautiful "Chesapeake," thou art still more famous for thy hospitality. The genuine welcome of the old English times is still cherished by thy sons. Free from the ostentation of opulence quickly achieved, Baltimore shows an example in social life, which it would be well for her wealthier sister-cities to follow.

CHAPTER V.

WASHINGTON.

The Capitol—Its Senate-Chamber, House of Representatives, Library of Congress, Supreme Court, &c.—View from the Capitol—Population of Washington—Facility of Admission to the Senate-Chamber—Commencement of Business—Dignity of the Senate, and great Respect paid to it by the People—Door-keeper in the Gallery of the English House of Commons—Want of Decorum in the American House of Representatives—Anecdote—Legislative Procrastination—Speech of one of the Representatives from Georgia—Bitter Attack on the Navy by another Member—Anecdote—Protracted Sitting of both Chambers—Smoking—Society at Washington—Anecdote—The British Minister and his Lady—The Patent Office—Sewing-machine—The Museum—Original "Declaration of Independence"—Printer's Press at which Franklin worked.

The Capitol at Washington, an imposing structure, is situated in the centre of a square on an eminence seventy-eight feet above the sea. It consists of a central edifice and two wings, the entire length being 352 feet. The height of the building to the top of the dome is 120 feet; and under the dome is the rotunda, 95 feet in diameter, adorned with sculpture and painting of a national character. A fine statue of Columbus stands at the entrance; and a colossal statue of Washington is placed in a temple in the east park.

Within the Capitol are the Senate Chamber, the House of Representatives, the Library of Congress, the Court-Room of the Supreme Court, and about seventy apartments for the accommodation of committees, &c. The building is surrounded by a park of twenty-two acres, ornamentally laid out with trees, shrubberies, fountains, &c.

The Capitol, from its commanding position, has an extensive view of undulating plains, bounded in the distance, on one side, by an amphitheatre of uplands, and on the other, by the muddy but placid Potomac. Several broad flights of steps lead through the park down the west side of the Capitol hill, and open upon Pennsylvania Avenue. In the distance, at the end of this broad and spacious vista, is the President's house; and in the vicinity are situated the various government offices. The population is about 40,000; but, like almost every city in the United States, it is rapidly increasing. The prosperity of Washington being due solely to its position as the seat of government, the population is of a very fluctuating character; in the session of Congress, it is crowded to excess, while in the intervals it is a very quiet place indeed. Social equality is here seen to perfection; and, as every one of the sovereign people has access to the head of the nation (the President), they think themselves, of course, equal to any one else.

The Supreme Court of the United States holds its sittings in the Capitol. This is indeed as dignified a body as can be presented by any tribunal whatever. It is composed of nine judges, the only persons in the States who sit in robes, a costume which adds to the dignity of their appearance.

The Senate and House of Representatives possess great interest for a stranger, particularly an Englishman who is acquainted with the British Houses of Parliament. Unfortunately, from some defect in the architectural arrangements, the voices of speakers in each chamber are very indistinctly heard.

Being extremely anxious to observe the proceedings in both Houses, I took care to arrive at the Capitol at half-past ten; and, after various inquiries, found my way, accompanied by a lady, into the ladies' gallery of the Senate Chamber. No door-keeper obstructed the entrance; and the sovereign people appeared to consider the House as part of their own property. The civility and kindness of manner exhibited to one another were remarkable, and formed a strong contrast to the conduct of the same class in England.

On taking my seat in the gallery, just opposite the Speaker, I watched with great interest the House as it became gradually filled with Senators. At eleven o'clock, the desks were about half-occupied; and the Speaker, rapping his desk with a hammer, exclaimed: "The House is in order."

A short prayer was then offered up; and the Senate, composed of sixty-two members, proceeded to business. As the first hour was devoted to the reception of petitions, I was fortunate enough to hear several Senators called for by name, in rotation, according to the Speaker's list. The first summoned was Mr. Clay, the Senator from Kentucky.

The Speaker's sonorous voice was heard with great effect, as he solemnly called forth:

"The Senator from Virginia;" "the Senator from Ohio;" "the Senator from Illinois," &c.

How could this fail deeply to interest an Englishman, particularly when he reflected that each of these Senators represented a "State" as large as, or larger than England; and with a soil and natural productions capable of supporting a much larger population.

The Senate is a remarkably dignified body, and may be favorably compared with any assembly in other countries. I remarked this to one of the Senators, who assured me that they had fallen off very much in this respect, and were not now so striking in appearance as they had been ten years ago. Still, it is impossible to avoid being struck by the unmistakable evidence in their physiognomies of intellectual power.

The sovereign people have a much greater respect for the

Senate than for the other House. I remarked that they invariably uncovered their heads, on entering the Senate Chamber. This was not the case in the House of Representatives.

On one occasion, I said to a tall, good-looking Yankee:

"Why don't you take your hat off in the presence of your Representatives?"

"Why, stranger," replied he, "I won't pay any respect to those who don't respect themselves."

At this moment, I could not avoid thinking of the usual scene in the Speaker's gallery of our House of Commons, on any interesting occasion, where, when the visitor becomes interested in hearing some statesman of celebrity, and leans forward a little, he is suddenly startled by the Cockney voice of the door-keeper, or other official in attendance, exclaiming, in a very grandiloquent manner: "'Eds hup, 'eds hup!" to the inexpressible annoyance and loss of the unfortunate listeners.

The Houses of Congress are perfectly free from all such impertinent and uncalled-for assumptions of "Jacks in office." In truth, the officials of every class in tho United States are as famous for their civility and attention as their contemporaries in England are for the reverse.

The House of Representatives is separated from the Senate by a large circular hall, called the Rotunda; but so conveniently placed, that the communication between the legislative bodies is simple and immediate.

The representative body, composed of about two hundred and forty members, does not give a stranger the idea of dignity or repose; as the constant and loud conversation is accompanied by a running fire of raps bestowed by honorable members on the desks before them, for the purpose of summoning the boys in attendance. These noises, coupled with the defective construction of the chamber, which causes five distinct echoes, render it necessary for the members to "roar again," if they intend to be audible. The consequence, as may be imagined, is an indescribable confusion of sounds; and the violent efforts of the orators to be heard, speedily excites them, particularly the Southern men, when the gesticulation at times becomes not only exaggerated, but absolutely ludicrous. I frequently heard abuse bandied about; such as, "I can not answer for that gentleman's obtuse intellect;" or, "I can not beat common sense into such a thick head," &c. Once, I regret to say, I heard "the lie" directly given. This outrage was answered by a greater outrage, in the shape of a rough push or blow. The belligerent parties were speedily separated, and order was restored, by all the members in the vicinity rushing forward to the rescue. The spectators were very indignant at this unseemly proceeding, especially as they knew that foreigners were spectators of the scene.

Toward the close of the session, great excitement is apt to be shown. This arises from the bad habit of procrastinating the Appropriation Bill and other important affairs to the last moment. It was said, by an American Senator, that more real business was transacted in fifteen minutes during the last two days, than for six weeks previously.

I listened with great interest to a speech by Mr. Toombs, one of the Representatives from Georgia. He was abusing the Army Appropriation Bill, and trying to have it reduced. With great command of language, and the voice of a Stentor, he was ably denouncing the expenditure; but the House appeared utterly careless and inattentive, and conversation was going on as usual. The loud flaps of the members' books or hands were not discontinued for a moment. Onward bellowed the orator, in what might be fairly termed an able discourse, but still without any person appearing to listen to one word that was said. At length, he began to compare the cost of each individual soldier of the American army with the soldiers of the English army. "Look at Great Britain," urged he; "look at that vast and magnificent empire, on whose territories it may be truly said, without exaggeration, that the sun never sets." This was a lucky hit. Instantaneously the noise ceased. All tongues were hushed at the allusion to Great Britain; and the orator proceeded with his harangue amidst comparative silence. Several members who were seated behind him, and could not hear distinctly, changed their places, and came round in front. Soon a little crowd was collected on the floor of the House, anxious to hear every word.

"How comes it," said he, "that the soldier of the United States army costs at this moment one hundred and fifty dollars a year more than he did in 1840? How comes it that a soldier of the United States army costs, in California, one thousand dollars per annum? If it be necessary, we can afford ten, twenty, fifty, nay, a hundred millions of dollars; but I consider this enormous expense totally unnecessary. How comes it that the soldier of the United States army costs more by a considerable sum than the most costly soldier in the world—the British soldier? What are these men? They are all hired and foreign mercenaries."

On the Navy Appropriation Bill, a member, whose name I forget, attacked the navy in a bitter and hostile spirit. Among other undignified and unstatesmanlike vituperation, he used the term, "Grog-soaked lieutenants."

I turned to an officer of rank in the American navy, standing close to me, and asked him what the navy would say to such language.

"They won't care a cent about it," replied he; "it is all Buncome: besides, it is well known in our navy that the man who is talking in this manner had his ear bitten off by a rowdy, some time ago. I saw the whole proceeding; and as I held a large stick in my hand, could easily have saved his ear, by knocking the rowdy down. But, of course, I wouldn't, as he was always abusing the navy. We can well afford to laugh at such a man's talking to Buncome. It is to gain credit with his constituents, and to create what we call political capital."

From the 3d of March, at noon, both Chambers sat until noon of the 4th. As most of the undignified scenes alluded to took place during protracted sittings, allowances must be made for the attendant fatigue, and consequent excitement and exhaustion. The easy access; the want of forms and ceremonies; the extremely polite and dignified bearing of the spectators, command the attention and admiration of a stranger.

In the evenings, numerous gentlemen were solacing themselves with cigars. The passages outside both Chambers were crammed with these fumigators, which rendered the air any thing but pure or agreeable. As, however, the ladies who crowded the galleries did not object to it, no other person had any business to complain.

The society at Washington is of a very mixed character; not nearly so select as any other city in the Union. The hotels are very uncomfortable, in consequence of the crowding together of persons of uncongenial habits. It was here that I first perceived an instance of social impropriety. I am bound to confess, however, that the American ladies, seated at the table, and cognizant of the affair, were infinitely more put out than myself. *I* was simply amused; but Americans are extremely annoyed and irritated, particularly when English persons are present.

A very beautiful young woman, seated near the top of one of the long dinner-tables, suddenly commenced a conversation with another young lady on the opposite side, who was divided from her by several sitters. She was forced to elevate her voice into a scream, to drown the clatter of waiters, knives and forks, &c. After a discordant dialogue of some minutes' duration, perfectly audible to the whole room, she turned suddenly to the subject of matrimony.

"As for me," she screamed, "as for me, I won't even *look* at any man (I don't care who he is) over the age of twenty-three. Oh, my!"

She then subsided into silence; and I could not avoid looking with interest on that expressive, innocent, and beautiful countenance. In repose, she seemed a perfect angel; but the moment her exquisite little mouth opened, and the delicate coral lips parted, what a sound! The illusion was dispelled, and the fable of the peacock singing, was forcibly recalled to my mind.

The entertainments at Washington are upon a less ostentatious, but infinitely more common-sense plan, than those in New York. In the fashionable society of New York, a display of wealth appeared to be the end in view. In Washington, mind and manner were in greater estimation; and comfort and economy of living bore the palm. Among the most hospitable and agreeable houses was that of the British minister.

"Never before did I see," was the observation of a keen and distinguished American, "a hostess with such exquisite tact—such keen, though quiet and observant manner. Are all your English ladies so unremitting and attentive to their guests?"

No person should leave Washington without a good look at the Patent Office, which contains countless inventions of the 'cute Yankee mind. These pour in with such abundance, that already the space allotted to them is so completely crammed as to preclude the possibility of any close investigation. By the kindness of Professor Renwick, I was enabled to examine the celebrated sewing-machine, and was informed that it had made *seventeen pair of inexpressibles* in one day; the only assistance required being a little girl to hook on the cloth.

"Alas! alas!" the assistant exclaimed, "it has been so mauled about since the ladies heard of its wonderful performance, that it is quite deranged, and won't work!"

The suit of clothes, worn by Washington on resigning his

commission as General-in-chief, is to be seen in the museum. I can not admire the manner in which these relics are exhibited. They are hung up, much like "old clothes" in a Jew's shop, and quite destroy the feeling of reverence and dignity attached to any memorials of so great and good a man.

An Englishman ought not to pass through this room without inspecting the original "Declaration of Independence"—the Magna Charta of the North American continent. Let him read it carefully through, and reflect upon its contents. It may not be generally known that, in the rough draft, as originally drawn out, a complaint against the mother-country was set forth, which is omitted in the present document. As it formerly stood, the British Government was charged with having forced *slavery* on the colonies, in spite of their entreaties and remonstrances.

An ancient and worm-eaten oaken printer's press attracts the stranger's eye. It is the self-same at which Franklin worked in London upward of one hundred years ago.

CHAPTER VI.

WASHINGTON DOCK-YARD.

Present use of the Dock-yard—Facility with which Foreigners may penetrate its Recesses, contrasted with the Difficulties to be encountered in gaining Admission into English National Dock-yards—Chain and Anchor Factory—Anecdote—Chain-cables—Superiority of American Iron—New Model for Anchors—English Dock-yard "Matee"—American Artillery—Remarkable Contrast—The Shell Factory—Rapid Manufacture of Musket and Pistol-balls—The Ordnance Laboratory—Shell Fuses—Percussion Caps—Congreve Rockets—Conversation at a Naval and Military Dinner-party.

THE Dock-yard, or Navy-yard, as the Americans are fond of calling it, situated on the banks of the Potomac, one mile south of the Capitol, is not now used for building, or even repairing, vessels; but exclusively for manufacturing boilers, steam machinery, anchors, tanks, and all the iron and metal fittings required in their ships of war. Buildings are now in progress to facilitate the manufacture of the very excellent copper recently discovered on the shores of Lake Superior. An ordnance laboratory is likewise attached to the dock-yard. This branch, unlike the ordnance in England, belongs to one and the same department. No person can visit the yard without being struck by the admirable arrangement, the nice adaptation, the order and regularity, displayed at every step, and on all sides.

Nothing of interest being concealed, it is impossible that any stranger, particularly one accustomed to the dock-yards in England, can avoid surprise at the readiness with which he can penetrate into this "sanctum" of Uncle Sam. Let me first describe the ceremonies of an entrance I once made into the English dock-yard at Portsmouth, and then contrast it with my entrance into the establishment at Washington. On a fine May afternoon, I strolled down Common Hard to the dock-yard gates, accompanied by a member of the House of Commons. Although well-known there, and asserting my companion to be an M.P., we were not allowed to enter without considerable difficulty and delay. At length, after sundry questions and a demand for signatures, the policeman was satisfied; a card was delivered to us, and the "people's representative" was *allowed* to walk in.

Now mark the contrast. On a misty and very English morning in the month of February, '51, I marched along Pennsylvania Avenue on my way to the naval workshop of Washington. The road led me through the Capitol, where I will only pause for a moment, to admire the fine marble monument erected to the memory of Somers, Caldwell, Decatur, and the American officers killed at Tripoli. Passing over the crest of the Capitol hill, and gradually descending south, toward the banks of the Potomac, I approached the gates of the dock-yard, when my mind misgave me a little. "What," thought I, "would be the reception of an American naval officer, if *he* were to march, thus boldly, into the jaws of Portsmouth, Plymouth, or Sheerness? A pretty civil reception he would meet with, truly."

Somewhat abashed by this idea, I rather halted on nearing the gate, particularly as I perceived a huge, grey-coated sentinel with an unmistakable Milesian countenance, staring fixedly at me. Putting the best face on the matter, I boldly advanced, and addressed my gray friend as follows:

"Is the Commodore in the yard?"

Not receiving any answer, and the sentry looking very wise, or fierce, I could not say which, I repeated the question.

"Is the Commodore in the yard, sentry?"

Without returning any verbal reply, he leisurely inclined his head on the right shoulder. This I correctly interpreted into "Yes; go ahead, stranger." So on I went.

Marching straight down the yard, I inquired the way to the Commodore's office, and was directed there with the greatest civility. The yard is composed of about a dozen large houses or factories, and one wooden ship-building shed (the latter old and apparently obsolete.) These buildings are scattered somewhat irregularly about the yard, covering nearly twenty-four acres of land, with a considerable frontage on the Potomac.

Let us first take the "chain-and-anchor" factory, and describe what is interesting and novel there. Before doing so, however, it may not be amiss to relate an anecdote told by a gallant Commodore in the American navy—a man who had a personal knowledge of Nelson and Bonaparte; and who is deservedly one of the most esteemed veterans in the service.

"Some years ago," said he, "I commanded one of our frigates. As we were going into Spithead, I unfortunately lost an anchor and chain. Of course I got it replaced at your dock-yard at Portsmouth. After a considerable stay, I sailed for Toulon, in France, and, by a curious coincidence, lost a second anchor and chain. Johnny Crapaud was as civil as John Bull, and immediately supplied me with another. On our return to the States, we determined to test the English chain and the French chain against one of ours of the same size. The trial took place at Boston, and resulted as follows. The Portsmouth chain gave out first; the French second; and the Yankee last."

It may be feared that some of the chain-cables served out to Her Majesty's ships are defective, in spite of the usual testing. This opinion is confirmed by my own experience. For instance, in the spring of 1830, the best bower of Her Majesty's ship "Childers," parted in the land-locked harbor of Cromartie, Scotland. Again, Her Majesty's ship, "Mastiff," August, 1847, was lying snugly moored in a bay, in the island of Sanday, Orkneys. At one o'clock, it was a dead calm. A heavy gale suddenly sprung up; and, although blowing off the land, the chains both parted in a few minutes. What makes this the more mysterious, is that, three days after, she rode out in quite as heavy a gale with her stream-anchor and chain. The sudden snapping of these three chains, with other reasons, might render one suspicious of all iron-work supplied from the Eastern Dock-yards.

The American iron, now furnished by contract, is found infinitely superior to any before used in Washington; a link of one and a half inch in diameter, of the new contract-iron, being found equal to a link two inches and an eighth of the old cables. In fact, so superior is the tenacity of the new iron, that the testing links were all broken on the first trial. There can be no doubt about the accuracy of this.

The model of anchors now manufactured in the United States yards, is an immense improvement on what is termed the "old establishment." The shank is much reduced in length, and more metal is used in the junction with the arms; thus strengthening the material part. The stock, likewise, is beginning to get credit in the States for holding power, bearing out the theory of Lieutenant Rogers, the patentee of the anchor of that name. The links of a chain-cable are all numbered. This, being a simple and easy process, under the forging hammer, and of obvious advantage to all naval men, ought to be generally adopted. The swivels for the largest moorings, are made so neat and compact, that they can be hove in through the ship's hawse-holes.

"And to whom do you suppose we are indebted for all these improvements, and many more too tedious to mention?" was the question put to me by my American chaperon. "Why, to an English dock-yard matee from Devonport. There he stands. Let me introduce you."

I was accordingly introduced, and found that my friend had been forty years in the Washington yard.

"He is worth 100,000 dollars," was whispered into my ear.

"Much more," I replied, "than he ever would have realized in Plymouth. What a lucky dog!"

Let us now examine the field and boat artillery. These admirable and exquisitely simple howitzer-guns are twelves and twenty-four pounders; the twelves averaging 750 cwt., and the twenty-fours 1300 cwt. It is impossible to describe the ease and celerity with which these guns are transferred from a boat's slide to a field carriage, and *vice versa*. At this time, the guns and slides and carriages were all lying in a confused mass on the floor of the store.

"Would you like to see the field-howitzer exercised?" was the polite offer made to me.

"Amazingly," I replied; "nothing better."

"Let us, then, walk down to the banks of the Potomac," continued my companion. And we leisurely advanced down the two hundred yards that separated us from the river. Before, however, the distance was passed, the twenty-four pound howitzer came racing after us, dragged by six, and pushed by two, dock-yard matees.

"Quick work," thought I, "quick work for matees."

"Now, sir, take out your watch, and mark time while they fire. Mind how you point her," added the Commodore, addressing the men; "see the shot don't hit that sloop in the bend. Now then, begin."

"These dock-yard matees are a pretty smart set of sailor chaps, I guess," said I. "Why, there were four discharges within thirty seconds; two shots were ricochetting at the same moment."

The intelligent officer who constructed these admirable field carriages, as well as many other ordnance improvements, was rewarded for his exertions the same day by a vote of Congress which secured to him one thousand five hundred dollars per annum extra.

Curveting at a sharp run round an old anchor, lying on the ground, the howitzer disappeared at a rapid pace. I am very much mistaken if this was not the simplest and most effective field-piece in the world—still more mistaken if the *majority* of the crew were not brought up in an English man-of-war.

These guns are cast from copper procured from Lake Superior. It is asserted that this metal is a considerable per centage more adhesive and tough than any other copper known.

A remarkable contrast was afforded in comparing this gun with one lying close by. The latter unsightly abortion was cast in England in 1777, and sent out to Cornwallis to assist in coercing Washington and the American colonies. Its exceeding ugliness merits a short description. Length, two feet ten inches. Ten inch bore, with several reinforce rings. Weight, about nine cwt. It is now looked upon more as if it were an antediluvian curiosity than a trophy. There is not the slightest chance of its ever coming into use again.

Let us now proceed to the shell-factory.

The first thing that strikes one is, that Brother Jonathan has succeeded in casting the "bushing" or case of fuse into the shell itself. This is a novel and extremely economical invention; and is a desideratum that all the "warlike powers of Europe" have been racking their brains for, this "many a year." The Yankees can not, however, manage it in any shell larger than a twelve pounder.

In this department, two men are employed, compressing musket and pistol balls with astonishing celerity. The lead is prepared in rods, about two feet long, and rapidly passed through a compressor. The usual day's work is twenty-five thousand; of course more than the present consumption.

The Ordnance Laboratory now was thrown open to my view, and fully kept pace with the other admirable arrangements for which our American brethren are so celebrated.

The uniformity with which the shell-fuses were pressed and filled, is extraordinary. A machine presses the composition gradually down, until the weight is 300 lbs. A bell then rings, giving notice to the operator, who is thus enabled to fill the fuse with exactly equal strength throughout. The percussion-caps, after completion, are covered with a coat of varnish, of such a nature that they resist the effect of soaking in water for many hours. The English and French caps are said to be useless after being immersed two hours. All the cartridges, in packages of a dozen, are likewise covered with a coating of the same varnish; this keeps them serviceable even after being under water. Cromwell's advice to his troopers has not been lost upon Jonathan: "Trust in the Lord, and keep your powder dry."

Congreve rockets, without sticks, are likewise used. They are so constructed that the back fire in escaping gives a rotatory motion, and thus keeps them in a direct line, without requiring the balance of a stick or bar behind. The rotatory motion must, however, greatly diminish their range from the lateral direction of the back fire. The cases are filled by means of an hydraulic press, capable of exerting a pressure of from seventy-five to eighty tons.

At a large dinner-party, the following day, composed of naval, ordnance, and scientific authorities, the conversation turned on the free and ready admission of foreigners to the American dock-yards, arsenals, &c.

"Your liberality is great," said I, "to permit an officer of a foreign service, like myself, to examine so minutely the interior of these establishments."

"Not so great as you imagine," replied an ordnance authority, "although we Americans know full well, that *you* do not allow such access to *yours*."

"Why then do you disavow your liberality?" I inquired.

"I will tell you," he replied. "It is a very simple affair; you will see it in a moment. We have accurate *descriptions*, and, what is more, *models*, of every thing of consequence in your dock-yards and arsenals. As *we* can procure these, we have no doubt that the English Government can do the same with regard to ours. In fact, we *know* they can. With this conviction, it would be only waste of time and money to endeavor to prevent that which is as inevitable as water finding its own level. You are at perfect liberty to examine into, and take notes of, any thing you please. We have no concealments; or, at least, very few indeed."

"This appears simple enough," I observed, "and in accordance with common-sense. But, although I don't doubt your assertion in the least, I should like you to produce some evidence to prove the fact of your possession of this knowledge."

"Let me see," said my Ordnance friend, pondering for a moment. "I have it, I have it, in one of the gunnery-books of questions and answers in use in her Majesty's ship 'Excellent.'

"The devil!" exclaimed I; "how did *you* get hold of that?"

"There is one proof, at any rate," continued my friend; "but in that book there is a question, No. 18, that has not received a satisfactory or correct answer. At least, it is not considered satisfactory or correct by our ordnance officers."

"Pray let me hear all about it," I exclaimed.

"Certainly," answered my intelligent informant; "I have great pleasure in doing so; particularly as it will tend to elucidate the truth—the great point we both have in view. The question runs thus:—'Are there any disadvantages in too great windage?' Answer,—'The deflection as well as the variation in the ranges of shot fired with the same charges and elevation, is partly attributable to the windage; for the shot, on its quitting the gun, is liable to strike against the sides of the bore. If the right side be the last part struck, the deflection will be to the left. If the under part, the range will be increased and *vice versa.*' In this answer to No. 18, you will therefore perceive that, although the word '*partly*' seems to recognize other causes of deflection and variation of range, the paramount or overruling cause is overlooked altogether. Certainly, the last blow of the ball at the mouth of the gun will have its influence, *for a time*, on the flight of the shot; but a variety of careful experiments have shown that the principal cause of deflection and variation of range, is attributable to want of uniformity in the density of the metal, inasmuch as very few, if any spherical projectiles have the centre of figure and the centre of gravity in the same point. From this circumstance, whatever may be the other causes of deflection, the shot or shell, on leaving the bore, assumes a rotary movement (the centre of figure revolving round the centre of gravity) the effect of which is to bring the *resistance of the air* in a direction more or less oblique with regard to the action of the powder, and thus produce greater or less deviation.

"In 1813, and since that time, numerous experiments have been made at Washington and elsewhere, which establish the governing cause of deflection beyond doubt. For example:—shells have been cast *positively* eccentric, and other methods have been resorted to, to give different degrees of eccentricity to shot. At our naval and experimental battery, where nice practice is required in ascertaining the ranges of guns, each projectile is floated in a bucket of quicksilver, by which means its preponderating part is ascertained. The shot or shell is then *spotted* at this point, and strapped to a wooden bottom, so as to place the heavy part in a uniform position, and avoid as much as possible the errors arising from variation in the position of the centre of gravity. I can assure you, from personal experience, that, by altering the position of the heavy side of a shot in its *sabot*, and carefully pushing it home, I can invariably predict the side of the target on which it will pass. Of course, this could not be done if the deviations were principally, or even materially, affected by the last blow of the ball on its leaving the bore. Mind you, I do not mean this as a criticism on the 'Excellent's' practice; it is more as a philosophical nicety than a point of great practical importance."

"Thank you," I replied. "You have at any rate proved that you procure as much information as you require from us Britishers. Pray what conclusions have you come to on this subject?"

"I will give you," answered my well informed American gunnery-officer, "a brief summary of the conclusions we have come to on this side of the Atlantic:

"First; if the centre of gravity of a projectile be in a vertical plane *above* the axis of the bore, its position will be the most favorable of any for length of range, and its lateral deviation will be diminished.

"Second; if the centre of gravity be placed *below the axis*, the range is uniformly less than that given by placing it in any other position.

"Third; if the centre of gravity be placed in a horizontal plane on the right or left of the axis of the bore, the effect is injurious to the range, and the ball will deflect to the right or left according to the position of its weight. The exceptions in lateral divergence are in the first graze of ricochet firing. Here, the striking of the ball probably influences the flight of the shot for a *short time*, and in cases where its eccentricity is not great. It is somewhat remarkable, that, although the law of deflection is known to the French artillerists (the theory being noticed and explained by Thioury), nothing is said about it in the publication of their experiments. In the *Manuel de Matelot Cannonier* (their gunnery catechism), the question is asked and answered much the same as in the 'Excellent's' exercises.

"In conclusion, I shall be extremely happy to exchange ideas with you on nautical subjects, in which sort of commerce, you know, we Yankees rather incline to free-trade principles."

"Thank you heartily," I rejoined, and concluded the conversation.

It is quite clear, from these facts and others that came under my notice, that the jealous restrictions at the Dock-yards in England, are equally ridiculous, useless, and annoying.

CHAPTER VII.

DOCK-YARD AT BOSTON.

The Dry Dock—The "Virginia," the "Franklin," the "Vermont" and the "Ohio"—Speech of Charles Sumner, Senator from Massachusetts—A few Words for Yankee Ears.

The Dock-yard at Boston, comprising eighty-five acres, is situated on a point of land at the confluence of the Charles and Mystic rivers. The dry dock is eighty-four feet broad, and two hundred and eighty-five feet long. Most of the rope used in the United States navy, is made here in a rope-walk twelve hundred feet long, and fitted with admirable machinery. Two building-sheds are also here, capable of covering first-class ships. In one of these is the "Virginia," 74, but mounting 80 guns. She is now nearly finished, but has been twenty years on the stocks Anchored in the Charles River are three fine two-deckers: the "Franklin," 74; "Vermont," 74; and "Ohio," 74. All these ships can mount upward of 80 guns of the heaviest calibre.

An American authority, the "Boston Courier" thus describes "three great ships of the line" under the head of Naval Intelligence.

"There are now in this harbor," says the Journal, "three great ships of the line: the 'Ohio,' the 'Vermont,' and the 'Virginia.' Each one them may be said to be remarkable for its model, its size, and accommodations; the excellence of the materials of which it is composed, its strength and fitness for sea and battle. They are called seventy-fours, but are capable of carrying one hundred and ten guns each, together with a complement of one thousand men, and all the provisions, stores, and munitions for a three years' cruise, not omitting twenty tons of powder for each vessel. These costly and splendid floating citadels are all at the navy-yard in Charlestown, under the command of the officers there; and never fail to attract the attention of strangers, and others in the Chelsea ferry-boats and other vessels plying in the upper harbor.

"Of such ample depth is the water in this navy-yard, that these immense line-of-battle ships can lie at its wharfs at low tide, without touching bottom; and indeed sail directly from the wharf with all hands on board, completely armed and provisioned for any voyage."

Such is the magnificence of some of the naval establishments in the United States. Yet though Americans can not but be proud of so unequivocal a display of power and grandeur, it is certain that public feeling among them is not wholly absorbed by the maritime and military might of the Confederation, but that they look with an anxious eye to the improvement of their universities, and other institutions tending to the elevation of intellect in science, art, and literature.

In one of the speeches of Charles Sumner, Senator from Massachusetts, the Republican orator utters the following noble sentiments:

"Within a short distance of this city (Boston) stands an institution of learning, which was one of the earliest cares of the early forefathers of the country: the conscientious English Puritans. Favored child of an age of trial and struggle, carefully nursed through a period of hardship and anxiety, endowed at that time by the oblations of men like Harvard, sustained from its first foundation by the paternal arm of the Commonwealth, by a constant succession of munificent bequests, and by the prayers of all good men, the University at Cambridge now invites our homage as the most ancient, the most interesting, and the most important seat of learning in the land; possessing the oldest and most valuable library—one of the largest museums ot mineralogy and natural history—a School of Law, which annually receives into its bosom more than one hundred and fifty sons from all parts of the Union, where they listen to instruction from professors whose names have become among the most valuable possessions of the land—a School of Divinity, the nurse of true learning and piety—one of the largest and most flourishing Schools of Medicine in the country; besides these, a general body of teachers, twenty-seven in number, many of whose names help to keep the name of the country respectable in every part of the globe, where science, learning, and taste are cherished: the whole presided over at this moment by a gentleman, early distinguished in public life by his unconquerable energies and his masculine eloquence, at a later period, by the unsurpassed ability with which he administered the affairs of our city, and now in a green old age, full of years and honors, preparing to lay down his present high trust:* such is Harvard University; and, as one of the humblest of her children, happy in the recollection of a youth nurtured in her classic retreats, I can not allude to her without an expression of filial affection and respect.

"It appears from the last Report of the Treasurer, that the whole available property of the University, the various accumulations of more than two centuries of generosity, amounts to 703,175 dollars (equal to about £140,000).

"Change the scene, and cast your eyes upon another object. There now swings idly at her moorings, in this harbor, a ship of the line, the 'Ohio,' carrying ninety guns, finished as late as 1836 for 547,888 dollars; repaired only two years afterward, in 1838, for $223,012; with an armament which has cost $53,945; making an amount of 834,845 dollars as the actual cost at this moment of that single ship; more than $100,000 beyond all the

* Hon. Josiah Quincy.

available accumulations of the richest and most ancient seat of learning in the land! Choose ye, my fellow-citizens of a Christian state, between the two caskets—that wherein is the loveliness of knowledge and truth, or that which contains the carrion death. I refer thus particularly to the 'Ohio,' because she happens to be in our waters. But in so doing I do not take the strongest case afforded by our navy. Other ships have absorbed still larger sums. The expense of the 'Delaware,' in 1842, had been 1,051,000 dollars. Pursue the comparison still further. The expenditure of the University during the last year, for the general purposes of the College, the instruction of the undergraduates, and for the Schools of Law and Divinity, amount to 46,949 dollars. The cost of the 'Ohio' for one year in service, in salaries, wages, and provisions, is $220,000; being 175,000 dollars more than the annual expenditures of the University—*more than four times as much.*

"In other words, for the annual sum which is lavished on one ship of the line, *four* institutions like Harvard University, might be sustained throughout the country!

"Still further let us pursue the comparison. The pay of the Captain of a ship like the 'Ohio,' is 4500 dollars when in service; $3500 when on leave of absence, or off duty. The salary of the President of the Harvard University is 2205 dollars, without leave of absence, and never being off duty."

I will conclude this slight sketch of a hasty trip to the four great sea-board cities, with a few words, intended solely for Yankee ears, on the price and quality of wine at the hotels, particularly at those of Washington. I can not imagine why, with such admirably conducted and enormous hotels; with such swarms of intelligent travelers; with such convenient common-sense arrangements in all the usual affairs of life in America, there should be one great fault; namely, the enormous price fleeced from travelers for very indifferent wine. Stuff, which in

England, with her enormous duties, would be dear at half-a-crown a bottle, is charged in the United States at from a dollar and a half (the lowest price) up to twelve dollars. And then, forsooth, the Yankees often boast of the price, and appear to think the extravagant cost a feather in their caps—something to be proud of—something to elevate themselves and country!

I have bought much better Cape Madeira in New York for two dollars and a half a gallon, than I have known a Yankee Boniface to supply at *five* dollars a bottle. I can not, for the life of me, understand how Jonathan can allow himself to be so gulled. Certes, he is green and soft on this point, or he would not be thus over-reached.

JOURNEY TO THE REMOTE SETTLEMENTS.

CHAPTER I.

The "Reindeer" Steamer—The Hudson Railroad Train *versus* Steamer—My Yankee Companions—Scenery on the Shores of the Hudson—Arrival at Albany—Unparalleled Facility of Intercommunication—Prodigious Traffic on the Hudson—Magnificence of the River Steamers—Permanent Residence of Families on Board the Steamers—Arrival at Utica—Interview with Mr. Fillmore, the President of the United States—Absence of Pomp—Mistaken "Independence"—Plank Roads—Trenton Falls—Lake Ontario—Approach to Niagara—The "meanest Railway in Creation"—"Snake-heads"—The "Maid of the Mist" and the Yankee Skipper—A violent Squall—Suspension-bridge below the Falls.

"Hie for the far West!" was my exclamation, as I walked aboard a beautiful and fleet steamer—the "Reindeer"—which was receiving her living freight for Albany.

While bustling passengers were hurriedly looking after the safety of their luggage, I hastily scanned the vessel and the surrounding scenery. The vessel was upward of three hundred feet long, and fitted up in the most elegant and useful manner. She was lying alongside a wharf in the North or Hudson River. The exquisite vegetation clothing the shores, and nearly concealing the villas of Hoboken, on the opposite banks of the river, formed a pleasing contrast to the busy hum on the New York side.

At seven o'clock exactly, the steamer shot out from her wharf, and began her rapid career. In spite of a strong adverse tide and wind, she appeared to fly past the land at railway pace. As I was hugging myself at her prodigious speed (sixteen miles an hour against the tide, according to my calculation, or, in still water, at least twenty), I was exceedingly mortified to see the train of the Hudson River Railroad overhauling us with great celerity. When the train was abeam of the steamer, it slackened pace to take up passengers at a station; and after a short pause, again proceeded, not only recovering the ground it had lost by the stoppage, but speedily ranging ahead of the steamer. At length, it shot round a point of land, and vanished from sight, with a hoarse and insulting scream. So much for the fastest steamer against the "iron horse."

At eight o'clock, the passengers sat down to an excellent breakfast, for which half a dollar was charged.

On lighting my cigar, after the morning meal, I was speedily discovered to be a "Britisher." Nothing could exceed the politeness of my Yankee companions, when they found it was my first voyage up the Hudson. Information was kindly given on every interesting point, and my admiration was forestalled for the Highlands. I was nevertheless disappointed with this part of the Hudson, as the Highlands are not half so grand, either in height or abruptness, as the sides of Loch Ness in Scotland.

Having been led to suppose that, after passing this part, the scenery would become tame and uninteresting, I was agreeably disappointed. The land undulates in an ever-varying and most pleasing manner, and is evidently depreciated by the Americans in the same proportion as the Highlands are over-valued.

A small party was assembled on the fore part of the upper deck, unsheltered from the wind. This attracted my attention, as Americans always carefully avoid fresh air, apparently deeming it poisonous. On a further inspection, I found the group to be "Britishers;" and, as they are always more sociable abroad than at home, I speedily became acquainted with them.

At four o'clock P.M. we arrived at Albany, having been nine hours in going one hundred and forty-five miles, against wind and tide.

The Hudson River is one of the first great links in the stupendous chain of inland transport. I say *one* of the great links, as several other lines of communication will soon be opened to Lake Erie, and share in the vast and unparalleled intercommunication. Well may it excite feelings of wonder, that, in a brief space of time, a goodly vessel may start from either New York or Quebec, almost circumnavigate the United States, and emerge from the Mississippi into the Gulf of Mexico. Two channels will soon be opened to the Mississippi for this purpose; one, already navigable from Chicago, on Lake Michigan; another, the best and shortest, through Green Bay, Lake Winnebago, and the Wisconsin River.

The enormous traffic on the Hudson is almost entirely monopolized by steamers; and there can be no sort of doubt that they are the swiftest and best arranged steam vessels known. The speed and size are improving so rapidly, that what is correct now, may be far behind the mark a year hence. The "Isaac Newton" is at present the largest river-steamer. She is three hundred and thirty-three feet long, forty feet beam. The saloon, which is gorgeously decorated, is one hundred yards long. In this vast, vaulted apartment, the huge mirrors elegant carving, and profuse gilding absolutely dazzle the eye. On first entering one of these magnificent floating saloons, it is difficult for the imagination to realize its position. All comparison is at once defied, as there is nothing equal afloat in the world. The old and slow boats are used for towing the commerce of the river, barges and canal-boats swarm about one of these vessels like bees round their queen. I have counted from fourteen to twenty vessels clinging in tiers to all parts of their concealed conductor. The funnels, and the queer-looking motion of the beam, are the only locomotive appearance visible through this shroud of canal-boats.

It is a very common occurrence, during hot weather, for families to reside permanently on board the steamers; thus enjoying the fresh air and changing scenery of their locomotive house, and avoiding the dullness of a stationary hotel on the bank of the river. A family can reside permanently on board, with a separate cabin and every luxury of living, including a voyage of one hundred and fifty miles, for about ten shillings a-head per diem. This is certainly the cheapest and best traveling in the world.

On arriving at Albany, I took the railway cars for Utica (ninety-three miles), and was safely deposited at Baggs' Hotel, in four and half hours. The house appeared remarkably quiet; and I was not aware, until the following morning, that the President himself—the head of the American nation—was in the hotel. Mr. Fillmore had stopped there since the previous evening, to rest and recruit after the festivities attending the opening of the great Erie Railroad. Nothing could exceed the calmness and placidity of the people. It was impossible to believe that the Chief Magistrate of so great a nation was among them.

As I was proceeding out of the front door, to engage a carriage for Trenton Falls, I was politely accosted by an American gentleman.

"The President," said he, "will receive this morning, Sir. Would you like to be presented?"

"Very much," I replied. Then, looking aghast at my shooting-jacket and careless costume, I added: "But will not this dress prevent my having that honor?"

"Not at all," replied the stranger who had accosted me; "your dress is quite good enough This is a free country. Come along. Let me introduce you to the Mayor of Utica, Colonel Hinman."

I was then led by the Colonel to the reception room. For some minutes, I was unaware that I had arrived in the presence of the President. About twenty grave-looking citizens were standing together, without the slightest ceremony. A voice at length exclaimed: "Please, Gentlemen, those who have been presented to the President, move on."

This bidding was followed by a grave and silent movement to the door. My turn at length came; and I had the great honor of shaking hands with Mr. Fillmore, who addressed me in a manner full of natural dignity.

"I am extremely sorry," said he, "that I was unable to receive you at Washington," alluding to a death in his family, which stopped his receptions.

The President is a portly man, with frank and simple manners. His countenance bears strong indications of amiability and kindness of heart.

On turning to retire, I was invited to remain, and gladly took advantage of the opportunity. The good citizens continued to pour in without the slightest bustle or confusion. Occasionally, a lady appeared; and all grasped the President's hand in a hearty and affectionate manner.

As this was the first time I had ever beheld such a sight, I looked on with intense interest. Although there was a considerable crowd, and no police, the utmost order and regularity prevailed. In the course of my experience, I never beheld so courteous and well-conducted a crowd, altogether forming a strong contrast to the demeanor of the "brilliant mob" in a similar ceremony in England. The only "military pomp" perceptible, was a military man at each door. These soldiers, who had quite enough to do in accommodating themselves and weapons to the pressure of the crowd, were infinitely more solicitous to assist the entrance of people than to bar them out. The ceremony lasted about an hour; after which, the President, taking the arms of two of the principal inhabitants of Utica, walked quietly down to the railroad-station, without the slightest fuss or parade.

This scene gave me a high sense of the propriety and self-possession of the American people. "Here," thought I, "is dignity without servility; a due sense of the people's own position, with a proper respect for their chief magistrate."

But a contrast was at hand. A few weeks later, I was standing among a large crowd in the principal street of Newport, Rhode Island, waiting to see the President, who had just arrived, pass by.

In a short time, an open carriage and pair approached, containing the President, bareheaded, and three gentlemen, likewise bareheaded. I gazed fixedly at his amiable and open countenance, and involuntary took off my hat, and made a low bow. Closely scanning the crowd, I was surprised to perceive that only one individual (an English boy) had the good feeling, or good manners, to remove his hat in token of respect to this bareheaded, dignified man—this head of a nation of so many millions!

Americans! This is said "more in sorrow than in anger." It is an occasional fault among you to sacrifice deference and consideration to false ideas of independence and dignity. I could not help thinking that the vilest and most ignorant rabble in Europe would, in point of politeness, have shamed this enlightened and grave crowd of American citizens. Incidents like these tempt ill-natured, short-sighted travelers to accuse the people of the United States of rude intention and ignorance, the more to be lamented as it arises merely from a morbid fear of looking servile or time-serving; for there was not a single person in that crowd who would not fiercely resent the slightest disrespect on the part of a foreigner to their President.

As Utica is only twelve miles from Trenton Falls, I determined to visit them. Great was my astonishment, on starting, to find how easily and swiftly my carriage rolled through the thick mud. At length curiosity prevailed; and I asked the driver the reason.

"I guess it's the plank road," said he. My eyes were immediately opened. As plank roads are now playing a very important part in the settlement of the West, I shall give a full account of them presently.

Trenton Falls disappointed me; my expectations had been highly excited by sanguine and enthusiastic Yankee friends.

Two hours and a half on the railway cars, the following morning, carried me to Syracuse through Rome. Here we left the Buffalo railroad, and entered the Oswego line. An hour and three quarters brought us to Oswego, on Lake Ontario, where conveyances were ready to take passengers and baggage free of expense on board the steamer. A very few minutes sufficed for this operation; and the magnificent steamer stood out on Lake Ontario, bound to Niagara Falls. A strong breeze and heavy sea somewhat retarded the vessel's speed; but the next morning, at five o'clock, after a thirteen hours' passage, including a stoppage at Genesee River, she was safely moored at Lewiston wharf. The travelers and their effects were transferred to what a tall Yankee described as "the meanest railway in creation." After a painful toil of an hour and a half, doing nine miles, the train at length came in sight of the Great Niagara.

With earnest haste, I thrust my head out of the car to catch a glimpse. An envious cluster of trees for the moment interrupted my gaze; I saw enough, however, to show that the train was in disagreeable proximity to the side of the precipice. My head was within a few inches of the edge of a crumbling cliff, peering over a fearful abyss.

To write about, or attempt to give, an adequate idea of Niagara, is impossible. I will content myself with describing (for the comfort of future visitors) the afore-mentioned "meanest railway in creation," with a few remarks upon its adjuncts, and my own personal encounter with Niagara itself.

First, the railway. From the single glimpse caught *en passant*, I determined to inspect it narrowly from the Falls to the suspension-bridge, and found that many of the sleepers are rotten, and the rail wedged in loosely with rotten wood. Several of the spike-nails, which ought to bind the strip of iron rail to the wood foundation, have worked out. Some of the ends of the rail are altogether loose, and raised up half an inch and more. These, I believe, are technically termed in Yankee language, "snake-heads." Fortunately, the speed is *no* speed, being only about ten or twelve miles an hour. At the edge of the precipice at this point, some one hundred and fifty feet high, I attempted, with a large stone, to drive the end of the rail firmly down. Vain were all my efforts, as the spike-nail was driven into decayed wood. I measured the distance of this part from the edge of the cliff, and found it barely two feet six. So careless and reprehensible a state of things admits of no excuse. The cars are usually crammed with passengers, not one of whom would ever trust his life to such "tender mercies," if he had investigated the road as carefully as I did.

The "Maid of the Mist" is a little steamer, about one hundred tons, whose limited sphere of action lies between the foot of the Falls and the narrow chasm which forms the rapids before tumbling into the whirpool—a distance of barely two thousand five hundred yards. Before describing my adventure under the Falls, it may be well to observe that the rush of water through the contracted passage or chasm, is intensely exciting. The whirlpool—so much vaunted—is not to be compared to Coryvreckan in Scotland; the Swelkie of Stroma, in the Pentland Firth; or many places in the Race of Alderney. The whirlpool is apparently a tame, exhausted, and sluggish movement of the fatigued element, after the "eternal catastrophe," to use a Yankeeism, of the appalling leap of Niagara.

The "Maid of the Mist" was lashed alongside the Yankee shore, a short distance above the suspension-bridge, which crosses the river about a mile and a half below the Falls. A party of twenty embarked in her, all in high glee to get close to the mighty "squash." Pushing off from the banks, she struggled up the stream, carefully taking advantage of the eddy along shore. I was highly amused at the Yankee skipper's account, to his anxious and excited passengers, of the strength of the current. All were desirous of carrying home every tittle of wonder they could gather.

"I guess," answered the Captain to one of the numerous questions, "I guess that the current runs fourteen knots."

This was swallowed by the passengers, many of whom were taking notes.

"Pray, what is the speed of this boat?" inquired I.

"Twenty knots," was the prompt reply.

Down went this answer in the tablets, particularly of the Yankee passengers, who, with proud and elated looks, seemed resolved to circulate the fact far and wide, to the glorification of Niagara and of Yankeedom.

I am sorry to dispel the poetical illusion. The utmost speed of the current is *seven* knots; and of the "Maid of the Mist," perhaps eight or nine, though she is mightily assisted in her upward course by the eddies.

Upward climbed the steamer, slowly struggling against the descending waters. At length she approached the lesser, or American Fall. At this moment, the gentlemen, enveloped in waterproof dresses, ascended the raised deck or platform, to enjoy a close, and of course, clear and admirable view of the Fall. As I considered my feelings on this occasion were similar to those of my companions, I will describe them.

"Now then," thought I, being, in the elation of the moment, smitten with a mock-heroical vein, "I will stare this stupendous gutter out of countenance! I will emulate the eagle and the sun! I will gaze, and be satisfied!"

Gradually the vessel drew alongside the falling waters. I was afterward informed by an overlooker on the cliffs that we did not come within fifty yards. Suddenly a violent squall, filled with spray, struck the steamer, causing her to heel over. I was completely drenched; the waterproof garments being forced from my tight embrace. I could hardly breathe, and could see nothing. Forgetting Niagara, my whole thoughts were occupied in tightly clinging to the benches. And thus I passed the outer and least violent edge of the spray, which is caused by a turbulent wind, generated by the weight and power of the falling water, and confined, as far as I could judge, to about seventy-five yards from the base of the cliff.

The suspension-bridge below the Falls affords the best view of the *chasm-rapids*, and is well worth crossing. I was rather astonished at the extravagant charge (25 cents, equal to 1*s.* 1*d.*); and in consequence made inquiries about the cost of erection. It is but fair to give the public the benefit of this investigation, although I do not pledge myself to exactness. I am, however, very near the mark.

Capital subscribed, 25,000 dollars; equal to about £5000. The average daily receipts, all the year round (the excess in the summer making up the deficiency in winter), are—carriages, twelve, at half a dollar (2*s.* 2*d.*) each. This would make six dollars (£1 5*s.*) The gate-keeper informed me that the passenger-traffic was three times this amount. Total, twenty-four dollars per diem, or nearly five pounds; equal, roughly, to £1825, or 9125 dollars.

It is said that the architect only required five per cent. in money down, taking six per cent. for the remainder. If this is the case, the greedy proprietors divide something like £1542 per annum, on an outlay of £250; and, be it remembered, with a constantly increasing traffic. This is worth the attention of English capitalists, as another bridge might be built in a more attractive position, nearer the base of the Fall.

CHAPTER II.

Buffalo—Wonderful Growth of the Western States—Embark in a Steamer for Michigan—Thirteen hundred Emigrants for the Far West—Arrival at Detroit—Lake Steamers bribed by the Michigan Central Railway—Statistics of the Lake Trade—Irish Emigrants—An American Settler in the Far West—Population of Detroit—Insane Spirit of Speculation—Extraordinary judicial Trial at Detroit.

From the Falls to Buffalo, the distance is twenty-two miles. Buffalo is the great port where the majority of emigrants concentrate to go to the fertile plains of the West, and it is one of the most extraordinary places on the face of the earth. The number of emigrants from this spot can not be well estimated, but a high authority has calculated that it could not be less than one million of human beings per annum, and still it is increasing. This gives some idea of the enormous growth of the Western States. I believe that the greatest emigration in ancient times was that of the Jews from Egypt. This emigration amounted, in the whole, to six hundred thousand adult men, or, perhaps, with women and children together, about two million; but here was an *annual* emigration of one million, and it is increasing year by year. It is likely, by-and-by, to increase to two million per annum. My great object was to get into the stream of emigration, and I went early in the morning to Buffalo, and took my passage in one of the largest steamers plying between Buffalo and Michigan. When I went on board at three o'clock in the afternoon, there were no less than five hundred passengers on board; and I had an admirable cabin, and large four-post bed in it, with a large window looking out on the sea. I thought that five hundred passengers must be a large cargo, but until nine at night they still continued coming in, and I was told that about thirteen hundred were on board. They were principally emigrants from Europe, who had concentrated from Boston, New York, Philadelphia, and other seaport cities; and at ten o'clock at night we sailed. I saw nine other steamers pass out before us, all apparently as crammed as we were. We arrived at Detroit, a distance of three hundred miles, at four o'clock the next evening; and in the meantime I ascertained something about these emigrants. A great number were from Ireland, very few from England, but many Norwegians, Germans and Dutch, and a great number from the Eastern States, Maine, New Hampshire, Massachusetts, and Connecticut; for they fancied that the climate and soil in the Western States was so much better than their own, that they had better leave a place where there was hardly elbow room, and repair to another where they could make their fortunes. Thus, it was not only the emigration from Europe, but that from the Eastern States, which caused the Western States to rise so rapidly.

I was informed that several of the finest lake steamers, which last year daily started to go round the great chain of lakes, namely, Erie, Huron, and Michigan, a distance of one thousand miles, had been bought off with a bribe of 70,000 dollars, by the Michigan Central Railway; whose interests were much improved by the stopping of the boats at their eastern terminus, Detroit.

A brief account of the lake trade will give some interesting particulars.

The following table, derived from an official source, affords a good idea of the magnitude of a portion of the internal trade of the United States. "The aggregate valuation of our lake trade," says the above-named document, "for the year 1850 (imports and exports) amounts, it will be seen, to the large sum of 186,-484,905 dollars; or more, by 40,000,000 dollars, than the whole foreign export trade of the country."

The aggregate tonnage employed on the lakes of the United States is equal to 203,041 tons, of which 167,137 tons is American, and 35,904 tons British. The commerce on Lakes Erie, Huron, Michigan, Ontario, Champlain, and St. Clair is as follows:

TOTAL VALUE OF EXPORTS AND IMPORTS.

	Dollars.		Dollars.
Erie	115,785,048	Ontario	28,141,000
Huron	848,152	Champlain	16,750,700
Michigan	24,320,481	St. Clair	639,524

Showing a total value of 186,484,905 dollars, as above stated. To this must be added the passenger trade of the lakes, valued at 1,000,000 dollars.

The aggregate value of the tonnage of:

	Dollars.
Lake Erie is	5,308,085
Lake Huron	75,000
Lake Michigan	564,435

The mind is lost in astonishment at so prodigious a commerce. It is not ten years since the first steamer ran round the chain of lakes. Population, and its commercial concomitants, are increasing so rapidly, that before twenty years the lake trade alone will be of greater extent and importance, than the whole trade of any other nation on the globe!

During the voyage I questioned several of the emigrants. Most of the natives and Canadians were bound for Wisconsin, Illinois, and Iowa. The Irish appeared uncertain and wayworn, and were huddled up in squalid masses, looking, as usual, utterly wretched.

Among the numerous stalwart rifle-bearers, I was much struck with the appearance of one, who, eighteen years ago, had shouldered his rifle, taking his young wife by the hand, and gone into the woods of Michigan.

"I have a nice farm now," said he; "but we still live in the settler's log-house. You will, however, have a hearty welcome, when you come, and the sooner the better."

In the course of conversation I found he was returning from the East, with some beautiful merino sheep. For four of these animals, which he had imported from France, he had paid 1000 dollars. This gentleman (for gentleman he was, both in manner and education) is a favorable specimen of the rising class of American farmers. Mr. Gale, of Ypsilanti, may, therefore, be taken as a type of what a great statesman calls "the ballast of the United States," or the educated and intelligent small landowners.

The population of the city of Detroit has increased, during the last ten years, from eleven thousand to twenty-six thousand; an advance which is mainly owing to the facilities afforded by the Michigan Central Railroad, for concentrating the emigrants from many routes on their way to the West. An absurd spirit of speculation has likewise contributed to the increase. Land, for building-lots, is now valued at higher prices than a city ten times as large could warrant. This spirit of speculation is now the curse of the Western States. Five years ago, the land in question was quite as well situated for building upon as at present; it has, however, increased from thirty dollars a lot to a thousand. So great an inflation and imaginary value, cause individuals to fancy themselves enormously wealthy. If pushed for money they will borrow at 10 and 12 per cent per annum. Nay, I have known from 4 to 8 per cent per *month* given to enable parties to hold lots, which will not be available as productive property for many years to come.

This mania is now (May, 1851) raging furiously all over the Union; but the chief madness appears to dwell in the far West. A fearful crash must ensue. In some parts, the farming lands are enveloped in the vortex of rash schemes; and so insane are some of the proprietors, that they have actually borrowed money at enormous interest for further speculations. The madness is similar (but with less foundation) to the railway mania in London of '45 and '46; and will be followed by as bad, if not worse results. I do not think the explosion can be far distant, as the absurd prices to which land has risen, is scaring the stream of emigration from the territory so cursed. The speculators are committing suicide with a vengeance. The only salvation for these speculators is the continued increase of vast swarms of emigrants, with money, from Europe, which may be the case, as a far superior and more wealthy class is beginning to appreciate the advantages to be derived from the rich alluvial plains of Wisconsin, Iowa, and other Western States.

During my brief stay at Detroit a singular trial was in progress; so singular and altogether unprecedented, that I could not refrain from attending the Court.

It appeared that an individual had conceived some spite against the newly opened Michigan Central Railway. To glut his violent and deadly animosity, he determined to destroy the whole concern, passengers and all; and, in the prosecution of his purpose, he formed a secret society of villains to the number of fifty-two. So skillfully was this society managed, that, for two years, the members were enabled to bid defiance to the law, although the existence of the infamous gang was well known. During this period they committed a series of depredations, such as burning the railway dépôt at Detroit, valued at upward of £20,000, and placing obstructions on the line, in hope of killing the passengers, in order to ruin the railway.

At length, the railway proprietors attacked them with their

own weapons, and got several shrewd officials to threaten vengeance for some imaginary grievance. The bait took with the gang, who, determined once again to burn down the newly-erected dépôt, entered into communication with some of the officials. After a long and cautious negotiation, the conspirators decided to admit one of the apparently disaffected officials into the gang, if he proved himself worthy such an honor. The test of his worth was, to burn down one of the buildings of the railroad company.

Having first communicated with the Directors, the building was set on fire ; but precautions had been taken to prevent any damage. An alarm was nevertheless bruited abroad, far and near.

The gang now considered their new associate sufficiently implicated to be part of themselves ; and, the proprietors speedily becoming acquainted with the names of all the conspirators, the whole gang, numbering fifty-two persons, were apprehended and thrown into prison. Among them were several, who up to this time had borne high characters, and were esteemed by their neighbors as persons of influence and consideration. All sorts of diabolical instruments were found ; principally to blow up trains, passengers and all.

Such blind and infernal wickedness in a civilized country is difficult to believe, or even imagine.

As the ramifications of this conspiracy extended far and wide, it was difficult to ascertain the real facts ; but some persons asserted, with an appearance of truth, that the conspirators felt aggrieved because their cattle and horses had been killed by the locomotives, and wanted not only payment for the cattle destroyed, but a bribe or indemnification of 100,000 dollars (£20,000), to withdraw their hostility. Others went still further, and actually took their part ! I was not much surprised at the latter, as I was once accidentally present at a serenade given to a notorious swindler, on his wriggling out of the hands of justice. This man, who had cheated several brokers in Wall-street, to the amount of £12,000, escaped through some technical flaw. These are the means by which Brother Jonathan gets a bad name, to his great loss, as the following anecdote will prove.

An English gentleman landed in New York on the day of the swindle. He had crossed the Atlantic with the intention of investing £100,000 in America; but hearing of the above knavish transaction, he waited cautiously for the result of the trial; when, finding that the law did not reach the swindler, he buttoned up his pocket, and took his passage home.

To return to the conspiracy case, which, previously to my departure from the United States, was concluded. The trial commenced the day I arrived at Detroit, and concluded on the 25th of September, lasting eighty days. Twelve of the prisoners were found guilty, and condemned to various terms of imprisonment, from five to ten years.

Some of the evidence is so extraordinary, and evinces such an infernal intention, that I have taken a few extracts.

At a place called the "Dry Marsh," there was a very sharp curve. This dry marsh was composed of a thin layer of earth, floating on the surface of a lake one hundred feet deep. Here, in the worst part of the curve, an obstruction was placed on the rail, with the intention of launching the passenger-train into this horrible abyss.

"Westcott, cross-examined by Senator Seward.—Have heard Filley, Corwin, Jack Freeland, and Woliver, speak of getting the cars off at the Dry Marsh. Filley spoke first, and said, 'It will bury the locomotive. It will bury the whole train. They won't want coffins, or sextons either.'"

A short passage from the admirable address of the counsel for the prosecution, is worth extraction.

"At the point," said he, "where this obstruction was placed, the railroad struck on a curve, with a descending grade, to the west. The curve obstructs the view of the road, while the descent renders it impossible to check the speed of a train approaching from the east. It is proved that at this point of the road, beneath a thin stratum of soft, marshy soil, slumbers a concealed lake of nearly one hundred feet in depth. At the sharpest point of the curve, on the most dangerous part of the marsh, just where the effect would be most fatal, was this obstruction placed. The freight-train, which, by a miracle, escaped destruction, came unexpectedly. This circumstance, as well as the admission of those found near the spot, proves that it was for the passenger-train, heavily laden as it is at this time of year, that this hellish snare was laid. . . . . When the 'Dexter' locomotive approached the Dry Marsh at a slow rate, the obstruction was discovered; but not in season to stop the train and avoid it. When the engine had been reversed, and the breaks put on with the energy of despair, it became evident that it was of no avail, and two men sprung off. By a miracle, the train was not thrown off the rail. The engineer, Spaulding, struggled bravely to stop the engines, and at last succeeded. At this moment, up comes Fitch, and says, 'What's the matter, Spaulding?' 'Some hyena,' replies he, 'has obstructed the road.' Fitch then remarks, 'By God, you never can run your cars over this road until you pay for cattle.' Spaulding remonstrates against this mode of obtaining redress, and urges his innocence of wrong, and the injustice of endangering his life. To this, one of the company replies, 'We would as soon kill you as any one.'"

Another redoubtable scheme was to *blow up* the train.

"Henry Phelps examined.—Fitch asked me if I had seen a new work of '*internal improvement*,' that Doctor Farnham was getting up. He showed me three tin tubes, one inch in diameter at one end, and one-fourth inch at the other, and sixteen or eighteen inches long. Said he, 'They are going to be placed in connection with a magazine under the road, to blow up the cars as they pass.'

"Henry Phelps, examined by Van Arman.—Filley described the match for burning the dépôt at Detroit. It was made of a tube, containing several holes lengthways, and filled with combustibles. There were small holes in the centre, glazed, and varnished, and filled with turpentine; then sealed up. When the fire penetrated the holes, or chimneys, from the other end, it would melt the wax, and communicate with the turpentine.

The observations of these ruffians, after throwing a train off the rail, have a dash of recklessness, at once ludicrous and grim.

"Great fun," says one, "to hunt coons; that coon ran away last night, but left its tail"—meaning the cars.

"I am very fond of coon-hunting," says another; "it is capital sport. A bar and a sledge are the best things in the world to hunt such game. Dry weather, very, when coons run off their track to drink"—alluding to a locomotive having been forced off the rail into a pond.

But enough of such frightful and reckless villainy.

CHAPTER III.

An "Irish Jontleman"—The Michigan Central Railway—Dreary Road—Unhealthiness of the Michigan Forest-land—The Fox and the Poultry—The inland Sea of Michigan—Arrival at Chicago—Wonderful Increase of Population in this City—Its advantageous Site in Respect of the Chain of Lakes—A rival Route—Handsome Villas in Chicago, and the horrible Odor to which they are exposed—Submerged Prairies—Luxuriant Growth—Pork Trade of the West—Lake-steamers—Embryo Cities—Arrival at Milwaukie—Wonderful Progress of that City—Fictitious Value of Land—Dangerous Harbor of Milwaukie—Practicability of floating Breakwaters in the Lake-harbors—Magnificent Position of Green Bay—Great Advantages appertaining to the town of Menasha.

THE following morning, as I was dressing to go by the railway, which was the scene of the villainy described in the last chapter, I was disturbed by a loud knocking at my door. Upon inquiry, I was thus answered:

"I'm an Irish jontleman, and want half a dollar."

"What for?" demanded I, opening the door.

"For cleaning them shoes," was the reply. "Come, give me the money."

The shoes in question were quite wet, and only a small portion of the dirt had been removed. I merely mention this as the only instance I ever met with of incivility, at an American hotel. Of course, I reported him to the proprietor.

The Michigan Central Railway is indeed a well-conducted and highly-creditable affair. With a uniform speed of eighteen miles an hour, it is punctual and safe. In the old countries of the world, it is very difficult to realize the fact of so good a railway through primeval forests. The road is extremely dreary. For miles, we swept through dark and dripping woods ; sometimes over half-cleared fields, rendered hideous by the remains of rotten and blackened stumps. Several neat and thriving villages were visible on the route, half-smothered in luxuriant foliage. The excessive exuberance of the vegetation, the oozy richness of the soil, and the flat, interminable plain, indicate to the most careless observer, that malaria, fever, and ague are indigenous to the Michigan forest-land.

Wild turkeys, quails, pigeons, and innumerable squirrels, were constantly seen, as the cars rushed roaring through the dismal solitudes.

On stopping at one of the stations, a loud cackling was heard in a baggage-truck. The poultry with which it was crammed appeared violently excited. Loud and incessant was the outcry. An immediate examination revealed a sly and cunning reynard, who, the moment the door was opened, frisked his brush, and levanted into the woods. He must have jumped in at the last station, without being perceived. No damage, however, had been done, as reynard had doubtless been too much frightened by the jar and motion to commence operations.

Twelve hours, at a steady uniform rate, brought the train to New Buffalo—a port on Lake Michigan. A steamer was ready to convey the travelers to Chicago. In half an hour, the freight was embarked, and the steamer stood out into the inland sea of Michigan. Having stopped a few minutes at a small port in Indiana, she resumed her course ; and, after three hours' steaming across the bottom of the lake, arrived at Chicago.

This city is one of those extraordinary phenomena peculiar to young America. It has increased in population from three thousand in 1840 to above twenty thousand in 1850. So enormous a growth is mainly owing to its advantageous site at the head of the navigation of the chain of lakes. At present, it possesses the only communication between the lakes and the Mississippi and has taken full advantage of its position in reference to these vast and comprehensive thoroughfares. I "guess," however, that its glory will be very much curtailed, if not eclipsed, by the new and far preferable route through Green Bay and Lake Winnebago.

The ground on which Chicago is built, is low and swampy—almost even with the waters of the lake. A long row of handsome villas has recently sprung into existence on the lake shore. These elegant buildings challenge the attention of a stranger, and would command his admiration if there was no sea-breeze. Unfortunately this wind was blowing at the time I took my first promenade, and the odor which it put into activity was horrible. I can compare it to nothing but the fish-market at Aberdeen, out of whose harbor I was once driven in my yacht from a similar cause. On examination, I found that all the offal, and other fetid matter, was usually deposited on the shore of the lake, invitingly close to the drawing-room windows of the Yankee aristocracy.

"Heavens, what a taste!" exclaimed I. "Let us be off. What queer people these Yankees are to endure such a nasty neighborhood!"

I have, however, remarked that when a nuisance arrives at a certain pitch, Brother Jonathan corrects it "pretty smart, I guess."

The prairies, with which Chicago is immediately surrounded, were at this time almost submerged. Vast droves of cattle were feeding on the rank and luxuriant grass; and I was informed that so thick is the growth that it is cut for hay, without being in the least deteriorated by the grazing of the kine.

Chicago is a remarkable example of the sudden and complete changes caused by quick transit, and modern legislation. This city is the chief commercial town of the State of Illinois. Within the last few years it has superseded the Irish producers of "Navy beef" for British consumption, to the amount of thirty-five per cent. This is only a foretaste of the extraordinary changes that will soon take place.

The annexed table will give some idea of the very large supply of hogs. The decrease in exports is, I believe, solely owing to the increased consumption arising from the immense flood of emigration continually pouring in. The produce can and will be multiplied in a ratio that is incalculable.

We give below returns from the West, keeping each State separate.

PORK TRADE OF THE WEST.

OHIO.	1851. Animals.	1850. Animals.
Previously reported, exclusive of Cincinnati	64,027	152,990
Cincinnati	324,529	401,755
Total	388,556	553,745

INDIANA.	1851. Animals	1850. Animals.
Previously reported, exclusive of Terre Haute	274,549	320,175
Terre Haute	65,548	60,000
Fort Wayne	2,000	none
Huntington	500	900
Lagro	1,500	2,000
Wabashtown	1,000	4,500
Americus	700	900
Durkee's Ferry	5,000	4,500
Darwin	1,200	3,300
York	1,500	1,000
Frankfort	2,500	1,900
Armesburgh	2,000	3,500
Carlisle	2,500	none
Evansville	12,000	14,000
Total	372,497	416,675

ILLINOIS RIVER.

	1851. Animals.	1850. Animals.
Beardstown	35,000	37,000
Alton	25,000	40,000
Meredosia	9,000	9,000
Naples	4,000	6,500
Peoria	30,000	21,000
Pekin	19,000	28,000
Canton	12,000	24,000
Liverpool	2,400	400
Springfield	8,000	19,500
Chillicothe	4,000	3,800
Lacon	13,000	11,600
Peru	4,000	15,000
Total	165,400	215,800

MISSISSIPPI RIVER.

	1851. Animals.	1850. Animals.
St. Louis (about)	85,000	124,000
Hannibal	17,000	24,000
Quincy	20,000	29,000
Keokuk	22,000	19,000
Burlington	19,000	29,000
Total	161,000	225,000

RECAPITULATION.

	1850–51. Animals.	1849–50. Animals.
Ohio	388,556	553,745
Indiana	372,497	416,675
Illinois	165,400	215,800
Mississippi	161,000	225,000
Cumberland Valley	30,000	40,000
Kentucky	205,414	201,000
Total	1,322,867	1,652,220
		1,322,867
Deficiency in number		329,353

There are yet a great many points in Missouri, Illinois, and Iowa not returned.

Not liking the appearance of Chicago, I stopped but a short time, and no doubt lost sight of many beautiful scenes on the more elevated ground inland.

From Chicago, steamers ply daily to Milwaukie, Wisconsin, and every port of importance round the lakes. The Milwaukie steamer coasts along the western shore, calling at several embryo cities; such as Waukegan, Racine, &c.

After a run of seven hours (ninety-six miles), we arrived at Milwaukie, a city beautifully situated on undulating ground, and having the advantage of a small river, the Menomonee, which forms the harbor. This is indeed a wonderful place, and perhaps the best example of progress in the Union. In 1835, there was not a single house on the spot, but in 1840 the inhabitants, including half-breeds, numbered 1700. At the last census (1850), the population amounted to 20,000.

To any one accustomed to the growth of cities in the old world, this appears incredible; but when one is actually a witness to the spacious and tasteful blocks of buildings, the wide and regular streets, the well-filled stores, abounding with customers no less than goods, the mind is lost in contemplating so marvelous and substantial an increase. It is, however, impossible to divest one's self of certain misgivings, generated by so rapid a growth. Twenty years ago, the land on which the city stands was not worth more than the government price, 1¼ dollars per acre (*5s. 5d.*) At present the lots are valued, in good locations, at 200 dollars a foot frontage. This astonishing augmentation of value has excited undue speculation, from the fact that individuals holding this land, suddenly became rich, and, having cleared immense sums, sold their lands to speculators, who immediately stimulated the public mind by means peculiar to the genus. Their efforts were seconded by the immense influx of emigration; and the lots rapidly rose far above their worth. This fictitious value had its effect upon the neighboring lands, which likewise became much inflated. The inhabitants are now likely to suffer from the mania of speculation, as the emigrants are becoming frightened at the high range of prices, and are stretching onward in other directions.

Milwaukie, for a great city, has a formidable disadvantage; namely, a bad and dangerous harbor. This vital defect is common to all the towns on the shores of Lake Michigan, from Chicago to the entrance of Green Bay; and it can only be rectified at a very heavy expense, as the small streams, that usually run through the harbors, are constantly forming bars, and thus damming up the entry. There being no tides to sweep away these accumulations, they become a serious annoyance.

The absolute want of a safe roadstead for so great a length of coast-line, must in future exercise an injurious influence in that quarter. Emigration is pouring in so rapidly, and the demand for water-transit accommodation is so pressing, that some harbors of refuge are imperatively demanded.

After a careful examination of most of the lake harbors I am convinced that any stationary or permanent breakwaters would be far too expensive to be attempted at present. A cheaper and simpler method must be adopted, and that speedily, or the losses will increase in a frightful proportion. Fully possessed by this idea, I had the satisfaction of proposing to the people of the lakes, through the columns of the Milwaukie Sentinel, the formation of floating breakwaters, which would be of inestimable service to the lake vessels, as numerous indentations are on the coast, where a floating breakwater would form a very fair and tolerably secure harbor. This proposal met with the approbation of the lake press; the writers in which at once perceived the economy and desirability of such a structure. Wood is a drug in this country; and the absence of tides renders the secure mooring of such a breakwater, comparatively easy and certain. I venture to prognosticate that these sea-defenses must be adopted in most, if not all, the lake harbors. Dunkirk, the present terminus of the great Erie Railroad, would be immensely benefited by such a breakwater.

Even with the assistance of the above structures, I do not think that all the engineering skill in the world will ever make a great shipping-port on the west side of Lake Michigan. Dame Nature has denied the facilities—nay, the essentials—for a good natural harbor; and, therefore, the labor of man will, in a great measure, be thrown away on such undertakings. Providence has, however, amply compensated humanity by the magnificent harbor of Green Bay, the head of which will eventually become the great *entrepôt* to supply the Mississippi, Western Wisconsin, Iowa, Minnesota, and the upper part of Illinois. I do not think the Americans have shown their usual acuteness in neglecting this part of Wisconsin, from which the water communication is nearly completed to the Mississippi, and begins to open the eyes of our translantic brethren, as the following extract from the "New York Herald," of December, 1851, plainly evinces.

"One of the remarkable characteristics of the present day, is the craving desire for new and cheap lines of transit for western demands. At present New York supplies the whole western world by the magnificent inland water-communication of the lakes.

"A rival spirit, of formidable character, has manifested itself in the Mississippi cities, St. Louis particularly. These cities begin to feel that their wealth and importance justify them in throwing off their dependence on the New York market, and that much greater profits can be realized by importing from Europe direct. Such a measure successfully carried out, would be a blow of no trifling importance to the interests of the Empire City.

"To avoid this premeditated blow, the New York merchants must carry the war into the enemy's camp, and supply not only the valley of the lakes, but likewise inundate the upper Mississippi. This can easily be effected by the route through Green Bay, Lake Winnebago, the Fox and Wisconsin rivers.

"On a careful personal survey, we find the distances in time as follows: Green Bay to Lake Winnebago (next spring when the communication is opened) five hours; Lake Winnebago, through Fox River to Fort Winnebago, forty-eight hours; Fort Winnebago to the Mississippi, sixteen hours; total, seventy hours.

"Green Bay has a decided advantage over every other port in Lake Michigan, from its perfect safety in any weather. This advantage secures not only a lower rate of insurance, but a certainty of punctuality, to which no port on Lake Michigan can pretend. It is likewise many miles nearer New York than Milwaukie, and vastly nearer than Chicago. Goods, therefore, dispatched from the Eastern cities *viâ* Green Bay, will be half-way across Wisconsin to the Mississippi before they can arrive at Milwaukie or Chicago. The complaints of delay at present, from the towns and villages *en route* are very bitter. Some of these places were supplied from Milwaukie, others from Sheboygan, and others from more remote distances. The time occupied in land carriage from these localities, varied from three to six weeks, and incurred an enormous expense in the freight and breakage. On approaching the Mississippi, we found many goods were sent from New Orleans; but the purchase and freightage were much more expensive.

"'What can we do?' asked the trader. 'Our expenses and losses are so great by land carriage from Lake Michigan that we are obliged to use the Mississippi.'

"We have carefully examined this route, and are of opinion that it is the best in the western world. We were particularly struck with the site of a small village, Menasha, at the end of

Lake Winnebago. From this place to the head of the navigation of Green Bay, a plank road was being constructed; which, when complete, will shorten the distance by four miles. As the grade is nearly level, we predict that the largest portion of goods-traffic, and all the passengers, will take advantage of this 'short cut,' instead of the roundabout delay of canals and locks. Menasha is similarly situated to the location of the Genesee Falls, but has a much finer water-power, sufficient, we believe, for one hundred and twenty mills. It is in fact the best water-power in the United States, for economy and adaptability. The soil likewise is similar to that in the vicinity of Rochester, New York, rather richer and deeper. With such exceeding advantages, we venture to anticipate at no distant date it will be a successful rival to the large cities on the shores of Lake Michigan.

"We can not understand why the Eastern capitalists should have overlooked such palpable advantages. It is out-and-out the best position in Wisconsin for a great city. The Green Bay route once open, it will be the fault of Eastern merchants if they do not command the traffic. The channel selected by the flood tide of supply will assuredly command the strong ebb of produce.

"Merchants of the 'Empire City,' how is it to be? It depends upon yourselves. Is this small stream (soon to expand into a vast tide of commerce) to flow for the benefit of New York or New Orleans?"

This extract is from one of the American papers, which, except that it sometimes defaces its columns with abuse of England, may be considered among the most able in the country. I have no doubt that a large and flourishing city must soon grow up somewhere on the Green Bay and Mississippi route. The town or village of Menasha, mentioned above, appears a likely place enough, as it is surrounded with as rich a country as the world produces. The water is supplied by Lake Winnebago, a vast and never-failing reservoir; and the climate is extremely healthy. The amazing quantity of fresh water in this vicinity modifies the extreme dryness of the air, peculiar to the United States. Here metal rusts rapidly; and guns, that, in six months' disuse in New York, were bright and free from the smallest particle of dust, were covered in this place with rust in twenty-four hours.

CHAPTER IV.

JOURNEY TO THE REMOTE SETTLEMENTS.

Embark for the Straits of Mackinaw—Crowded Steamer: its uncomfortable Condition, except as to the Food of the Passengers—Gigantic Strides of the Far West—Cupidity of a Colored Waiter—Shores of Wisconsin—"The Sleeping Bear"—The Manitou Islands—Singular Circumstances in Natural History—Island of Mackinaw—Large Companies of Fish—The Straits of Mackinaw—Optical Delusions—A Mirage—The Light-house of War-e-chance—Fishing for Mackinaw Trout—Spontaneous Vegetation on Fox Island—Embark for Green Bay—Approach the Mormon Settlement at Beaver Island—Threat of Vengeance against the Mormons—Attempt to vindicate them—A Visit to the "Gentiles"—Polygamy—Fugitive Saints—Great Increase and Prosperity of the Mormons—The Promised Land—Scene in the House of Representatives—Recent Intelligence respecting the Mormons—Mormon Poetry.

Daily steamers ply from Chicago to Buffalo, calling at Milwaukie. I took advantage of one of these, and embarked in the evening for the Straits of Mackinaw—the connecting link of the two huge "fresh-water seas," Michigan and Huron.

The steamer was crowded with passengers; the cabin, as usual, at fever heat, and full of squalling children. I can not speak well of these steamers from the specimen I took passage in. They are a sad contrast to the beautiful vessels in the Eastern States, whose perfect cleanliness, comfort, and luxury, are the admiration of all. This vessel was filthily dirty; and the courtesy scant. A *single towel* was allowed for the use of hundreds; and was (as may be imagined) an exceedingly disgusting clout. There was no excuse for this as the vessel was coining money by her large freight; and the number of passengers was so great, that three dinners were necessary to satisfy them all. In this respect, the appointments were not deficient. The dining-table extended the whole length of the vessel, except the slight interruption (perhaps fifteen feet) caused by the engine protruding from below. This vast table had room for about two hundred and fifty people, and was literally covered with little dishes—two at least for each person.

I was much interested and amused to scan carefully this crowd of western passengers; and could not help thinking how few years had elapsed since the land had been redeemed from its Indian inhabitants. What gigantic strides the Far West has taken in five years! and what a prospect is before it! Not *an old man* was to be seen, because time enough had not passed to silver the hair of the first settlers!

I was sitting in a large arm-chair, musing on this wonderful people and country, when my attention was attracted by a whispered conversation between one of the passengers and a colored waiter. I soon perceived that a bright quarter-dollar had passed into the dingy hand of the waiter, who advanced toward me.

"That arm-chair is engaged, sir," said he.

As there were six or eight more of these esteemed seats, I quietly moved to another. Still following me up, my knowing *darkey* managed to pocket from different passengers a quarter-dollar for each arm-chair, and oust me from them all.

I was too much amused at the fellow's impudence and dexterity to be angry, and quietly submitted to this anti-republican wrong. The steamer's name shall not be mentioned, as I am sure the owners do not countenance this sort of "*black-mail.*" Perceiving that I was aware of his tricks, the rascal cast at me queer looks, as much as to say, "There now, only see what a nice seat you might have had for a quarter-dollar."

Coasting along the shores of Wisconsin, we called at two ports, Sheboygan and Manitowoc; then steered diagonally across the lake toward Michigan, continuing north along the shores of that State.

A remarkable projection now became visible, called by the Indians, "The Sleeping Bear," from its fancied resemblance to that animal. We soon arrived at the Manitou Islands, which are of extremely curious formation. Densely covered with wood, they are, nevertheless, apparently composed entirely of sand. I was informed by Captain M'Comb, of the U. S. Topographical Engineers, that when employed in surveying this group, he desired to plant a surveying station on the crest of a sand hill. On attempting to cut down certain bushes for the purpose, he was much astonished to find that they were the tops of some cotton-wood trees. From the still living foliage, he came to the conclusion that the drifting sand had completely buried them alive; and believed that two years, at the utmost, was the period of time required to envelop them to the depth of sixty feet. It was very difficult, if not impossible, to conceive whence the sand was derived, as the island is extremely limited in extent, not being twelve miles in circumference, and at least the same distance from the nearest shores.

After wooding at this station, we proceeded for the Straits of Mackinaw, arriving at the island of that name the same evening. I perambulated the beach the following morning, and was struck by large companies of fish close to the shore. Several hundred in a dense mass were crowded close together, with their noses on the edge of the shelving beach. I watched this animated mass with great interest, and concluded my survey with a discharge from a duck gun. This secured several fine fish, weighing from three to seven pounds.

The following day, by invitation from my esteemed friend Captain M'Comb, the chief of the Lake Survey, we embarked in the steam vessel "Surveyor," and proceeded through the Straits of Mackinaw to inspect the new light-house off the Fox Islands.

The optical delusion in the Strait, during certain conditions of the atmosphere, caused by refraction, presents a mirage which is ever varying and eminently beautiful. Sudden and extraordinary changes astound the most experienced. On this occasion the phenomena was seen to perfection. At one moment, seemed to arise vast sandy cliffs, exhibiting huge chasms, gullies, and caverns. Fallen timber and water-courses appeared so clear and natural, that the most experienced were deceived. Anon, the cliffs "melted into thin air," and a vision of a large inverted forest took its place. This phase of the delusion disappeared, and vast savannas, and apparently interminable grassy plains, arose as if by enchantment.

The lighthouse of War-e-chance is situated about two miles from the Fox Islands, and is a remarkable structure. Before commencing the foundation, an accurate model was taken of the crest of the reef. A wooden frame, one hundred feet by ninety, was then built on a neighboring island, St. Helena, and towed to the reef. This huge structure was divided into compartments, leaving a large hollow space in the centre for the lighthouse. By the aid of several cables and anchors, the frame was adjusted in its place, and then sunk by filling the compartments with ponderous stones. So well was the shape fitted to the bottom, that it sank exactly square, all parts bearing evenly on the reef. This was a task of great difficulty, as the north side was in four feet, and the south in fifteen feet water.

During the progress of the work, a singular circumstance occurred; so singular that, unless witnessed by persons whose testimony is beyond all doubt, I should hardly like to mention it. A huge boulder, estimated to weigh sixty tons, was rolled a distance of fifty yards, grazing the corner of the frame of the above structure in its course. This Herculean performance was

achieved in one night, during a severe gale from the northwest. As heavy ice was moving at the time, it was imagined that it had considerable influence on this Titanic movement. Long before the ponderous masses are in motion, the structure is completely fortified by the ice that forms from the spray. The building is therefore now substantially fixed. The hollow centre is completely filled in with hydraulic cement, and raised some feet above the surface of the water. A massive brick tower, sixty feet high, then rises from this solid foundation. On the top is a powerful lantern, visible at an amazing distance in this clear and transparent atmosphere.

"Would you like to see how we catch Mackinaw trout?" inquired my worthy host.

"Amazingly," I replied, delighted at the chance of sport.

Jumping into the 'Surveyor's' boat, we pushed off in the direction of the Fox Islands. Two large cod-lines were unrolled, and allowed to drag about two hundred feet behind the boat. To these lines were fastened large cod-hooks; one baited with a piece of pork, the other with a shining strip of tin.

"Now look out for a bite!" exclaimed our host; "we must secure a dozen at least before we land."

I had not much faith in this rough method of catching so delicate a fish as trout, and held the line with some degree of incredulity. My host perceived my skepticism, and smiled benignantly at such fresh-water ignorance. Suddenly, I felt a violent jerk, and the line slipped several feet through my fingers before I was on the alert. I then began to tug with "might and main," and after considerable difficulty lugged in a huge lake trout, weighing thirty pounds. Before we arrived at the island, the bottom of our boat was alive with flapping silvery fins and tails.

War-e-chance, on Fox Island, is densely covered with wood. On the small prairies or natural clearings, many beautiful wild

flowers flourish. Wild gooseberries, cherries, currants, and raspberries were likewise scattered about in great profusion. I was informed that the destructive potato disease was quite unknown in this region.

While forming my plans for a thorough exploration of Mackinaw and its vicinity, I was taken with a lake-warning; that is to say, the steamer was approaching to convey passengers to Green Bay. A few minutes sufficed for hasty preparations, and I found myself steaming through the Straits in the good vessel "Julius Morton." In this steamer I experienced great comfort, cleanliness, and civility. The cabins are excellent; a small sitting-room being attached to each sleeping cabin. Calling at St. Helena, the vessel again commenced plowing the dark blue water of the lake; so clear, so blue, that it compared advantageously with the tropical seas. I discovered that we were approaching the famed Mormon settlement at Beaver Island.

A group was assembled on the forecastle, discussing the recent outrages among the Mormons, who were violently abused by a pale attenuated man, in the garb of a sailor. He spoke of a murderous attack made by them upon himself and brother. Elevating his wounded arm, he described the onslaught in animated terms. "They fired five balls through my brother's body!" exclaimed he. "I will pursue them to the world's end, until I get vengeance."

His story had a wonderful effect upon the listeners, who became excited, and even threatened to raise a body of men to exterminate the rascally fanatics.

After listening for some time, I ventured to say:

"Well, gentlemen, this appears very dreadful; but it would be as well to hear the other side, and not make up your minds on an *ex parte* statement."

This observation was assented to, particularly by a couple of persons who had been silent listeners to all that had passed. As the vessel was now approaching the island, one of these persons addressed me, and strongly took the Mormons' part.

"Let me introduce you," said he, "to some of the chiefs; you will see, as an intelligent stranger, how falsely they are accused."

This assertion certainly staggered the impression previously made, and I determined to judge for myself.

"Do you think," inquired he, "that a party of intelligent, industrious, and careful men, with considerable property at stake, would willfully commit such blind and foolish atrocities? There is a conspiracy against them."

Soon afterward we ran into a beautiful land-locked bay—very similar in appearance to the coral lagoons in the South Seas, and the vessel was lashed alongside a projecting wharf. In a few moments the space between the vessel's side and the wharf was swarming with fish from one to three feet long.

I landed, and strolled into the village. On my way, I entered into conversation with several of the inhabitants, but found them all, as they expressed it, Gentiles. This is the name given by the Mormons to those who do not belong to their sect. The Gentiles positively affirmed that each of the Mormons had more than one wife. Several were mentioned to us by name, who were asserted to have from four to six each! If this be true, it is certainly an astounding fact in a civilized country. My suspicions were rather strengthened on learning from an officer of the steamboat that a large party of Mormons were anxious to take passage in the vessel. As the officer expressed it, "they wanted to make a bolt of it," because the sheriff of the State was on his way to arrest them.

The Mormons of Beaver Island are only an off-shoot or branch from the main body, who have migrated far inland. The movement of these singular religionists has assumed the condition of an important popular agitation; and after much suffering and many reverses, the sect has achieved a condition of eminent industrial prosperity. The name of the mock-hero—his ignorance, and want of character—the low cunning of his accomplices—the open vices in which they indulged, and the extraordinary success of the sect they founded, is one of the most singular incidents of the present age. In twenty years, the sect or company has increased to nearly half a million. They occupy one of the richest portions of the United States, have a regularly organized government, and are represented in Congress by a delegate.

With missions in every part of the States, in every capital in Europe, in Mecca, Jerusalem, and among the islands of the Indian and Pacific Oceans, all the disciples are charged with the duty of making converts, and gathering them to the Promised Land of Utah, or Deseret. They must soon have a sufficient population to claim admission to the Union.

The promised land is situated in the valley of Sanpeech, and they have settled the country two hundred and forty miles north. The principal part of their territory is situated on the banks of a beautiful river, named by them the Western Jordan. It was on the right bank of this stream, on a rich table-land, traversed by exhaustless waters falling from the highlands, that the Mormon pioneers, on the 24th of July, 1847, pitched their first camp in their present locality, and consecrated the ground. The Mormon wheat-farms in this district are said already to cover as large an extent of land as Rhode Island.

Recent information (December, 1851) from the New Jerusalem, justifies apprehension that the ambition of the territorial governor, Brigham Young, will cause great difficulty. A considerable portion of the territorial officers, who are appointed by the United States government, are preparing to leave for the Atlantic States.

There are seven counties in Utah, respectively named Davis, Great Salt Lake, Iron, San Pete, Tooele, Utah, and Weber.

During a recent debate in the House of Representatives at Washington, as reported in the "New York Herald," on the question of the legality of the election of Mr. Bernheisel, the delegate from Utah, Mr. Briggs, of New York, remarked that he had good reason for asserting that Mr. Bernheisel had received his certificate of election through fraud and corruption; and that he paid Brigham Young, the Governor of the Territory, and chief saint of the Mormons, the sum of 3000 dollars (£600) to secure his seat in Congress.

This announcement created extraordinary excitement and confusion; members rose upon their feet, and the Speaker had much difficulty in quelling the disturbance. One member wished to know whether polygamy was really countenanced; another, whether the delegate himself was a polygamist? Several members averred that if Mr. Bernheisel was guilty of any such abominable conduct, he or they must leave the house; they could not, and would not, associate with any such men.

After great noise and confusion, the subject was postponed to another day, when it is expected that developments of a most astounding character will be made.

One of the initiated Mormons, named M'Gee van Dusen, disliking their mummeries, left them in disgust, and published a pamphlet, entitled "The Spiritual Wife-dogma of Mormonism." This contains a curious revelation of the profane secrets and initiation of these deluded and ignorant people.

Should any of my readers desire to be acquainted with the peculiar ceremonies and tenets of these fanatics, they may be found in a recent number of a weekly religious paper published in London.

In the beginning of the present year, the Speaker of the House of Representatives laid before the house a report relative to Utah, from the judges and Secretary of that Territory, dated on the 19th day of December, 1851, giving an account of the deplorable state of things in the district in question. Among the documents is a resolution of the Legislature of Utah, passed in September, 1851, stating, that "As B. D. Harris, Secretary of the Territory, is about to leave, abscond, or absent himself from the said territory, in case he shall refuse, neglect, or in anywise fail to deliver the papers, records, documents, money, or any other property or articles pertaining to said office, it shall be the duty of the United States marshal for Utah to arrest the said Harris, and him safely keep in custody, until he shall comply with the resolution."

"Mr. Bernheisel, delegate from Utah, stated that the communications to the President contained grave charges and exaggerations, not to say falsehoods. He knew his constituents to be loyal to the Government, and they should not be disparaged, and charged with gross crimes and enormities."

House adjourned.

It appears, therefore, that the Mormons have commenced open hostilities with the United States.

The most recent intelligence respecting the Mormons, is given in a letter, dated Deseret, 15th November, 1851.

"The affairs of Deseret are in a very flourishing condition. The crops generally have been good, though the beets and potatoes are rather light. Wheat is cheaper than ever before known in the mountains. The foundation of the Tabernacle is laid and the only hindrance is for timbers. The joiners have been in their new shop on Temple block a week or two. The railroad is progressing; the grading completed to a considerable extent. The public barn, also Presidents Young and Kimbal's barns, are inclosed. Many cattle, horses, and much produce have been received as tithing. The hearts of all rejoice that they have done their duty in paying their tithing. Parent schools are established, in which persons of both sexes are to be qualified for teachers in the common schools; and to improve themselves in the higher branches of education, such as algebra, astronomy, &c.

"At the first District Court for the Territory of Utah. Howard Egan was tried for killing James Munro, who it seems had seduced his wife.

"George Smith, counsel for prisoner, urged as argument in favor of his client, that the prisoner had acted in accordance with 'mountain-law.' In relation to this mountain-law, he demands, What is natural justice with this people? The principle, the only one that beats and throbs through the hearts of the entire inhabitants of this Territory, is simply this: The man who seduces his neighbor's wife must die, and her nearest relative must kill him."

The following is given as a specimen of Salt Lake poetry. Like every thing else connected with the singular people to whom the writer belongs, the stanzas of Mr. Phelps are wild and eccentric. Of meaning, they are certainly not destitute; but no metrical writer, except a disciple of the arch-mountebank, Joseph Smith (founder of the preposterous sect of Mormons, or "Latter Day Saints") would have adopted so queer a style as characterizes the verses now quoted. How do the Mormon fanatics reconcile the licentious practices imputed to them, with the gloom of Mr. Phelps's muse, rendered more oppressive by the grotesque familiarity of its utterance, which seems to fondle, in a half-jocose spirit, the mysteries of the charnel-house.

WHAT NEXT.

BY W. W. PHELPS.

What next? They say
There is a spot of real quiet,
Where ne'er an one doth fret and riot;
And yet all flesh is great to shy it,
And would, by wealth or art, defy it;
But ah! they can't.

What next? 'Tis said
The king and courtier, full of treasure,
The priest and people, by long measure,

The judge and lawyer, at their leisure,
Have tried to snub such dreadful pleasure,
But all have failed.

What next? Oh, there
No whisp'ring tongue can speak it,
Or shrinky tub doth leak it;
The vilest one, or purest meek-wit,
In perfect peace lies there a secret—
And will a while.

What next? Oh, tell
Me where is such a place of sleeping,
Where every thing, in perfect keeping,
Is free from pain, and free from weeping?
For age and life for it are leaping—
Among the tombs.

What next? My friends,
Ye goodly wise, or fools who err it—
The grave takes all by common merit,
For there's no false, contending spirit;
The finest dust "grave-worms" inherit—
The Grave is next.

CHAPTER V.

Transparence and deep blue of the Lake Water—Arrival at Green Bay—An embryo City—Offers for Sale of Land—Steaming up the Fox River—Interesting View—Spacious Lock—Pursuit of Deer swimming across the River—Numerous Rapids—Gigantic Chain of Water-communication—Village of Appleton—Water-power—Critical Situation—Village of Nenah—Governor Doty—Lake Winnebago—Exquisite Scenery—Eligible District for Emigrants—Wisconsin—Fond-du-lac—Clear Fountains Natural Advantages of the District—New Plank Road—Chain of Lakes—Extraordinary Progress of Wisconsin—great Increase of Population——Favorite Haunt of the Menomenee Indians.

Leaving Beaver Island, the steamer stood toward Green Bay, in the smoothest and clearest water I ever beheld. The deep blue of the transparent element forcibly reminded me of the intertropical ocean. The illusion was almost perfect, and was varied only by the solemn stillness of the surface, and absence of Mother Ocean's ceaseless and majestic roll, even in her deepest slumber.

On rising in the morning, we were running up Green Bay; well named from its appearance. At noon, the vessel was lashed alongside the wharf at the village, an embryo city.

I was accosted by several persons, anxious to sell farms. Curious to know their prices, I led them on; and was much amused at their exorbitant demands—about three times more than they would gladly accept. From mistaken judgment, or rather mistaken interest, the good citizens of the "Far West" will never allow any place to be eligible for the supposed emigrant, but their own. This partial feeling renders it almost impossible for a stranger to form a true opinion without a personal inspection.

After an hour's delay, I embarked in a wretched little steamer, and steamed up the strong current of the Fox River. The engines were placed on deck, quite uncovered. The view was interesting, from the fact, that only four years had elapsed since its cession to the United States. The right bank, going up, is still occupied by wild Indians. Wild woods and rich farms were rapidly passed on the one hand ; while the rough land on the other, still in a state of nature, clearly indicated the wild man's abode.

Six miles above Green Bay there is a spacious lock, which enables the steamer to proceed above the first rapids. Wonderful work for a State only three years old. On proceeding, the scenery became wilder; the woods closing to the water's edge. Suddenly a cry on deck called my attention; a fat buck was discerned, swimming across the river. The movement on deck, slight as it was, attracted the attention of the concealed Indians. In a moment, a bark canoe shot out toward the deer, frantically propelled by its dusky crew. The animal wavered for a moment, turned toward the nearest shore, landed, and disappeared.

This incident excited the emulation of a sportsman on board, and, immediately after, a huge duck-gun made its appearance. In a short time, another deer was descried ahead, taking his evening's bath. He did not appear intimidated by the approaching steamer, but floated about with the utmost unconcern. Soon, however, the loud snorting of the high-pressure escape-pipe, appeared to rouse his attention; when, turning his antlered head, he strove hard to gain the nearest shore. Alas ! alas ! the huge duck-gun is rising to the eye. The suspense is horrible ! Mingled feelings of hope for the noble stag, and anxiety for the successful shot, are combating in the minds of all.

F*

A loud report, and the poor stag disappears; driven under water by a huge charge of No. 3 shot. Again he rises; strikes vigorously for the strand—achieves it—bounds over a prostrate tree, and falls dead!

The steamer now struggles hard to overcome the numerous rapids. Occasionally, a loud and startling roar is heard—and a plug is blown out of the cylinder. The engineer coolly sticks it in, and taps it down, smoking his pipe as usual. Eight miles on is another lock; enabling the vessel to ascend six miles farther to Kaukanau.

We have been particular in describing the Fox River thus far, as the portage of nine miles to Appleton is, at this moment, the only break in the line of inland navigation between the Mississippi and St. Lawrence. When the canal (now in rapid progress) is completed, there will be another link in the most gigantic and wonderful chain of water-communication the world ever beheld. On the strength of this communication being opened, villages are springing up on the banks with unexampled rapidity. Appleton, for instance, has now upward of one thousand inhabitants. It is exactly eighteen months since the first tree was felled!

The water-power on this river must render it a place of some importance. At Kaukanau, the river falls forty-four feet in a mile, and the bed is full of small islands. This gives great advantage for applying the falling water. At Appleton the fall is thirty-four feet in one mile. We journeyed the nine miles of portage in a wagon, through the dense woods. No person can understand the perils and dangers, from stumps and swamps, unless he has had experience.

Fortunately, Mr. Blood, our Jehu, was an exceedingly careful and expert driver. After two hours and a half of torment, we were brought up all standing, by running against a stump, still sticking out of the swamp. For a brief space we rested to give the horses breath. In the interval the following dialogue took place.

First Passenger.—"Pray, driver, are there any wolves about here?"

"Plenty," answered Mr. Blood, "and bears, too."

At this reply the passengers wriggled uneasily; and, in truth, the prospect was dreary enough: the wagon was at a dead lock; the night dark as pitch, with the certainty that all the bridges were broken, and the lowlands overflowed.

"I guess I'll get out and *feel* for the road," said the driver.

Suiting the action to the word, out he jumped, throwing the reins on the horses' backs. They, poor creatures, either jaded with their labors, or cowed by the distant howling of wolves, now distinctly heard, remained perfectly still.

Here was a nice position for an English lady, one of the passengers.

"Are you not afraid?" I heard her husband whisper in her ear.

"No," replied she; "not while you are with me."

At this moment the driver returned, exclaiming that he knew where he was.

At his "*git up*," intended as encouragement to the horses, they slowly drew us through the swampy soil; at length, after several hair-breadth 'scapes we arrived at Appleton.

The steamer for Winnebago Lake, not being quite ready for service, we were obliged to take the usual conveyance; namely, the ferry boat.

Two hours' hard work enabled our lusty rowers to take us to the little village of Nenah, on the banks of Lake Winnebago. After a hurried dinner I got on board the lake steamer, little prepared for what was to open on my unprepared vision. Fortunately, I met an esteemed friend, Mr. Doty, the Governor of the State of Wisconsin, who invited me to mount the upper deck, and see the view.

At the rate of thirteen miles an hour, the high-pressure little steamer shot out of the creek; and revealed to our astonished sight the most enchanting scenery.

Lake Winnebago is about thirty miles long, and ten to twelve broad. A high ridge of limestone bounds it on the east, trending at each end of the lake to the west, nearly as far as the Mississippi. The eastern shores of the lake, therefore, slope gradually down to the edge of the water. Numerous natural clearings, or prairies, relieve the sameness of the luxuriant forests. On the western side the land invades the lake in long low capes and peninsulas. The fragrance of the air; the exquisite verdure of the trees; the gorgeous colors of the prairie-flowers; and the artist-like arrangements of the "oak openings," and wild meadows, are delights never to be forgotten. The most elaborate and cultivated scenery in Europe falls into insignificance in comparison.

I was struck with astonishment that such a "garden of Eden" should be so little known, even in the Eastern States. That such extraordinary advantages should be neglected! After a careful examination of many places in the western portion of the United States, I advisedly assert that the Lake Winnebago district is the most desirable and the finest in the world for emigrants.

My reasons are as follow: first, the district in question has communication with the Atlantic on each border of the State. The Mississippi on the west; Lake Michigan on the east. There is likewise a water passage, before described, running diagonally across the State from Green Bay to the Mississippi. The soil is equal to any in America, and the climate remarkably healthy. The extent of water-power is very great; the numerous rivers give admirable and cheap facilities for transport of goods in all directions. It is very rare for animal and vegetable life to flourish luxuriantly together. In the Winnebago district of Wisconsin, this combination of advantages is quite remarkable. We attribute the rude health of the inhabitants partly to the admirable water, amply supplied by small borings or artesian wells. Almost every house at Fond-du-lac, has its own crystal fountain spouting from the earth. The greatest depth to procure water is ninety feet; the least sixty-five. These delicious fountains rush up several feet above the surface, and are so remarkably clear, that it is difficult to perceive whether a vessel filled with it contains water or not. The whole limestone valley is said to be blest with the same bounteous privilege. No wonder the inhabitants enjoy such rude health; for, besides this great advantage, the climate is not of that wearing and exhausting character peculiar to most parts of the United States. Numerous villages are rising up all round the lake. No doubt, ere long, they are destined to be populous and wealthy cities. During the present year, a plank road will be completed from Lake Winnebago to Kaukanau. This line will shorten the distance to navigable water; being only nine miles. The canal previously alluded to, is compelled to take a circuitous route, with great natural disadvantages.

A chain of lakes are joined to Lake Winnebago by the Fox and Wolf rivers; all enjoying similar advantages. The climate is much more equable than the same latitude on the sea-board, and is quite free from fever or ague.

This country has an extraordinary effect upon the imagination. Nearly all the ramblers from the other States of the Union settle in the district. This is one of the reasons of the extraordinary progress of Wisconsin, which was first settled by Americans, chiefly from the Northern and Eastern States, and since largely augmented by emigrants from Europe. It was created into a territorial government in 1836, and admitted into the Union in 1848. Area 53,984 square miles. Population in 1840, 30,000. In 1847, 212,000. It is now estimated at nearly half a million.

At the outlet of the Lake Winnebago is an island, containing eight hundred acres, the favorite haunt, for ages, of the Menomenee Indians; and in truth they are capital judges of locations. I was fortunate enough to receive an invitation to this favored spot; and by the great kindness, and assistance of my host, the Governor of Wisconsin, the Honorable James Duane Doty, I was enabled, not only to enjoy the finest sport, but likewise to investigate the best means of securing "first-rate shooting" for any adventurous English spirit that may despise the narrow, and very expensive limits of the "sea girt isles."

Not to interfere with the continuity of my narrative, I will commence a fresh chapter, with my adventures on leaving Milwaukie, bound on a visit to Governor Doty.

SPORTING EXCURSION.

CHAPTER I.

Preparation for Shooting and Angling—Embark in a Lake Steamer fc Sheboygan—A young English Emigrant—Abundance of Game—Formation of a Plank-road—Origin and Effects of this new Kind of Highway—Travelling Disasters—Hospitality in the Wilderness—Approach to Fond-du-lac—A rolling Prairie—Rapid Rise of the Village of Fond-du-lac—Indians driven from their Land—Abundance of Sturgeon—Town of Oskosh—A Lake Island—Agriculture of the Wild Man—Wild Vines and Cucumbers—Bears attracted by the Abundance of Fruit—A Bear Battue—Sad Catastrophe—Interview with a Tribe of Indians—Visit to their Encampment—Their Cookery.

HEAVILY laden with guns, ammunition, and fishing gear, I was glad to find myself on board the steamer lying at the Milwaukie quay, and bound to Sheboygan.

In a few moments, the vessel glided out into Lake Michigan, cutting the smooth and glass-like surface as she ran along the densely-wooded cliffs. After a run of six hours, we arrived at Sheboygan, the nearest point to any practicable road to Lake Winnebago.

After a short delay, I engaged a wagon and team, sharing the conveyance with a young Englishman from Ringwood, in Hampshire, who was proceeding west to try his fortune * as a

* We have since heard that he settled at Menasha, and is on the high-road to fortune.

painter and glazier. All the baggage, about seven hundred weight, being carefully stowed away, we started at a smart pace on a capital plank road. In high spirits at this favorable commencement, I loaded my gun, lighted a fragrant Havanna, and kept my eyes on the alert for a shot. I was not disappointed, as quails, pigeons, ducks, and other birds were constantly exposing themselves as we drove along.

After twelve miles of this easy work the wagon came to the end of the plank, where a party of men were engaged with a locomotive saw-mill ; the engine sawing up the trees that were cut ready for the men to lay as fast as the road was graded. The usual dimensions of the plank are eight feet long, three inches thick, and varying in breadth.

The effect of these roads on the western woods, is quite marvelous.* It is said that the first of them was made by a private gentleman in Canada, to remedy a few rods of swampy bottom on a road adjoining his estate, through which he had often to travel. As this road likewise benefited travelers in general, he nailed a box to a tree, soliciting contributions to keep the road in repair. The benefit of the plank road was generally acknowledged, and the box not only received voluntary contributions sufficient to repair the road, but to pay a very handsome interest. This first gave the idea of the plank-road, which is now very generally adopted in Canada and the United States. It is allowed, that if a plank-road is only projected with a certainty of being carried out, the lands adjacent rise in value one hundred per cent ; and that when completed, it is difficult to estimate the rise in the value of land, it is so immense. The whole neighborhood becomes settled immediately. The companies or individuals who construct the roads, procure charters from the government, and generally receive a large dividend. The tolls vary from half a cent to two cents a mile (or from a farthing to a penny.)

* See Appendix.

The first plunge of the horses from the smooth plank to the common rough road was sad indeed. A box of glass, part of our young Englishman's venture, was shot out of the wagon, and smashed to pieces. All the travelers jumped out to assist in "the strait," and found one wheel up to the axle in a mud hole. A violent effort of all hands extricated the wagon, and we attempted to proceed. But, alas! every yard was a mud-hole or a stump; and in a few minutes we were all shot clean out into the mud, and the wagon capsized. This second disaster took a considerable time to repair, and the young Englishman lost a large can of varnish.

When the wagon was once more loaded, we found that the horses were unable to drag it out of the mire. As the evening was approaching, we left the "ship fast anchored" in the mud, and sought a shelter for the night, which was afforded us in a frank and hospitable manner by a Vermont man. His wife spread before us excellent tea, bread, butter, and bacon, and made us as comfortable as possible.

The following morning at day-light we were afoot; and as we heard that the road did not improve, a team of oxen was hired to aid our progress. With this addition to our power, we succeeded in dragging the wagon from its "mud bed," and advanced about three miles. Here the heavy vehicle again sank in a mud-hole, and appeared to be gradually settling down. All hands were hastily engaged in unloading the goods, and placing them on firm ground; but every effort to drag out the wagon was useless, and the unfortunate machine was gradually sinking out of sight. One of the party was now dispatched for more aid, and the remainder made a fire and prepared to dress some game. Our messenger fortunately discovered, at no great distance, an Irishman at plow with two teams of fine oxen. A promise of liberal payment induced him to leave his plow and come to our assistance.

The four teams, three of oxen and one of horses, were now attached, and with a liberal allowance of "oxen-talk" and whip, the unfortunate wagon was drawn out of its oozy bed.

In this manner the cavalcade proceeded until once more it gained the plank road, about four miles from Fond-du-lac. The unplanked part of the road was twenty-four miles, and occupied two days in passing with six upsettings. The planked remainder (sixteen miles) was easily passed over by a single team of horses in two hours.

This will give some idea of the immense advantage of these plank roads. In fact, the new country that is without them, has little or no value, as the farmer can not carry his produce to market, or get his supplies.

Ten miles from Fond-du-lac, the dense forests begin to separate, and small prairies are visible. Gradually as the lake is approached, the trees get still wider apart; and, at last, from a small thicket, the beautiful rolling prairie bursts upon the view, stretching along with a gradual descent, until it joins, in a verdant lawn, the silvery waters of Lake Winnebago. The numerous and variegated wild flowers, the exceeding richness of the soil, and the appearance of a highly-cultivated landscape, produce an extraordinary effect on the traveler.

Fond-du-lac is a small village, with a population of about 2400. Five years ago it was a desert! I was walking in the streets of this town with one of the principal men of the State, who led me to a particular spot, and pointed to a very slight indication of a path.

"Listen to me," said he, "listen to that which will hereafter be considered an historical marvel. Seven years ago, in an official capacity, I landed from the lake, and attempted to follow this indistinct path, which at that time was well beaten and well defined—it was the great Indian trail to the Mississippi. On this spot" (pointing to the ground whereon he stood), "I was met by a large party of Indian warriors, headed by their chief, who addressed me as follows: 'White man, thou canst not pass; we know that a pale face, once allowed to see our country, will bring swarms after him, and drive us out. Go in peace, but do not attempt to return.' "

My companion, balked for the moment, returned to his canoe, and pretended to retire. Making a long *détour*, he surveyed the country from several elevated positions, and finally succeeded in his object. Two years after, the tide of immigration set in, and the effects are now one of the wonders of the age.

The poor Indians, quite right in their anticipations, are long since removed beyond the Mississippi. Numerous bands, however, constantly return to see once more the "loved spot." It is said that they are so intensely attached to this district, that the tribe are gradually pining away. They look upon it as a "Paradise Lost." Truly it has every advantage to make it the wild man's Eden.

The following morning I embarked for the other extremity of the lake, and, during the voyage, was astonished at the number of large fish constantly leaping out of the water. On inquiry, I found they were sturgeon. This fish, described as being in quality infinitely superior to any that are found in other lakes, constituted the principal article of winter food for the Indians, and were extensively used by them for purposes of traffic with distant tribes.

Fifteen miles coasting along the western shores brought us to Oskosh, a small town of 1600 inhabitants. Nothing can exceed the beauty of this coast, nor the effect of the prairie openings (gracefully timbered), as they extend in long, low points. Occasionally a small copse completely smothered with vines and creepers, and fringed with fantastic shrubberies of sumac-gum, gemmed the prairie.

Oskosh is built at the mouth of Fox River, which now communicates with the Wisconsin and Mississippi. A few miles above the lake, a branch (the Wolf) runs one hundred and fifty miles northerly, into extensive pine lands, thus rendering Lake Winnebago the centre of a vast field of commerce. These advantages will, no doubt, soon render it a place of considerable importance.

Leaving Oskosh, the steamer still coasted the western shores, which became fringed with dense woods, and arrived at the end of the lake, where it discharges its waters by two channels into the Fox River. The island, which the two outlets form, is the beau ideal" of an Indian's habitation. Divided from the mainland on each side by a channel about one hundred and fifty yards broad, they unite at the northern end, forming a miniature lake, the little "Butte des Morts." As the water has a descent of ten feet along the shore of the island, it is admirably adapted for fishing. Indeed the Indians often travel hundreds of miles to enjoy this sport in their old and favorite home. I never beheld such swarms of fish in my experience; and from the numerous "rises" after flies, I should think it must be a first-rate place for fly-fishing.

The island is now named after its owner, J. D. Doty, the Governor of Wisconsin. It was fondly called "Menasha," literally "The Island," *par excellence*, of the poor fugitive Indians. And truly it speaks well for the wild man's taste, as a more beautiful location would be impossible to find.

In his own untutored way, the wild man has been for thousands of years, trying to decorate this favorite place. Numerous wild fruits of every description abound on the diminutive prairies and oak openings; and although neglect has fallen on this island since the departure of the Indians, which has not yet been rectified by civilization, the quantity of wild fruit in the autumn is prodigious.

The lake shore, looking south, is fringed occasionally with trees, both large and small, some of the latter of which are smothered with wild vines, loaded with fruit. The grapes, of course, for want of cultivation, are rather sour. Wild cucumbers vie with the vines in excluding the sun's rays from the unfortunate trees, and frequently stifle them with parasitical embraces. In some instances, an ambitious vine has exclusively devoted itself and succeeded in entwining the trunk, with its huge folds, to the height of forty or fifty feet; then thrusting out its arms, unfolds its flaunting foliage amidst the leafy garments of its supporter, and strives to gain the greatest share of heat and light: its purple bunches aloft give a singular tropical appearance to the scene. I found the stem of one of these vines as large as a stout man's thigh; no doubt many are larger.

This abundance of fruit attracts the wild animals, far and near. The bears regard it as a pet place, and the alarm was constantly sounded that a huge Bruin was swimming from the main land. If he was perceived in time, men were posted behind a sumac-bush, affording a convenient ambush at the point for which he steered. Many bears were shot in this manner, but some passed over in the night, and played sad havoc in the hog-sties and gardens. A small and jungly swamp, in the middle of the island, afforded a secure asylum, out of which it would be extremely difficult to dislodge these brutes.

I attended one of these bear battues, but was significantly warned, by the frequent unpleasant proximity of the whistle of a rifle ball, that juvenile Yankees with rifles, in a cover, are more dangerous neighbors than one cares to be with. Thinking prudence the better part of valor, I shouldered my rifle, and marched home, albeit rather lingeringly, being excited by the loud and exhilarating shouts and repeated crack of rifles. Perhaps this was fortunate for me, for a sad catastrophe finished the battue. A young man shot his own brother through the heart, mistaking him, as he stooped in the brushwood, for a bear.

Returning by a bridge that spans the eastern river, I perceived a "withered atomy" crouching on her hams, angling. She was an old Indian crone, just arrived with her tribe from a journey of several hundred miles, to revisit once more the loved scenes of their youth.

Grounding my rifle, and lighting a cigar, I stood quite still, watching the old woman. She did not pay the slightest regard to me, but tended her line with eager expectation. I did not know which to admire most—her wonderful skill, or the profusion of strange (to me) and beautiful fish that, hooked by her, were speedily flapping at our feet; large fish and small fish, white fish and dark fish; all of which were quite novel to me, in fresh water, at all events.

In the height of her success, I perceived the approach of a small cavalcade. It consisted of a tall, handsome, mounted Indian, followed by his squaw, likewise mounted, with her child at her back, and another, of seven years old, also on horseback. In rear of the three Indian ponies and their riders, some ugly curs, of decidedly "hang-dog" expression, advanced in sullen silence; looking neither right nor left, nor taking the slightest notice of any one. This piqued my curiosity.

After the wild procession had passed to some distance, I shouted, as a signal to stop, and hastened forward to address them. Signs and gestures were, however, the only means of communication; and I and my savage friends walked on together in silence. As I wished to conciliate the Indian, and examine his wigwam, I thought it might be politic to attack him through the organ of philoprogenitiveness. Accordingly, I pulled a silk handkerchief from my neck, walked close up to the squaw's pony, and tied it round the child's throat. This did not alter the demeanor of the Indians in the slightest perceptible degree; but I determined to accompany them, and examine their domestic arrangements.

The dingy little "red-skin" was extremely delighted; it eyed the colored silk with the greatest eagerness, and thrust the end in its mother's face, who, although she must have felt the greatest joy in possessing so choice a piece of finery, was true to her Indian nature, and did not exhibit the slightest emotion.

Feeling by this time, secure of a favorable reception at their encampment, I determined to partake of their hospitality, should it be proffered. We soon arrived at the lodges, numbering three, and composed of long sticks, entwined, and covered with skins, &c. A fire was soon made, gipsy fashion, and a large pot suspended over the embers.

On the arrival of the old crone from her fishing, the bunch of fish was carelessly pitched into the dirt, and the cookery commenced. At this moment, another Indian came in with a stock of squirrels, larger and fatter than I ever beheld; black, gray, mouse-colored, red, and though last, not least, a fine specimen of the flying squirrel, were among the store. I seized hold of this last, and examined it with great interest; while the cook was busily employed in skinning his brethren, and popping them into the pot. At length she looked for the one I was examining. I held it out to her by the tail, suspended over the cooking mess; when, with a dextrous movement of her knife, she severed the body, which fell plump into the seething caldron.

I now began to doubt the prudence of dining with such companions, although the mess smelt very invitingly. My doubts were speedily changed to certainty, by seeing fish, scales, entrails, and all thrown into the caldron, and to cap the climax, some rats were pulled from a heap of rubbish, and actually added to the stew. My stomach began to mutiny, and I was peremptorily compelled to run off.

But let me not be partial in my animadversions on the Indian *cuisine*. Truth compels me to declare, that the cookery of many white people among the western folks is quite as crude, though much cleaner. Their waste and extravagance is painful to behold. I am inclined to believe that no civilized people in the world are so utterly careless in their preparation of food as the new settlers in the Far West. Their method of treating the grouse is worth relating, as a notable instance of the perversion of delicate edibles. The housewife, on receiving the birds, throws them (whole) into water, and lets them soak till wanted; sometimes thirty-six hours. They are then cut apart, as if to stew, or curry, and put in a saucepan to boil. The meat is sodden, and utterly spoiled, and the "gude-wife" is indignant if the dish is not relished.

CHAPTER II.

Fine Ground for Deer-shooting and other Sport—Preparation for an Orchard—Nature of the Soil—Turtle's Eggs—Grove of Sugar-maples—Earth-mounds in the Shape of Animals—Evidences of a civilised but extinct Race—Remarks in Corroboration of this Theory—Curious Conversation with a Scottish Emigrant—The Advantages of settling in Wisconsin—A six Weeks' Exploration—A vast Prairie covered by a Mist—Singular Mode of steering across it by the aid of Resin-grass.

THE eastern shore of this lake is, perhaps, the finest ground for deer-shooting in the States. It is covered with a heavy growth of the finest and largest trees we have seen in North America. These woods are intersected at all points with deer paths, most of which terminate on the shores of the lake. By placing a boat, or boats, at certain points, and putting two or three stanch, but slow hounds in the woods, any number of deer may be driven into the lake. This method of shooting is of course used only in the summer. The small creeks, and sloughs, are absolutely swarming with wild fowl in the autumn, when they congregate in vast quantities, preparing to migrate south in the beginning of winter. Here they get fat upon the wild rice, and are delicious eating. Woodcocks breed in this part of Wisconsin, and are to be found in vast numbers. In a small garden, attached to the Governor's house, of not more than one acre, it was usual to kill three couple of woodcocks every morning before breakfast. But the chief glory, in a sporting sense, I conceive to be the grouse-shooting. The vast prairies on the west side of the lake, must be swarming with these great fat fellows. I say "must be," as I had not the means to decide positively. I went frequently with one slow and pottering but very good pointer, and generally took a straight course to some spot which captivated my fancy. I never failed killing as many as I required on whatever course I chose.

With proper dogs, the sport on the western prairies would greatly surpass any afforded on the best moors in Scotland. The few settlers who have recently taken up land on these wild meadows, complain much of the increase of grouse. It is indeed a singular fact, that game increases rapidly with the first settlement of a new country. When, however, the population arrives at a certain point, the game as rapidly decreases, and often in America disappears altogether.

During a stroll on the south side of Doty Island, I was much interested in watching the proceedings of a number of Irishmen, who were busily engaged in digging up for an orchard some virgin ground scantily covered with prairie grass, of which the roots hardly penetrated a quarter of an inch. The soil, when turned, was black and unctuous, and looked almost like chocolate. These clods are extremely friable after a few days' exposure to the air; and, although the first plowing takes from three to six teams of oxen, it can easily be worked afterward by one team.

While examining this grain-teeming earth, I perceived several curiously shaped eggs turned up with the spade. On inquiry, I was informed by the Irish diggers that they were snakes' eggs. Not readily believing this statement, I broke one, and to my infinite astonishment, found a fully developed little turtle, or terrapin, which fell struggling to the earth, and immediately made an effort to walk down to the lake. This was a novel discovery, and I had much difficulty to persuade the inhabitants of the fact, until the little animal was produced from my pocket.

Still continuing my stroll, I entered a magnificent grove of sugar-maples without any underwood. On admiring the size and growth of these venerable trees, my companion called my attention to some earth-mounds in the shape of prostrate animals such as beavers, bears, deer, squirrels, &c. These were of gigantic proportions, very distinctly marked and discriminated, evidently the work of some ancient and unknown race. Much speculation has been already induced by the discovery of singular architectural and sculptured remains in Central America, which can not possibly be ascribed to the red Indians. May not the evidences I have just mentioned offer an additional testimony to the existence of a race of inhabitants, possessing some civilization, which has now entirely passed away? Over a vast amount of ground, including these figures of animals, and covered by dense forests, the remains of ancient Indian corn-hills may be traced, clearly indicating that two distinct races have been masters of the land before the maple trees above alluded to had rooted themselves.

The following remarks (from the "Ancient Monuments of the Mississippi Valley") thoroughly corroborate our assertions on this singular subject.

"The strongest and most indisputable evidence in favor of the antiquity of these works of man is, however, afforded by the monuments which nature has raised on their ruins. In numerous cases, where the forest-trees, which now cover the majority of these mounds and embankments, have been examined, annual rings, denoting a growth of from six hundred to eight hundred years, have been counted on their trunks. But even these eight hundred years do not bring us near to the date of the erection of these works; for it has been observed by those who have given attention to these matters, that a homogeneity of character is peculiar to the first growth of trees on lands once cleared and then abandoned to nature, whereas the sites of the ancient works which we have been describing present the same appearance as the circumjacent forests, being covered with the same beautiful varieties of trees.

"In a discourse on the aborigines of Ohio, the late President Harrison of the United States, after having stated, that upon the first clearing of the forest certain trees of strong and rapid growth spring up in such profusion as entirely to smother the others of more weakly nature which attempt to grow in their shade, expresses himself as follows: This state of things will not, however, always continue; the preference of the soil for its first growth ceases with its maturity; it admits of no succession on the principle of legitimacy: the long undisputed masters of the forest may be thinned by the lightning, tempests, or by diseases peculiar to themselves; and whenever this is the case, one of the oft-rejected of another family will find between its decaying roots shelter and appropriate food; and, springing into vigorous growth will soon push its green foliage to the sky, through the withered limbs of its blasted and dying adversary; the soil itself yielding a more liberal support than any scion from the former occupants. It will easily be conceived what a length of time will be required for a denuded tract of land, by a process so slow, again to clothe itself with the amazing variety of foliage which is the characteristic of the forests of these regions. Of what immense age, then, must be these works, so often recurred to, covered *with the second growth after the ancient forest state had been regained!*

"In the north and northwestern part of the territory over which these ancient remains spread, in Wisconsin, and also Michigan, Iowa, &c., the earth-works assume a character so different from any we have as yet surveyed, as almost to induce a belief that they must be the productions of a distinct race.

"The animal-shaped mounds are situated upon undulating prairies and level plains; and although of inconsiderable height, averaging four feet, are distinctly visible, and the imagination is not taxed to trace in them the resemblance of bears, alligators, foxes, pigs, men, monkeys, and birds. They principally occur in the vicinity of large water-courses, and are always placed above the reach of the annual inundations."

One of these embossed figures in Wisconsin is described as follows:

"It represents a human figure having two heads, which gracefully recline over the shoulders. It is well preserved. The arms are disproportionately long. The various portions of the figure are gracefully rounded; the stomach and breasts are full, and well proportioned. Its dimensions are, from one armpit over the breast to the other, 25 feet; across the arms at the shoulders, 12 feet, and tapering to 4 feet at the extremities. Over the hips, the breadth is 20 feet; and over the legs, near the body, 8. The figure above the shoulders measures in width, 15 feet; each neck 8, and the circumference of both, 10. Length of body, 50 feet. Some of these mounds have been excavated, and found to contain human remains."

While on this spot, I was much amused at falling in with an old acquaintance, in the shape of an under-keeper from one of the Scottish moors. He had emigrated two years, and had become owner of a small farm. His remarks were shrewd and entertaining.

"Ah, Sir," said he, "if the quality in England only knew there was a place like this, do you think they would go and pay such extravagant rents for the mere shooting in Scotland? No, Sir, not they. My old master paid £500 a year for his moor adjacent to Loch Ness."

"And pray what did he get for it?"

"Why not half such sport as he can get here," replied he.

"Truly," I rejoined; "but remember the distance, and expense of coming here."

"As for the distance," responded he, "you can, at present, be here from London in fourteen days. In two years the rail will be finished to Fond-du-lac, and you will be enabled to get here in *eleven* days. The expense, as I will prove, will not only be far less, but it may be turned into a positive gain."

I pricked up my ears at this assertion, and requested my old acquaintance, the ex-keeper, to proceed.

"Well, Sir, look'ee here: suppose a party of five gentlemen subscribe £500 apiece, that will be £2500. With £1500 they can purchase a quantity of land, and build an excellent house, stable, and offices, on Doty Island, in a position which, in ten years' time, will increase greatly in value as an eligible site for building allotments. The very fact of such an establishment by wealthy English gentlemen will cause the land to rise in value enormously; and I will warrant that in five years it will be worth ten times the present cost."

"Suppose such to be the case," I observed, "and from my knowledge of the wonderful progress of this country, I think it very probable, where are the gentlemen to shoot?"

"I'm coming to that, Sir," said the ex-keeper. "From their location on Doty Island, they would have the finest fresh-water fishing in the world. They would have thirty miles lake-shore for deer-shooting; and dense woods, forty miles back to Lake Michigan, where bears and catamounts, and other wild animals, are plentiful. Abundance of wild fowl, quail, and woodcocks would be found every where."

"Stop," exclaimed I, interrupting him; "what are we to do about the main point—the grouse-shooting? besides, remember there is another £1000 to account for."

"Don't interrupt, please, Sir; I am coming to that. I know several districts of country in this neighborhood with natural boundaries; such as creeks, rivers, thick belts of trees, &c. These districts vary from five thousand to twenty thousand acres, and are so fertile, the Europeans can not even imagine such richness. Well, Sir, the farmers, who are thinly scattered about, are very poor. A little money on mortgage of their land would enable them to get more than double its value; but I propose that you take £500, equal to 2500 dollars, and lend it them in small sums, say 100 dollars each on mortgage, at the rate of 12 per cent. per annum."

"Why, you are a regular Jew," exclaimed I. "Twelve per cent. is horrible usury."

"Usury or not," returned he, "many of these poor men pay from 2 to 8 per cent. *per month.* With a hundred dollars at the moderate interest of 12 per cent. per annum, they could relieve themselves from the burden of excessive interest, and preserve the game on their own and neighboring lands. You would, by thus accommodating the farmers, have better stocked preserves, and more friendly occupiers of the soil, than can elsewhere be found. The remaining £500 you might keep to improve your lands; or invest at 12 per cent, as the other half. If thus invested, you would get 12 per cent on £1000, nearly equal to 5 per cent upon the whole sum laid out, and the land increasing in value in a prodigious ratio."

"Wonderful!" thought I, with enthusiasm. "I will pop you in print, my lad. You ought to have been a financier. Let us see what the 'Quality,' as you call them, will say to this."

"Don't forget," continued he, "to report that a single individual can do as well. I have put my finger in a similar pie with great success."

I was wonderfully struck with the man's ability at figures, and ventured to ask him for an outline of his life.

"I was born," said he, "and bred to agriculture in Caithness: and at the age of twenty-two, became grieve or bailiff to Mr. —— A little love affair drove me off South, where I first met you, with the Quality party from Dochfour. I was then an extra gamekeeper at —— House, in the expectation that Prince Albert, after his visit to Dochfour, of Dochfour, would honor my master's moor by shooting over it. As this expectation was not gratified, I was discharged, with only ten pounds in my pocket. I then remembered the conversation I had with you the half hour we took shelter from the rain together; and particularly one observation: 'Intelligence like yours,' you said, 'has much better chances West, over the Atlantic, than here.' Thank Heaven, Sir, I took your advice. I am now an independent man."

"Well, my friend," I said, "you are not the only acquaintance I have met with on this continent, and I must say they generally appear to succeed; but what are your future intentions?"

"My great object in life is to get my friends and relations out here; but they are careful, suspicious people, and I have not the faculty of putting things down in writing. Will you, Sir, do me one more favor, and add to your publication the offer I have had from Governor Doty? It will explain exactly to my friends what I can not do, and be of great interest to a large class of small capitalists in England, who would jump at such a chance, if they were only aware of it."

"Show me the offer you mention," said I; "and if I can do it conscientiously I will, and give it publicity."

On perusing the manuscript alluded to, I came to the conclusion that it might be of inestimable service to persons desirous of emigrating. The advantages are so obvious to all, that I merely give the offer of ex-Governor Doty, and present member of Congress.

COPY OF MEMORANDUM, BY J. D. DOTY, MENASHA.

"I have some land, the soil of which is composed of a rich black loam. It is situated on the banks of the river Nenah, close to the outlet of Winnabago Lake, where steamboats pass daily. Two villages are within a mile: Nenah on the one hand, and Menasha on the other. A good market is at hand for agricultural produce, particularly culinary vegetables; also pigs and poultry. The soil is a rich limestone, capable of producing any crops in great perfection. It is part of an island of 850 acres. Several flour-mills and saw-mills, beside other kinds of machinery moved by water, are in the vicinity.

"Schools, and well-established religious societies, are in each of the villages. The country is settling rapidly, and respectable female 'helps' are in great demand. I am now erecting several houses, with parlor, kitchen, and bed-room below, and two chambers above, with a brick chimney and oven in the kitchen. Each of these houses will be surrounded by a secure fence to inclose five acres of cleared land.

"I will let these lots to tenants, whose characters are satisfactory, for one or five years as they prefer, taking as rent one half the produce of the land. I will likewise give the accepted tenant a range for a cow and a pig on the adjoining land, and as much wood as he can use for fuel."

For six weeks I amused myself exploring in all directions; and the more I roamed through this beautiful country, the more I was delighted with it. Sometimes I climbed the range of limestone hills, and traversed deserted Indian clearings; at others I rambled through boundless flowery meadows and oak openings.

On one of these rambles I found myself in a vast prairie, several miles in extent. I was thinking of the difficulty of "steering" over this interminable plain, in a dark night or foggy day. My thoughts were prophetic, as a thick mist, a very unusual occurrence, crept instantly over the scene, shrouding the undulating landscape in an impenetrable and hoary mantle.

"How am I to get home?" was the question I put to my companion.

"That is an easy matter," replied he. "There is plenty of rosin-grass here."

Looking intently on the pasturage at his feet, he led me steadily in the proper direction. As I thought that this was a mere

"Yankee trick," no notice was directed to the grass, and I followed him in silence. When too late to examine this curious matter, I found that he had spoken the truth, and that the rosin-grass, or weed, had peculiar leaves which always grew in the same direction, namely, north and south. This simple fact makes the prairies as easy to travel over as the best marked plains.

CHAPTER III.

Endless Variety of Scenery—Beautiful Vegetation and abundant Wild-fowl—A huge Muscalonge—Difficult Capture of one of them—Profitable Investment in Land—Captain Marryat's Remarks—Extraordinary Energy of the Western Men—Magnanimous Offer by one of them to put an End to our War with the Kaffirs—The British Musket and the Yankee Rifle—Sharp-shooting from the Tops—A new Town—How to build a Road—Plank Roads in the United States.

THE endless variety of scenery in this district is quite beyond description. Sometimes a stately avenue of burr-oaks half encircled an eminence covered with small, but dense copses. Suddenly the avenue would cease on a plateau, the very site for a castle, or magnificent mansion. Let us wend our way across this plateau; the grouse rising right and left, disturbing the silence with the loud whirring of numerous wings: we will, by-and-by, examine the view, now momentarily concealed from our sight by the ground in advance. At length, the prospect is unvailed; Heavens! how beautiful. A winding, silvery lake is before us, studded with islands. All the ornament that money or art could furnish, would not improve the beauty one jot.

On approaching the margin of the lake, the effect was absolutely enchanting. Wild flowers and climbers in some places struggled to conceal the dense foliage on the banks. In others, the ripple of water on the smooth beach joined with a gentle kiss the rich and unctuous black prairie soil. Strange and ornamental wild fowl here dressed their plumage in security. The fierce and fiend-eyed fish, the Muscalonge, glided steadily and closely past. Every movement of his huge and savage shape was strangely distinct in the crystal water.

A few days after this adventure, a birch-bark canoe was launched, and the surface of this sylvan retreat was disturbed, perhaps for the first time, by man. By the kind forethought of my enthusiastic angling friend, George Trott, Esq., of Philadelphia, who had furnished me with the new-improved Anglo-Yankee spoon-bait, I was well prepared for a "raid" against the Muscalonge. With a stout cod-line two hundred feet long, to which this admirable bait was attached, we paddled into the lake. In a moment, the "glittering deceit" was caught in the jaws of a monster, who would have made old Izaak Walton open his eyes in rapture, and the canoe was nearly upset with the violent jerk. Careful management was necessary until the first furious efforts of the fish were over. The canoe was then paddled to the bank, and the line taken on *terra firma*. Considerable care was still needful to secure our prey; and it was nearly half an hour before the huge Muscalonge was high and dry. No means were at hand to ascertain his weight, but he was pronounced by competent judges to be nearly one hundred-weight. Several more were taken, and the sport was voted to be prodigious.

One of the party, in a furor of excitement and admiration, started off next morning, to purchase the lake and land adjoining. I afterward heard that he had bought two quarter sections (three hundred and twenty acres) for six hundred and forty dollars, about £130. There are thousands of similar situations. The next visit I pay there I expect to see a small town; so rapid is the growth of a new country possessing such wonderful advantages.

This eulogy, I feel, must appear exaggerated. Fortunately,

Captain Marryat went over nearly the same ground, and speaks as follows: *

"I consider the Wisconsin Territory as the finest portion of North America, not only from its soil, but its climate. The air is pure, and the winters, although severe, are dry and bracing; very different from, and more healing than those of the Eastern States. The country is, as I have described it in my route from Green Bay, alternate prairie, oak opening, and forest; and the same may be said of the major part of the Territory. Limestone quarries abound; indeed, the whole of this beautiful and fertile region appears as if nature had so arranged it that man should have all difficulties cleared from before him, and have little to do but to take possession, and enjoy. There is no clearing of timber requisite; on the contrary, you have just as much as you can desire, whether for use or ornament. Prairies of fine rich grass, upon which cattle fatten in three or four months, lie spread in every direction. The soil is so fertile that you have but to turn it up to make it yield grain to any extent; and the climate is healthy, at the same time that there is more than sufficient sun in the summer and autumn to bring every crop to perfection. Add to all this, that the western lands possess an inexhaustible supply of minerals, only a few feet under the surface of their rich soil—a singular and wonderful provision, as, in general, where minerals are found below, the soil above is usually arid and ungrateful."

The extraordinary energy of the Western men is the true secret of success.

These 'cute Yankees have seen strange adventures; they have not thrown away the advantages thus acquired, and are full of anecdote and information. I had several curious conversations with some of them, as the following anecdote will fully prove.

* Marryat, vol. ii. p. 72.

I may here observe that I speedily became known to all the neighbors for miles.

I was once strolling on the beautiful prairies, and perceived in my path, a little in advance, a tall, gaunt Yankee. He stood erect, leaning on his rifle, watching my approach. As I never met any thing but the utmost civility and attention on my rambles, I went up to him with my usual confidence. On approaching, he addressed me as follows:

"Well, *Captin.* How are you?"

"Very well," replied I, "how does the world wag with you?"

"I have a duty to perform, Captin," he replied.

"Fire away, and do your duty," rejoined I, wondering what duty my stalwart Yankee friend had to perform.

"Well, Captin," he continued, "you are not at all starched up, as I thought all Britishers were. You wear tow breeches, and don't think more of yourself than any of us. Moreover, I *see* you carry a large jar the other day, and I know you have lots of dollars. Well, then, it is my duty to ask you to take a drink."

"With all my heart," returned I; and we repaired to my friend's log-house.

After a social glass and sundry shaking of hands, my Yankee friend told me his history.

"I *fit* in Mexico," said he. "I likewise *fit* the *Injuns* in Californy, and have had a good deal of experience in savage warfare. My name is Captin Ezekiah Conclin Brum, and I think you are the best Yankee Britisher I ever seed. Now, then, Captin, I have a proposal to make to the British Government; but before I tell it you, I'll explain what made me *fust* think of it. When I returned from *fitting* the Injuns in Californy, I read in the papers the accounts of your *fitting* the Injuns at the Cape of Good Hope. Well, I wanted to find out all about it, so I sent to England, by a relation of mine who is mate of a liner, for a British infantry musket, with all the *fixins.* About six weeks ago it arrived here, and here it is, Captin" (going to a corner and bringing out a regulation musket). "Well, Captin, did ever you see such a clumsy varment in all your born days? Now, Captin, look out of the doorway. Do you see that *blazed* stump? It is seven feet high, and broader than any man. It's exactly one hundred and fifty yards from my door. I have fired that clumsy varment at the stump till my head ached, and my shoulder was quite sore, and have hardly hit it once. Now, then, Captin, look'ee here" (taking up his seven-barreled, revolving rifle, and letting fly one barrel after the other). "I guess you will find seven bullets in the *blazed* stump. I will, however, stick seven playing cards on the stump, in different places, and if you choose will hit them all."

"You are very skillful," I exclaimed.

"There are plenty more quite as skillful as me," he responded; "but, Captin, let me ask you, would you *fit* me with that machine, bagnet and all, against my rifle at one hundred and fifty yards?"

"No, thank you," I hastily answered, "I had rather not."

"Would you like to be one of two, or three, or even six, with bagnet fixed and all?" urged he.

"No," I replied, "certainly not. You would have the best chance by far."

"Now then comes my offer to the British Government. Will you make it to them from me?"

"No," replied I. "If I made the finest offer in the world to the British Government, the chances are, they would not read it. If they did, they would only sneer at me, and call me officious and impertinent, and very likely put a black mark against my name. I can not, therefore, present your offer; but I will put it in print, if you like, and the public can judge of its merits."

"That's the very thing, Captin," returned he in an animated voice; "and that will stir up public opinion—at least it would in the States, where, when once a thing is made plain, it is adopted, never mind who the recommender might be.

"My offer to the British Government is as follows: I, Ezekiah Conclin Brum, have learned by the papers, that the last war at the Cape of Good Hope cost ten million dollars (two millions sterling) to the British Government; and that it is likely the present war will cost quite as much, and be a protracted affair. I, Ezekiah Conclin Brum, have a high opinion of the bravery of the British soldiers, but a very contemptuous opinion of their arms. I, Ezekiah Conclin Brum, will undertake to enlist five thousand Yankee marksmen, each armed with a seven-barreled revolving rifle, or any better weapon that may turn up, and kill, or disperse all the Injuns on the British territory at the Cape of Good Hope, within six months of our landing there; conditionally, that the survivors are paid the sum of five million dollars, on the extirpation of the Injuns, and settlement of peace; thus saving half the expense, and great numbers of British soldiers. In course, the British Government must send us over in their brass-bottomed sarpents. This will be easy, as we can stow very close, having little or no baggage."

"You think your five thousand 'marksmen' could do it in six months," said I.

"Sartain," he replied; "we should be ekal to thirty thousand troops with such tarnal, stiff, clumsy consarns, as them reg'lation muskets is. We should do it slick, right away."

"Suppose you were successful," I rejoined, "what would you and your Yankee marksmen do afterward?"

"Do afterward," echoed he: "why, many would settle in the country, and show them how to go ahead."

"And," added I, "turn it into a republic before long."

"In course," that is sure to follow afore long, whether we go or stay. But I tell'ee what it is, Captin; this here gold in Australy will bring on a republic there while you Britishers are dreaming about it."

"Good-by, Captain Ezekiah Conclin Brum," I exclaimed, as I shook hands heartily at parting. "I will print your proposal. It will have the advantage of novelty, at any rate."

"Good-by, Captin. Wont you take a chaw? But mind you write, and tell me all about it."

And thus we parted

This proposal of our Yankee friend gives rise to grave reflections, not only as to land fighting, but naval engagements.

In England we rely too much on precedent, and antiquated maxims. As an example of this reverence for whatever is established, we will take an axiom of one of the most celebrated men of any age—an axiom which invention and science have superseded. We allude to the opinion of the great Nelson, that small arms in tops, though fatal to a few men, never decided an action. To this mistaken, though humane notion, he owed his death; for after he had twice ordered the fire on the "Redoubtable" to cease, because she seemed to have struck, a ball fired from the mizen-top killed him.

Now let us ask, What would have been the state of the "Victory's" upper deck, five minutes after she was alongside the "Redoubtable," if the tops of the latter had been manned by good marksmen, armed with such seven-barreled revolvers as excited the enthusiasm of our friend Ezekiah? The result would have been, that every man on the "Victory's" uppor deck would have been killed in a few minutes. This fatal result may be confidently anticipated in any future war with America or France. In America especially they are preparing rifles that will discharge twenty-four times without loading; the only preparation required, being the usual one of cocking.

The following calculation we will base on the seven-barreled revolver, leaving the reader to calculate the effects of the new Yankee rifle, which discharges twenty-four shot without loading.

Let us then suppose the " Victory " closing with the " Redoubtable," whose tops should be armed as follows : " Victory," as is the custom at present, *nil;* or at best short ships' muskets. " Redoubtable," ten men in each top, armed with the seven-barreled revolver.

These ten men can fairly be estimated to disable in one minute and a half seven men on the opponent's deck. Thus, seventy men will probably be *hors de combat* from the fire of each top; or the frightful loss, in this brief space, of two hundred and ten men from the three tops combined.

This would amount to the destruction of the whole crew stationed on the upper deck.

If any fighting ever does occur between English and American, or French ships, these new and wonderful rifles will be disastrously tested.

We pity the unprepared, as the chances are that they *must be vanquished.*

There can be no doubt, that although we are equal to the best in artillery and gunnery, we are far behind most nations in small arms.

During my various ramblings I had the good fortune to secure the confidence of several most able and energetic men—an advantage which enabled me to peep behind the scenes in many of the Western movements. The following incident came under my own knowledge.

Not one hundred miles from Green Bay, in an admirable situation, a small village suddenly peered out from the woods. The site was chosen by one of those extraordinary men (educated pioneers), who had silently selected a position, and established himself as proprietor, before any persons, even his most intimate friends, were aware of his object. As soon as this became known, the working pioneers of the West, well aware of the talent, perseverance, and sagacity of their leader, began to drop in likewise. In a few months, a town was laid out, and people began to flock in. When the place was a year old it was perceived that a road was absolutely necessary; and immediate steps were taken to obtain a charter from the Government. This being soon effected, a public meeting was called of all persons who might be interested in the said road, to which I will give the fictitious name of the Nesacoochera and Chittenango Plank Road Company, with branches from Gubbinsville to Hogskinsville, by Smithsville and Thomsonville. The main branch was ten miles long.

About one hundred persons attended, and the terms of the charter were read to them. It specified that at least five hundred shares should be subscribed for, and one dollar each paid up, before the charter became a valid instrument. The whole capital required was £10,000.

This appeared to be a complete "stopper over all," as probably that sum, in cash, could not be mustered within a hundred miles.

After a considerable pause, one citizen got up, and spoke as follows:

"I guess money arn't to be stumpt up here. I'll write to mother, who owns a fine location in the Genesee valley, and get the five hundred dollars. My note will do for the cash."

This knotty point being decided, the chairman next asked the meeting who would take stock, and supply the sinews of war. A dead silence ensued. There was not ten dollars (cash) in the township. At length, up got a citizen from Gubbinsville, and expatiated on the absolute necessity of an immediate formation of the road.

"I have not," said he, "any cash at my command; but I have

credit with a provision merchant down East. I will supply the workmen with pork, molasses, tea, and sugar, out of my friend's store."

This speech was received with immense applause; and it was followed by others, who pledged their credit for shoes, soap, clothing, &c.

The greatest number of the assembly, who were hard-working landowners, undertook to go to work immediately; taking for part payment the necessaries of life, and receiving road-stock for the balance. These energetic fellows immediately began to labor at this great work, which would eventually cost fifty thousand dollars, without a cent of capital. The most extraordinary thing was, the unfailing confidence felt by every one that something would turn up to procure the wherewithal; more extraordinary still was the complete success of the project. The road has not only quadrupled the value of property all around but it bids fair to pay a dividend, in five years, of fifty per cent.

If a steamboat is wanted, it is acquired in the same way. I have known large vessels completely built and equipped, without the owners possessing one farthing, and which have not only paid for themselves, but have made handsome fortunes for the lucky and enterprising projectors.

What country can attempt to cope with such energy and enterprise as this? It is frequently a subject of remark, that men born in England, and educated in the States, are among the foremost in these enterprising projects.

The reader, who is unacquainted with plank roads, and their wonderful utility in the Far West, may well be astonished at the high rate of interest mentioned above. It must, however, be remembered that the tolls in America are very high (charged both ways)—from one to two cents a mile for a single team; and that the wood (the main point) costs ten times less than in England.

The plank roads, throughout the States, vary in price from

£300 to £800 a mile, and do not require any repair for three years. The sooner, therefore, that these roads are worn out by traffic, the greater profit will be realized by the proprietor. We consider them one of the safest and most profitable investments in the United States.

CHAPTER IV.

TRAWLING.

Fish Markets in America—Their Inferiority to those in Europe—Cause of this—Abundance in America of the best Kinds of Fish not available for want of proper Means to secure them—The Trawl-net—Yankee Ridicule of this Expedient—Experiment—Its Effects—Prejudice—Queer Expression of the Newport (United States) Fishermen—Great Expediency of the Trawl-net in America.

THE fish-markets in America are not at all in keeping with the size and wealth of the cities. This probably arises from the scanty variety of fish caught, compared to any large city markets in Europe. And yet a greater quantity and more variety of fish may be found on the shores of the United States than in any other country I have ever visited. The reason America is not as plentifully supplied as any other part of the world, is simply because the people do not use the means. In the first place, the trawl-net is unknown in the New World. This is glaringly visible to a European on first visiting their markets, where may be seen every variety of what in England and France are termed coarse fish—in contradistinction to the finer kinds of white fish caught in the trawl. For example, the "bass," though considered an inferior fish in England, is highly esteemed in the States. Many others, which are disdained in Europe, are very differently estimated across the Atlantic. This "standard of taste" may originate in the want of knowledge of the better kinds, generally, if not invariably, caught by the "trawl."

One of my visits after arriving in New York, was to the Fulton, Washington, and other fish-markets. I must confess I was sadly disappointed at the markets and the supply. On carefully examining the small fry, caught by seines on the beach, I was astonished to perceive the young of all the esteemed fish of Europe, such as turbot, sole, brill, plaice, &c. On mentioning the circumstance to the market-men, they doubted the correctness of my assertion; but, after pointing out the characteristics in shape, color, fins, mouth, &c., they speedily acknowledged that I was right.

I do not mean to assert that these fish were precisely similar to their namesakes in Europe. Not so; some slight modifications in color and shape were perceptible; but to all intents and purposes they were of the same genus. The only strange flat-fish, which seemed to puzzle the market-men, was termed a fluke. Upon a careful examination, I found this to be a species of common English sole. After repeated observation, and careful inquiry, I came to the conclusion that the shores of the United States were swarming with fine and delicate flat fish; but, as by some extraordinary oversight for such keen and clever people, they did not use the trawl, they could not catch them.

My assertion that the finest flat-fish in the world, including turbot, were within the grasp of Yankeedom, was variously met. Some became immediate converts to my opinion; and one—a wealthy American gentleman—accepted my offer to procure a proper trawl from England, to try the experiment thoroughly Others ridiculed the "Britisher" who should come over from Europe to teach the Yankees to catch fish; and made affecting allusions touching the supererogation of instructing one's grandmother in the art of making extracts from eggs; to say nothing of other language, more expressive than elegant

At this attack, my indignation overcame my coolness, and I retorted that the Yankees had not improved in fishing since the time of the Indians, but used precisely the same means, without any change.

The "turbot controversy" was thus prolonged until the trawl should come from England.

On the arrival of the trawl, I was disappointed at not being able to make an experiment with it. Fortunately, I met an American gentleman (Elnathan Smith, Esq.,) who, holding opinions similar to mine, had, ten years previously, imported nets of this description; but, not finding any fishermen who knew how to use them, the nets had remained among other stores until they had become almost useless. One of them, less decayed than the rest, was selected for a first trial, although little better than a plaything, being only twelve feet in breadth. This net was taken to Newport, Rhode Island, with a view of testing its efficiency Several difficulties, however, supervened. First, I was ignorant of the ground and bottom; secondly, I could not use such a small and decayed net in deep water; thirdly, I had nothing but an open boat; and lastly, the Newport fishermen beheld the novel machine with derision.

"That thing catch a fish!" exclaimed one.

"I guess I'll put 'em all in my eye!" observed another.

The miserable "turn-out" almost warranted their contempt. Fortunately, I had secured the co-operation of some intelligent inhabitants, who accompanied me.

Although limited to shallow water, and within a mile from the shore, the success was conclusive. Seventeen varieties of fish were caught, nearly all quite young; but of these, seven were flat fish, including a small species of American turbot. The trial was prolonged for three days, during which several hundred-weight were caught.

But the shortness of the hauls in shallow water, the foulness of the ground, both from rocks and sea-weed, rendered the experiment a very poor criterion of the success that may be looked foi with a competent apparatus in deep water. The fish are so plentiful, that, when the proper grounds are discovered and explored by experienced trawlers, turbot, sole, and all the European varieties of fish will be more plentiful in the States than they now are in England and France.

After the success of the trawl had been fully demonstrated to the Newport fishermen, they took refuge in an expression far beyond what might be expected from the most bigoted and prejudiced John Bull. "Oh!" ejaculated they, "oh, after all, it is a very *mean* way of catching fish!"

A good Brixham trawler would make a fortune in America, and increase the variety and amount of food for human beings. A great proportion of the best kinds of fish consumed in England is derived from the trawl-net; and it is extraordinary that Ameri cans should neglect this mine of wealth, lying in abundance on their coasts. I venture to call to this subject the attention of the chief magistrates of New York, Boston, and other American seaboard cities; and I do not see why the American markets should not be supplied with as great a variety of fish as those of England, which is not the case at present, merely for want of the trawl-net. I should be very happy to give my advice and assistance in this matter, and to offer my personal superintendence to add a new and important branch of commerce to the United States. As a certain amount of experience is requisite both to manage the net and discover the grounds which different kinds of fish frequent, I strongly advise that a few experienced trawlers, with their nets, be imported from Brixham or other English ports, where this species of fishing is carried to great perfection. It is not possible to anticipate the effect such a measure would produce on the fish-trade of America; but it can hardly fail to be very beneficial. If we estimate the value and amount of fish taken only by the trawl, as evidenced at Billingsgate in London, we may well be astounded at the sum total, where three kinds alone, namely, turbot, soles, and plaice, are valued at several million dollars per annum. What an extraordinary gain would this be to a country whence this vast source of wealth may be secured without any drain on the land, and with no other expense than the labor of securing the fish. In this point, Americans are certainly behind Englishmen; and it does seem rather supine on their part to allow such opportunities to continue unavailable.

CHAPTER V.

KIDD, THE PIRATE.

New View of this so-called Buccaneer—William III. in Partnership with Kidd—Phipps, the supposed Founder of the House of Normanby—His Discovery of sunken Treasures—Kidd's Expedition against Pirates—His Commission from William III. to make Reprisals against the French—His Success as a Sea-rover—The English Government urged by the East India Company to stop Kidd's Depredations—Order for his Arrest—Gold, Silver, and Precious Stones buried by him in Gardiner's Island—His Apprehension at Boston, Massachusetts—He is sent to England—His Trial, Sentence, and Execution—Anecdote—Account of the Treasure found on the Island—Attempts now in Progress to recover a large Amount of Gold and Silver supposed to be sunk near the Shore in a Vessel formerly belonging to Kidd.

Among the many admirable institutions with which New York abounds, the Historical Society holds a distinguished place. Through the kindness of my American friends, I frequently attended the lectures delivered at this establishment. On one occasion Kidd, the famous pirate, was the subject under discussion. The Hon. William Campbell, Judge of the Superior Court of New York, had spent much labor and research in ascertaining the facts of Kidd's career; and, having consulted many old and rare documents, he formed the following history of the so called buccaneer. By Mr. Campbell's account it appears that Kidd was no pirate at all; or, if he was one, King William III. was his partner, together with many of the chief officers of his government.

It is difficult to understand, at the present day, why the Dutch monarch of England should ever dream of going shares with such a man as Kidd. But the wonderful stories, current at that time, of the buccaneers—their excessive plunder, and secret stores of wealth—had violently excited the public mind, and this excitement extended even to His Majesty.

Among many other popular stories of this nature, was that of the celebrated Phipps. As this bears upon the case in point, and is interesting and authentic, we will venture to insert it as a kind of apology for the rather loose morality of King William III. Phipps was born on a despicable plantation on the banks of the Kennebec. That is to say, the founder of the House of Normanby was a Yankee. Ill educated as he was, he contrived to attain great wealth and consideration. The foundation of his fortune, and successful career, hinges on the following story. This, we will hope, was the leading cause of King William's rumored partnership with Kidd.

"Phipps," says a recent chronicler (Mr. Craik), "had obtained information that somewhere in the neighborhood of the Bahamas, lay a Spanish wreck, wherein was lost a mighty treasure hitherto undiscovered ; and, having a strong impression that he was destined to be the discoverer, he hoped to be able to persuade some persons of wealth in England to advance the necessary funds, and, all unknown as he had hitherto been, to get himself appointed to conduct the search under a commission from the Government.

"At length, in the year 1683, he was successful in the representations he had made at Whitehall, and found himself captain of a King's ship, the 'Algier Rose,' a frigate of eighteen guns and ninety-five men. He sought for the sunken treasure long in vain. Once his men, losing all hope, rose in mutiny, and, assembling on the quarter-deck, with their swords drawn, demanded that he should join with them in running off with the ship, and take to the trade of piracy on the South Seas. Phipps, rushed in among them; and, with nothing but his bare hand. felled many of them, and quelled the mutiny. His men, nevertheless, continued so mutinous that he was obliged to bear up for Jamaica, and ship another crew. With the fresh and honester hands, he proceeded to Hispaniola, and there, by his policy and address, he contrived to worm out, from a very old Spaniard, more authentic information as to where the lost treasure-ship lay. Not succeeding, he returned to England, where, we are told, so proper was his behavior that the best noblemen in the kingdom, admitted him into their conversation.

"At length, he prevailed upon the Duke of Albemarle, to run the pecuniary risk necessary for the adventure, and again set sail for the fishing ground that had been so well baited half a hundred years before. Among other novel instruments invented by Phipps, for the successful prosecution of the search, was the diving-bell. Anderson, in his 'Origin of Commerce,' makes mention, under the year 1680, of a diving machine, or engine, used by Phipps. He quotes no authority. It must have been in 1684 or 1685 that Phipps set out on this expedition.

"For a long time he was unsuccessful, and could make nothing of their 'peeping among the boilers,' as the shoals were called. But at last one of his men, looking down into the calm water, from the periagua, or canoe, perceived a plant or weed growing, called a 'sea-feather.' That they might not return to the ship empty-handed, one of the Indians was ordered to dive and fetch it. The diver, bringing up the feather, brought therewith a surprising story—that he perceived a number of great guns lying round. This report at once turned their despondencies into brilliant anticipations, and they were immediately confirmed in these assurances by the diver ascending with a *sow*, or lump of silver, worth three hundred pounds.

"When Phipps heard this, he exclaimed: 'Thanks be to God, we are made!'

"Away now went all hands to work. In a short time, without the loss of a man, they brought up thirty-two tons of silver, besides six tons appropriated by Captain Adderly of Providence.

"Upon much of the coined silver, there was grown a crust like limestone; this, when broken with instruments, revealed whole bushels of discolored pieces of eight, which came tumbling out. There were also great quantities of gold, pearls, and other precious stones. In fine, the treasure recovered by Phipps amounted in value to nearly £300,000, although the adventurers were obliged to leave without a clear sweep, as their provisions ran short. In consequence of this sudden departure, considerable gleanings were discovered and gathered by other explorers.

"Now came the difficulty. His men seeing such vast litters of silver sows and pigs come aboard, were naturally little disposed to be satisfied with ordinary seamen's wages, and were tempted to seize the whole for themselves. After various dangers, arising mainly from this feeling of cupidity, which Phipps surmounted with great address, he got safe to England with the treasure. The Duke of Albemarle was so well satisfied, that he presented him with a gold cup for his wife, valued at £1000. The King (James II.) likewise was so delighted at his success, that he knighted him, and made him Governor of Massachusetts."*

The above story will, we trust, fully account for King William's partiality for supporting naval enterprise and adventure.

William Kidd was an Englishman by birth, and had been commander of a merchant-vessel that sailed between London and New York. He was so celebrated for nautical skill and enterprise, that he was recommended by Colonel Richard Livingstone, of New York, then in London, as a proper person to command a vessel which Lord Romney and others had pur-

* "Romance of the Peerage."

chased and were fitting out against the hordes of robbers and pirates, which preyed upon the commerce of all nations in the Indian seas.

The expense of the expedition was £6000, provided by a joint fund, to which the King, Lord Somers, Earl of Romney, Duke of Shrewsbury, Earl of Oxford, Lord Belmont, and Colonel Livingstone were subscribers.

Kidd agreed to be concerned to the amount of one-fifth of the whole, and Colonel Livingstone became his surety for a certain sum.

Hume says the King promised to contribute one-half the expense, and reserved to himself one-tenth of the profits. However, he never advanced the money.

To give character to this expedition, two commissions were issued: one against the pirates in the Indian seas, not interesting enough to insert, and the other as follows:

"William the Third, by the grace of God, of England, Scotland, France, and Ireland, King, Defender of the Faith, &c.

"Whereas, we have taken into our consideration the injuries, spoils, and acts of hostility committed by the French King and his subjects, unto and upon ships, goods, and persons of our subjects, extending to their grievous damages, and amounting to great sums, &c. We did, therefore, with the advice of our privy council, think fit, and ordered, that general reprisals be granted against the ships, goods, and subjects of the French King, &c. And whereas, William Kidd is thought fitly qualified, and hath equipped, furnished, and victualed a ship, called the 'Adventure,' galley, of the burden of two hundred eighty-seven tons, &c. Know ye, therefore, that we, by these presents, grant commission to, and do authorize and license the said William Kidd to set forth in warlike manner, and therewith by force of arms, apprehend, seize, and take the ships and goods belonging to the French King, &c.

"In witness whereof, We have caused the great seal of our High Court of Admiralty of England to be thereunto affixed. Dated, 11th day of December, 1695."

Kidd sailed from Plymouth in April, 1696; and, after taking a valuable French ship on the voyage, arrived on the American coast. Here he was held in high estimation, for the protection he had afforded to the colonial commerce. The Assembly were so well satisfied with his services, that they granted him £250 as an acknowledgement.

After three months' delay at New York, in completing his crew to one hundred and fifty-five men, he sailed for the East Indies. On his arrival, in July, 1697, he selected a convenient station, called Bob's Key, at the entrance of the Red Sea, a place admirably situated for waylaying and robbing the trade to and from the East Indies.

Kidd's first attempt was against a fleet of Moorish vessels, but he was forced to quit his prey by several well armed galleys. Still cruising about, he made a fruitless and unprofitable attack on some Portuguese men-of-war.

At length, fortune was more propitious. On the 30th of January, 1697, about thirty miles off Cutsheen, he fell in with a large Moorish ship, "The Quedagh Merchant," and speedily captured her. She was a large and very valuable prize, above four hundred tons. Her owners were Armenian merchants, and the vessel was on her voyage from Surat to Bengal. The owners offered 30,000 rupees as ransom, which was refused by Kidd, who sold a small portion of the cargo for £12,000; also supplying both ships with ammunition and provisions, besides dividing plenty of gold among the crews.

Various other captures were made as they roamed about in company. At length, the "Adventure" galley becoming leaky, they repaired to Madagascar, where they arrived in May, 1698. The "Adventure" was now abandoned and burned, and the plunder was divided into shares, as per agreement. This booty was enormous. Each man had three bales of rich goods, besides considerable amounts of gold and silver. The name of Kidd's prize, "The Quedah Merchant," was now changed into "Scuddee Merchant," and recommenced ranging the Indian Ocean from the Red Sea to Malabar, and his depredations extended along the Atlantic coast of South America, through the Bahama Islands to the shores of Long Island; this last being selected as the fittest for depositing his ill-gotten wealth.

It is believed, that among numerous other valuable ships, he captured two Spanish galleons, and that he returned from the East with a greater amount of treasure, than has ever been contained in any floating vessel.

The East India Company, furious at the idea of the disturbance of commercial relations with the neighboring potentates, urged the Government to put a stop to such lawless depredations upon the commerce of the world, in which they asserted England, as well as other nations, suffered. They declared, moreover, that it became necessary, for the character of the Government, and the immunity of the merchants, to take effectual measures to suppress the widely extended evil, and to punish the individual who had so grossly violated his commission, his plighted faith, and the laws of the civilized world.

A hot debate ensued in the English Parliament, in which the most bitter charges were made against the chancellor (Lord Somers), and the Duke of Shrewsbury, as co-partners in a piratical scheme; and an order was issued for Kidd's apprehension, by one of His Majesty's Secretaries of State, as follows:

"Whitehall, Nov. 23, 1698.

"The Lords Justices being informed by several advices from the East Indies, of the notorious piracies committed by Captain Kidd, Commander of the 'Adventure' galley, and of his having seized and plundered divers ships in those seas, their Excellencies have given order to the commander of the squadron fitted out for the East Indies, that he use his utmost endeavors to pursue and seize the said Kidd, if he continue still in those parts, so likewise they have commanded me to signify their directions to the respective governors of the colonies under his Majesty's obedience in America, that they give strict orders and take particular care for apprehending the said Kidd and his accomplices, whenever he or they shall arrive in any of the said plantations; as likewise that they secure his ship and all the effects therein, it being their Excellencies' intention, that right be done to those who have been injured and robbed by the said Kidd, and that he and his associates be prosecuted with the utmost rigor of the law. You are to be careful, therefore, duly to observe the said directions, and if the said Kidd or any of his accomplices happened to be seized within the province under your government, you are forthwith to transmit an account thereof hither, and take care that the said persons, ship, and effects be secured till his Majesty's pleasure be known concerning them.

"I am, Gentlemen,
"Your most faithful, humble servant,
"JA. VERNON."

Kidd's accusers asserted that the first piratical act of this bold marauder was at Malabar, on the Red Sea, where he took a quantity of corn; after which, he continued his depredations. A more bloody, daring, and cruel pirate, according to their account never infested the ocean. The King finally offered a reward for his apprehension, and a free pardon, by proclamation, to every pirate who should surrender himself before the 30th of April, 1699.

On Kidd's homeward passage from the West Indies to Boston, he anchored in Gardener's Bay, at the east end of Long Island, where he went on shore; and in the presence of Mr. John Gardener, owner of the island, and, under the most solemn injunctions of secrecy, buried a quantity of gold, silver and precious stones. He then sailed to Boston, where, on the 3d July, he was summoned before Lord Belmont (a party to the original adventure), and was required to give an account of his proceedings, while in the service of the company; which he obstinately refused to do. On the same day, the Assembly of Massachusetts examined him; and on the 6th ordered his apprehension. His wife, Sarah, came from New York, and claimed some plate, which had been seized, as her property; this was restored to her. A letter from the King and Council, of February 10th, 1699, having required all pirates to be sent to England for trial, Kidd, with Joseph Bradish, and several others, was transported thence.

Kidd was put on trial for the murder of William Moore, gunner of the ship, whom he had killed by striking him on the head with a bucket. The trial was conducted with great severity and injustice; Bradenham, the doctor of Kidd's ship, being the chief witness against him. Moore, the gunner, was proved to have attempted a mutiny against Kidd. In the altercation that ensued Kidd threw a bucket, and fractured Moore's skull. From the evidence, published at length in Hargrave's State Trials, 1777, we can not arrive at any other conclusion than that given by Kidd himself, namely: "that it was an accident, for which he was heartily sorry." He was, however, found guilty, sentenced to death, and executed at Execution Dock, May 12th, 1701. On his previous visit to Gardener's Island, in the absence of Mr. Gardener, he presented his wife with two small blankets of gold cloth, rich and beautiful. In a letter from the present proprietor of the island, he says: "We have a small piece, a sample of *cloth of gold*, which my father received from Mrs. Wetmore, mother of the wife of Captain Mather of New London. I send you an extract from her letter, giving an account of Captain Kidd's having been on this island."

"I remember," she says, "when very young, hearing my mother say that her grandmother was wife to Lord Gardener, when the pirate Kidd came to Gardener's Island. The captain wanted Mrs. Gardener to roast him a pig: she being afraid to refuse him, cooked it very nice, and he was much pleased with it; he then made her a present of this silk, which she gave to her two daughters. Where the other went, or whether it is in being, I know not; but this was handed down to me; it has been kept very nice, and, I believe, is now as good as when first given, which must be upward of a hundred years."

It having been ascertained, in some way, that he had buried treasures upon this island, commissioners were dispatched from Boston, by Governor Belmont, to secure the same. Having taken possession of it, they gave to Mr. Gardener a receipt therefor, the original of which is still preserved by the family, and is as follows:

"A true account of all such gold, silver, jewels, and merchandise, late in the possession of Captain William Kidd, which have been seized and secured by us in pursuance of an order from his Excellency, Richard, Earl of Belmont, bearing date July 7, 1699:

"Received, the 17th instant, of Mr. John Gardener, viz.:

	oz.
1. One bag of dust-gold	$63\frac{3}{4}$
2. One bag of coined gold	11
" one in silver	124
3. One bag of dust-gold	$24\frac{3}{4}$
4. One bag of silver rings and sundry precious stones	$4\frac{7}{8}$
5. One bag of unpolished stones	$12\frac{1}{2}$
6. One piece of crystal, cornelian rings, two agates, two amethysts.	
7. One bag of silver buttons and lamps.	
8. One bag of broken silver	$173\frac{1}{2}$
9. One bag of gold bars	$353\frac{1}{4}$

	oz.
10. One bag of gold bars	238½
11. One bag of dust-gold	59½
12. One bag of silver bars	309

"SAMUEL SEWELL,
"NATHANIEL BYFIELD,
"JEREMIAH DUMMER,
"ANDREW BELCHER.
"*Commissioners.*"

The inventory of the whole property obtained by the commissioners, shows a more considerable sum than is included in the above receipt. Some was found in the prisoner's chest, and more in the possession of Duncan Campbell, of New York, which had been landed from on board the sloop "Antonio," the last vessel commanded by the pirate. The schedule, in possession of Mr. Gardener, exhibits the amount to be 1111 ounces of gold, 2350 ounces of silver, seventeen ounces of jewels and precious stones, sixty-nine precious stones, fifty-seven bars of sugar, forty-one bales of merchandise, seventeen pieces of canvas, one large loadstone, sundry silver candlesticks, and other articles of value.

The Quedah, or Scuddee Merchant, with the main portion of the treasure, disappeared, and was apparently lost forever. But some years ago, a very old man, having acquired a competence, bought a portion of land at the entrance of the Highlands on the banks of the Hudson River. This was considered a strange location at the time, as it was far from the habitation of men. Shortly before his death, he informed some relatives that his father had revealed to him that, when he was a young man, he was witness to the arrival of a large Moorish ship, the "Scuddee Merchant," which had been chased up the Hudson River by the king's cruisers. When she arrived at the entrance of the Highlands, the wind suddenly shifted to the north, preventing her further progress up the Hudson, and the crew, afraid of being captured, ran her close to a steep bank, and set her on fire. She speedily foundered, and the crew escaped on shore.

Informant's father had likewise explained to him that the vessel was loaded with gold and silver, and that the crew had received directions from Kidd (who had gone to Boston, with about £10,000, to make terms with the governor, Lord Belmont), to take the vessel to Livingstone Manor, the property of Colonel Livingstone, his partner.

These rich tidings were corroborated by sundry other circumstances, and excited the public mind exceedingly. Moreover, the land adjacent had been purchased by the old man, with the intention of trying, at some future time, to rescue the treasure.

At length, a company was organized to search, and active proceedings were commenced. First, they bored at the spot indicated with long augurs, and were speedily assured that a large ship lay there. After boring through a certain thickness of wood, they came to some metallic substance. This encouraged them amazingly, and they increased their outlay, to enable them to build a coffer-dam round the vessel—no easy task, as the river was fifty feet deep; moreover, the soil had been washed down from the banks in the lapse of so many years, sufficient to cover the wreck to the depth of many feet.

After overcoming the natural difficulties they completed the coffer-dam, and set a powerful engine at work to pump the water out. With incredible exertion they succeeded in lowering the water considerably, and began to look forward to a successful result to their labors. Suddenly, however, they discovered that the pump not only did not lower the water, but that they had the greatest difficulty in holding their own. On a careful examination, for this provoking leak, they ascertained that it was caused by a subterranean stream rushing in beneath the coffer-dam with great force. This checked the enterprise, almost at the point of success. Differences arose between the parties, and the case is now in the law courts.

From all we have heard and read on this subject, we are inclined to believe that this is the richest and most remarkable instance of treasure-trove that ever interested the public mind. We have heard, from good authority, that parties are now organizing, and preparing very powerful and effective means to carry on the project.

We fully believe that the Quedagh, or Scuddee Merchant lies there; and do not see why, with such skill and energy as Brother Jonathan will bring to bear on such a project, it should not be successful, and prove as profitable a venture as that of Phipps.

MISCELLANEOUS NARRATIVES.

A HURRICANE IN ANTIGUA.

The mists, that late involved the hill,
Disperse. The mid-day sun looks red: strange burrs
Surround the stars, which vaster fill the eye.
A night of vapor, closing fast around,
Snatches the golden noon. Each wind appeased,
The north flies forth, and hurls the frighted air:
Not all the brazen engineries of man,
At once exploded, the wild burst surpass.
Yet thunder, yoked with lightning and with rain,
Water with fire, increase the infernal din:
Canes, shrubs, trees, huts, are whirled aloft in air.

GRAINGER.

READER, were you ever in a West-Indian hurricane? If such has been your lot, I am sure you will agree with me in heartily and anxiously wishing never to behold one again; for though there is something strangely fascinating in scenes of terror, few desire to renew their acquaintance with them.

Tho following description of an unusually severe elemental convulsion, is derived from notes taken while on a visit, in August, a few years ago, to a friend at Dry-Hill House, in the vicinity of St. John's, the capital of Antigua. It is the faint record of a calamity which will be memorable in the annals of that unfortunate island.

The inmates of my friend's mansion were one morning early

astir, and actively employed in preparations for a marriage-feast. With the happy, careless air, peculiar to their race, negro women and children were bustling among the large and luxuriant foliage which, if it every now and then concealed them from view, could not stifle the sound of their rapid chattering, their giggling laughter, and snatches of songs, conveyed in the queer negro dialect. This irrepressible animation, reckless gayety, and vivacious defiance of care, can hardly be imagined by the inhabitants of our northern climate. The merriment of negroes surpasses that of any other branch of the great human family.

I also had risen early on this festive occasion, being unwilling to lose any portion of the hilarity which I knew would commence with the earliest light of morning. Never shall I forget the splendor with which the day broke—a splendor to be witnessed only in the tropics. The sun slowly rose from the glass-like sea, first glancing on a few clouds which had congregated, then

"Flattering the mountain-tops with sovereign eye,"

and gradually revealing the gorgeous colors of the vegetation. I gazed with rapture on the serene magnificence, and the language of the Psalmist was not unremembered: "The heavens declare the glory of God; and the firmament showeth his handywork."

My ruminations, at this moment, were disturbed by one of the servants (a black girl), who brought me a cup of coffee and a cigar—the usual morning-custom on a West-Indian plantation. It struck me that something uncommon, nay, even ominous, was observable in the expression of her countenance, and I waited, with no little curiosity, to hear what she had to communicate.

"Hy, massa," said she, "here de coffee. How do you do dis morning?" Then, with a significant glance, she added, "Ole massa, he say, will nyung massa look at 'rometer?"

"Thank you, Nancy," I replied, "it will be time enough to inspect the weather-glass when I have finished my coffee. How are *you*, Nancy?"

"So-so, rader poorly, tank God, massa," rejoined the girl as, with a sigh, she left me.

"Very mysterious," thought I, "is this message about the barometer with my morning coffee. It never occurred before during my visit here. Something strange must be in the weather. Let me see if I can find it out."

I accordingly looked carefully round at all points of the compass; but nothing extraordinary was perceptible, excepting that a dull haze crept languidly over the scene, and that the silence was awful.

In a few minutes, having finished my cigar, I went into my friend's bedroom. Though generally an early riser, he was, on this occasion, still in bed.

"Hallo!" exclaimed I, "why are you still there? Up, man, up, and set to work: you have plenty to do this day."

"Heaven grant," responded he, "that I may not have *too* much to do before a few hours are past! There's a hurricane in the air—I am sure of it."

"Stuff and nonsense!" I rejoined. "The barometer stands firmly at 30°; it has rather gone up since yesterday."

"My dear boy," returned he, emphatically, "I have been thirty years a resident in the West Indies. During that time I have witnessed eight hurricanes. The last three were foreshadowed by my own sensations. These sensations are now aggravated tenfold. A terrible day is before us."

That forebodings like those under which my friend then suffered, are unerring, I have since that time ascertained. They are produced by two causes, namely, physical derangement, and observation of meteorological peculiarities. In his treatise on European Colonies, Mr. Howison observes, "Persons long resident in the West Indian Islands are able to foretell the approach of hurricanes with tolerable accuracy, by the observation of certain atmospherical phenomena; but this kind of knowledge proves, unfortunately, of little avail, either on shore or at sea; the violence of the tempest generally rendering impotent all precautions that may be employed against its destructive effects. On the day preceding the hurricane, the weather is almost always calm and sultry, and the sea-breeze does not set in at the usual hour, or, perhaps, is not felt at all; the sky is red and hazy, and the horizon surcharged with clouds; the noise of the surf seems particularly loud and distinct; and thunder, more or less distant, is heard incessantly. At length, the wind begins to blow in shifting gusts, and to lull again; these increase in strength and frequency, and ere long the blast comes roaring from one quarter with concentrated fury." This, no doubt, is generally correct; but it does not precisely describe the morning witnessed by me.

As I perceived my friend to be really in earnest, and that he was suffering greatly under his apprehensions, I gave in to his humor, and promised to note accurately the appearances of the weather, and the movements of the mercury in the barometer.

This assurance seemed a little to relieve him.

"I shall leave all preparations and precautions to you," said he. "I am quite unnerved, as is always the case when these fearful tempests are breeding in the air. The tornado will be upon us within twenty-four hours."

It can not be supposed that a young man who, for five years previously, had been knocking about in all parts of the world in small vessels, could sympathize with the climate-worn and sensitive planter. I, therefore, left the bedroom in excellent spirits; not only without apprehension, but actually longing for the hurricane to arrive, as excellent fun; so rash and thoughtless is youth.

Outside the house I met Betsey, the staid black housekeeper, feeding the poultry.

"Well, Betsey," said I, "massa say hurricane come to-day."

Never did a few words produce such a change in the person who heard them. The woman's gabble to the cocks and hens ceased suddenly. A grave, disconcerted look supplanted the good-humored smile which had played about her thick lips. I might almost say she turned *pale;* and the measure of corn fell from her hands. It was evident that until now she had heard nothing of her master's prognostications.

"Oh, ky, ky!" sobbed she. "Massa always right." And off she ran, in violent perturbation.

"The devil!" exclaimed I, "here's a pretty kettle of fish!"

In a few minutes, the whole household was in violent commotion. Messengers were instantly dispatched to the sugar-works (about half a mile inland), and also to the cove, where an establishment of small vessels was kept for various purposes, such as sugar-droghing, collecting coral to burn into lime, &c. Meantime, the table in the dining-room was removed, disclosing a huge trap-door leading down to a spacious cellar. Into this chasm, contrived as a place of refuge during hurricanes, the scared nigger-kind conveyed all the most portable articles of value.

By nine o'clock, all needful preparations were completed, and a hurried breakfast was snatched. The barometer certainly had a downward tendency, having fallen ·03° but there was no other perceptible indication of a change. A light air from E.N.E. had now set in—the usual trade-wind; but all was placid and beautiful as before. In the yard grew a magnificent tamarind-tree, loaded with nearly ripe fruit. The pods hung in large and tempting clusters; and the foliage, gently agitated by the breeze, gracefully waved to and fro.

The domestic animals were evidently disturbed: their manner was hurried and uneasy. They clearly had a knowledge of impending evil.

Not being so skeptical as to disbelieve these signs, slight as they were, I kept all my senses on the alert, watching alternately the mercury in the barometer, and the signs of the weather. By eleven o'clock, a more decided fall in the glass was evident; it had gone down to 29·80°. To the northward the horizon had darkened considerably. The trade-wind, however, still swept gently and refreshingly over us; but at two P.M. it died away, and then the mercury fell considerably.

All doubt about the approaching tempest was now dispelled The black inhabitants of the small cottages in the vicinity, belonging to the estate, flocked up to Dry-Hill House, to seek consolation from companionship with the white people.

A light breeze soon sprang up from the north, and, as it rose, the mercury fell. At three o'clock a furious gale was raging. Being anxious to observe the proceedings of the shipping, I slipped out of the back part of the house, and went down toward a cliff overlooking the anchorage. To my great disgust as a sailor, I perceived among the twelve merchant-vessels, lying in the roads, that only four were making any preparations to withstand the typhoon. Three were at single anchor, with a short scope of chain, and top-gallant yards across, and one brig with royal-yards and head-sails loosed. Such bare-faced and lubberly carelessness is almost incredible. "Old Columbus" knew better. *He* soon made himself master of the signs preceding a hurricane in the West Indies.

"When he was off the principal Spanish West Indian settlement at St. Domingo, he foresaw that a hurricane would shortly arise, and sent to Ovando, the governor of the place, to request that he might be allowed to take refuge in the harbor; but this being refused, he was obliged to stand out to sea, and face the storm. 'What man, without excepting even Job, would not have died of despair,' says Columbus, 'to find that, at the crisis when the lives of myself, my son, my brother, and my friends were in danger, I was prohibited from approaching that country, and those ports, which, under the blessing of God, I had purchased for Spain at the expense of my blood!' At this time a fleet of twenty-four ships was about to sail for Spain, carrying large quantities of gold and pearls, partly the revenues of the king, and partly the property of those private individuals who were passengers on board. Columbus, notwithstanding Ovando's inhumanity, advised him to detain the fleet a few days, because a tornado was likely soon to occur; but his warnings were treated with contempt, and the vessels were suffered to proceed on their voyage. Before the close of the following day, twenty of their number, with fifteen hundred persons had foundered in the hurricane. The loss of treasure on this occasion was so great as to affect the financial resources of Spain for several years after."*

As the wind still steadily increased, I considered it best to get back to the shelter of the house. To enable me to do this conveniently, it was necessary I should creep along under the garden bank, which offered some protection against the gale. Not having the slightest idea that the force of the wind would be so enormous in this early stage of the hurricane, I attempted to walk past a gateway, and being instantly struck by the full power of the blast, was rolled over, and driven, as by a giant's strength, violently along the ground. For a moment I gave myself up for lost, as the harbor of St. John was directly in my compelled course. Fortunately, before coming to the open water, the land declined into a bushy marsh. Here, assisted by the underwood, I clung firmly to Mother Earth.

After resting awhile and collecting my thoughts, I succeeded, by taking advantage of the nature of the ground, which sheltered

* Howison's "Colonies."

me in some measure from the wind, in regaining the yard of Dry-Hill House. The stunning roar of the blast continued, and the noble tamarind-tree, writhing, seemingly in agony, was grinding its huge limbs, whipping off large branches, and throwing them and the fruit violently about, as if by this oblation it hoped to appease the demon of the gale. Alas! the sacrifice appeared only to incense and provoke its rage.

I entered the mansion, and sat down to regain my breath. It now became necessary to close and barricade every door in the house, and nail the windows firmly down. A crowd of women and children were huddled together on the floor in silence. Conversation was impossible, on account of the furious noise.

My imagination had been very much excited by the dismemberment of my favorite tamarind. The idea of its apparent torture held me in thrall. Through a crevice in one of the shutters, I painfully watched its throes. Its main branches (the growth of a hundred years) wrestled obstinately with the opposing force: their groaning was heard above the mighty wind; and soon nothing was left but a few jagged stumps on the blackened trunk.

Darkness now closed upon us. The violence of the tempest waxed stronger and stronger: the noise increased to such an overwhelming roar, that the strongest efforts of the human voice, in closest proximity, became totally useless: they were "as a whisper in the ears of death, unheard." Loud cracks now gave notice that the house began to complain. The women and children were immediately roused from their sitting position, and, by signs, desired to go below. This movement was speedily effected, and the ground floor was left in possession of the manager and myself. Our attention was now divided between the barometer, which fortunately hung near the open trap-door (our last retreat) and the perilous vibration of the building. The walls appeared to bend and give before the raging blast.

Suddenly, a violent shock was felt, sending a thrill to our

hearts. This was afterward ascertained to be caused by the demolition of the kitchen, stables, and outhouses adjoining the dwelling, which, with all their contents, had flown away on the wings of the wind. Not a vestige was ever recovered or seen. Numerous smaller shocks succeeded, like reports of cannon. Huge stones were hurled through the air, battering and tearing away the verandas that surrounded the house.

To crown our dismay, a large spout of heavy wood, intended to convey the cane-juice from the mill to the boiling-house of a neighboring estate, two miles to the northward, came spear-like, through the air, penetrating the roof, piercing the table, and fixing itself into the floor close to us. The part which projected above the roof caught the gale, and acted as a powerful lever, shaking the house as if it were pasteboard. In a moment more it parted, leaving the lower portion still fixed.

At this time, the barometer had fallen to 28·50. We felt, or fancied we felt, the house giving way. Taking a farewell look at our faithful monitor, we prepared to descend into the cellar. To my intense astonishment, the mercury suddenly fell a quarter of an inch. In the excitement of the moment, I seized hold of the manager, roaring the information in his ear; but, as before, the human voice was of no avail in such a turmoil. By dumb show, I succeeded.

On a sudden, we were aware of a marvelous change in the state of things.

"Great Heaven!" I ejaculated, "what can this mean?"

There was a dead calm—a profound silence, disturbed only by the low, wailing sobs and incoherent prayers of the women and children in the cellar. *We were in the vortex of the hurricane!* It is impossible to describe the horror of this period. A door was unbarred and opened, and, with a lighted candle, I stepped out. The flame took its upward course steadily. All around was black, and calm, and silent.

But the stillness was of brief duration. In a short time, a distant rumbling noise was heard, when I quickly re-entered the house, drawing bolt and bar. A slight tremor shook the ground: an earthquake was added to our ills. Again came the hurricane from the opposite quarter, overwhelming our senses with its fierce impetuosity. The house, already shaken, now rocked to and fro, threatening instant destruction. We immediately descended into the cellar, fastening down the trap-door with a strong lashing. During several dreary hours, we remained in suspense, stunned by the hellish disturbance overhead, while our feelings were occasionally varied by the horrible and sickening sensation of the earthquake. Some bottles were thrown down by the agitation of the ground, and the long rows of rum-casks grotesquely heaved, as if instinct with life, and tottered and fell in the most approved style of German demon-pranks.

At four A.M., there was a sensible diminution of the gale. We proceeded carefully to unfasten the trap-door. On its falling back, *the moon was plainly visible,* throwing light on groups of dense, black clouds driving furiously across the heavens. Nothing was above us but the sky! The upper part of the house was gone!

My friend proceeded with me to a rising ground, waiting in anxious expectation for daylight. His agitation was extreme. Dawn was in the east.

"Look toward the mill," he said. "I can not do it. It must be gone. Nothing could withstand such a night. I am a ruined man!"

My eyes were strained anxiously in the direction of the mill. At length I exclaimed:

"Cheer up: The work stands firm and strong. All yonder seems to be right."

The sun now appeared with the serenity which marked its rise on the preceding day; but the scene of devastation that met our eyes baffles all power of description. Had a hot blast from hell passed over the whole island, the effect could not have been more destructive. Vegetation, human habitations, animal life, all had vanished.

On our return to the house, we passed through what had been a group of lofty cocoa-nut trees, of which nothing remained but stumps, standing only a few feet from the earth. The huge tops, foliage, fruit, and remainder of the trunk, were gone. A solid stone wall, two feet high, surmounted by iron railings, had surrounded the house. This, railings and all, were blown away in masses; some of two hundred weight were afterward found a mile off.

The previous day we were in the midst of plenty and luxury, now we were glad to banquet on a decayed ham luckily found in the cellar.

Reports soon came in from the different parts of the property. We understood that the cove-house was blown down, and that all the small vessels were driven high and dry far above high-water mark into the jungle on Rat Island. The overseer of the works, a black, reported all destroyed except the boiling-house, which, however, had sustained serious injury. Its steam-engine chimney was blown down, and the earthquake had made a rent in its wall.

"Is any one killed?" asked I.

"Yes, massa," returned the overseer, "three nigger missing."

"But is any one *killed?*" I repeated.

"Oh, no massa, nobody kill," replied the overseer, "only big rock 'tone mash up poor Peggy head."

"You don't mean to say she's dead?" persisted I.

"Um head mash quite up, massa," responded the negro. "Big rock 'tone come tro de air, tro de roof, hit um so," added he, with a queer gesticulation, "kill um dead."

I ascertained afterward, that the poor woman had been killed in the manner described.

The natural anxiety of a sailor again led me down to view the shipping. Never did I behold such a scene of wreck! Two of the largest craft had foundered with all hands; the lower mast-heads still sticking above the water. The small vessels, as already stated, I found a long way above high-water mark. Three had ridden out the storm, and among them, to my surprise, the brig. There she lay, still at single anchor, the main royal-yard still crossed, but the fore top-mast-head twisted off, and all the upper gear gone. Who can account for this?

The poor steamer to which I was attached in English Harbor had fared very badly. In the first part of the gale she had dragged the huge moorings, and gone broadside on to the wharf. On the gale shifting, not being able to snap the numerous fastenings by which she was secured to the buried guns, she had torn down the whole length of the wharf whereto she was attached, and dragged huge masses of debris into the harbor. Several ponderous stone buildings in the dockyard were blown down, and a Dutch corvette, strongly secured in English Harbor, was driven up into six feet water; her usual draft being seventeen feet.

It may, perhaps be consoling to our lady-readers to be informed that the wedding to which allusion is made at the commencement of this narrative, took place a few days after, as soon as the roads could be cleared of the numerous and heavy masses of wreck, blown on them by this fearful hurricane.

It is believed that the happy couple are still "a happy couple," with numerous children, living in affluence at St. John's, Antigua.

CRUISE OF THE "FLAME."

CHAPTER I.

Port Royal Harbor, Jamaica—The Palisades—Exploits of a Guard-fish—Chasing a Sun-fish—Prodigious Strength of this Creature—Ferocity of a Shark, and Death of his Victim—An extempore Steam-bath—Convoy Signal for Chagres—Weighing the Anchor—A mysterious Impediment—An old Tar's Explanation—The Discovery—Dolly Johnson, the Negro Bum-boat Woman—Premonition—Dolly's critical Situation—Deluging Rain—The Chagres River—Perpetual Rain—Gigantic Lizards—Town of Chagres—Exploring Party—Balboa's first View of the South Seas—Modern Improvement in the Airiness of Ships.

On the 10th of April, 18—, H.M.S. "Flame" was lying in Port Royal Harbor, Jamaica. The awning had just been spread, and the recently-washed decks, even at the early hour of 7-30 A.M., were perfectly dry and even hot under the scorching and nearly vertical sun. The Mid. of the morning watch, feeling exhausted with his exertions (since 4 A.M.) in holy-stoning the decks, was too glad to pipe the ship's company to breakfast, and get a little rest. Seating himself in the gangway, he looked anxiously to the eastward, in eager expectation of the sea-breeze.

Vain were his longings. The whole surface of the sea, as far as eye could reach, was like a mirror. From the burial-ground, called "The Palisades" (a spot justly dreaded by all whites as being the receptacle of victims of the yellow fever), a transparent vapor arose, flickering a few feet above the surface: this was apparently an evaporation from the numerous bodies there deposited—a most sickening and horrible exhalation.

Through this haze, which trembled and vibrated as it hung over the ground, the diminutive islets, guarding the entrance to Port Royal, appeared to be agitated into sandy wavelets. So strange a contrast to the perfect repose of the ocean, presented an effect which, once beheld, can never be forgotten. It suggested to the imagination, a group of unquiet spirits transformed into islets, and imprisoned in a sea of molten brass. Not a sound was to be heard. Even insect life, usually so brisk and active in tropical climates, appeared to have withdrawn from the intolerable and unmitigated solar heat. Every thing in animated nature was unwilling, if not unable, to appear until a cooling breeze should refresh the air and abate the tyranny of a cloudless sun.

In the narrow shade caused by the hull and awning of the vessel, a numerous shoal of small fish had taken refuge. Clustering closely to the coppered side, they appeared to fancy themselves in perfect security. Our Mid., a lover of natural history, watched them with interest, and wondered at their boldness. Suddenly, he was startled by a splash. A guard-fish, four feet long, had sprung a distance of at least twenty feet, and, with unerring aim, seized a victim. This was frequently repeated without a single failure. If human dexterity may vaunt its frequent successes, instinct can truly boast that it *never* fails.

The strength of some, and the ferocity of other members of the finny tribe frequenting the coast of Jamaica are almost beyond belief. A few remarkable instances fell under the author's observation, and may be considered worthy of note. A gentleman, famous for his exploits among the fish of these waters, was taking a cruise in his little yacht of seven tons. While sailing about the spacious harbor of Port Royal, his attention was attracted by a large substance floating and slowly revolving like the motion of a wheel.

"Hallo!" exclaimed he, "that answers to the description I have read of a sun-fish. Here's at him."

As the little vessel approached the huge creature, a man was stationed at the boltsprit end, poising a harpoon. The yacht soon luffed up, head to wind. Bringing the boltsprit gently over the unconscious sea-monster, a splashing commotion in the water proved, plainly enough, that the harpoon had been driven well home.

It might be supposed that victory was now achieved: no such thing. To reckon without one's host, has, time immemorial, been denounced as egregious folly; and, on the present occasion, "the host" strongly differed in his reckoning from the guest who would fain, like Paul Pry, have intruded on him. If it might be permitted, for only a single moment, to compare a specimen of Nature's most uncouth productions with another which is marked by consummate perfection and loveliness, one might say that this ill-favored creature, like the adored Celia of the poet,

"Was coy, and hard to win."

Indignant at the mere idea of captivity, the sun-fish immediately made for the sea, choosing the deepest channel, and towed the little craft rapidly after him. Sails were promptly taken in; and the barb-harnessed fish was left to his own devices. The rate at which he towed the boat was pleasant enough, and, indeed, very exhilarating as long as his efforts were confined to the harbor. When, however, it appeared that the open sea was the creature's object, the affair assumed a different aspect. The vessel contained but little water; hardly any provisions. Still, away she went from the land at the rate of six miles an hour, without the assistance of a stitch of canvas!

"Let us haul up by the harpoon line, and kill the beggar with a lance," angrily exclaimed the owner. "I never had the luck to bag a sun-fish before."*

* "The sun-fish (*Orthagoriscus*)," say the naturalists, "grows to an immense size, sometimes attaining the diameter of eight feet."

Accordingly, all hands (a scanty crew, unfortunately,) clapped on, and tried hard to haul the vessel up alongside the fish. But their best efforts were of no avail, their strength being unequal to the task. Still onward went the monster with unabated speed! At length, the land growing dim and distant, our adventurers had no alternative but to cut the tow-rope and free themselves, after being towed nearly twenty miles.

The prodigious strength evinced by this sun-fish, if sun-fish it was, in tugging the yacht so far to sea, proves its size to have been far greater than is generally imagined; and may afford some approach to an explanation of the supposed fabulous kraken of the Scandinavian seas.

During our stay in Port Royal harbor, we had fearful evidence of the ferocity of the shark, in an incident which occurred the day before the brig sailed for Chagres. A sergeant of the army, his trowsers tucked up above his knees, had been employed washing clothes. As the guard-house, where his duty called him, was close to the point leading into the harbor, he naturally walked on the shallow tongue of the point to rinse the soap-suds from his bare legs.

While engaged in his ablutions, a shark seized him by the calf of his leg, and tried to drag him into deep water. His fearful screams speedily brought his comrades to the rescue, but they were only just in time to catch him by the hand, as he was disappearing under water, and drag him toward the beach. Even then, the shark fought hard for his victim. The taste of human blood seemed to madden his ravenous nature into desperation; and for a short time, it was doubtful if the "Vampire of the sea" would not have been drawn forth from his element, hanging to his victim's leg. The horror of the spectators was further excited by the appearance of numerous other sharks closing in from all quarters, and trying to force themselves alongside their too successful kindred murderer.

At length, after a harrowing struggle, the bleeding and mangled man was torn from the jaws of the shark, and laid gently on the beach.

Alas, it was evident that life was ebbing fast away. The poor fellow had received two awful wounds. From the calf of the leg, where he was first seized and held with the tenacity of a bull-dog, the flesh was completely torn off; but the fatal wound was in the thigh, which, presenting a huge gap in the fleshy part, showed plainly that the femoral artery had been divided. Affectionately shaded from the blazing sun by his comrades, the sufferer gasped heavily once or twice, and then all was over. The general supposition was that, while one shark held him by the lower part of the leg, another gave the fatal bite.

This shocking occurrence sent the Mids. (for once serious and reflective) off to their brig. Many a good resolution was made as they turned into their hammocks.

The following morning at 8 A.M. a gun was fired and the convoy-flag hoisted for Chagres. So unusually profound, however, was the calm, that the flag drooped without the slightest movement, and the smoke hung like a shroud over the vessel; fitting symbols for so deadly a place. Our Mid. was shortly relieved from his morning watch, and gladly descended to breakfast.

In a cabin only eight feet by six, and destitute of ventilation, were assembled a jolly crew of ten young fellows. The place was a sort of extempore steam-bath, and its effects on the occupants may easily be imagined. To make matters worse, the ship's allowance of scalding tea for breakfast, was produced in a large tea-pot, and carefully stowed in the centre of a small table, as if to insure an impartial distribution of its steam. The thermometer was at 108 !

"Well, old fellow," said one of the party, "what was the cause of that bark on deck just now ?"

"Only that horrid convoy signal for Chagres," replied our midshipman. "What a dreadful place it is: This is our fourth trip running. We *deserve* to be sickly. Confound it!"

In order to take advantage of the land-breeze, every preparation was now made for sailing. The convoy consisted only of one schooner. She parted company willfully the first night, and was never seen afterward.

Fragrant and delicious, though laden with malaria and death, were the light land-breezes from the north. Sweeping over the swamps on which Fort Augusta was situated, they fanned with treacherous dalliance the heated frames of the crew laboring at the capstan.

"Cheerly, cheerly, men!" was the animating cry of the officer in command, as the massive links of the chain-cable came slowly, as if with obstinate reluctance, through the hawse-hole.

"Up with the anchor, lads; toss him up to the bow!" vociferated the officer.

Merrily revolved the capstan-wheel, while muscles and sinews were energetically strained to keep time to a lively tune from the fife. A hundred men concentrated their powers to weigh the anchor. Gay was their measured tramp, and irresistible appeared their strength as they rapidly circumambulated the great mechanical purchase. Suddenly however, the movement was stopped.

"Heave lads, heave together; tear him out of the ground!" exclaimed the officer.

With a simultaneous effort, every man exerted himself to the utmost: another heave, and yet another. All was in vain. The anchor appeared to be enchanted. A double purchase was then applied, and the mechanical skill of the vessel tried to the utmost. It was no use. The men might as well have endeavored to uproot Olympus.

As it was now clear that some uncommon cause prevented the purchase of the anchor, a requisition was dispatched to the dockyard for assistance, and the ship's company were sent to breakfast. Numerous were the surmises on this singular event. It was well known that the bottom of Port Royal harbor was composed of black mud, which, assuredly, could not present any formidable resistance. What could be the mysterious cause?

At length, an old tar, remarkable for taciturnity and good conduct as a seaman, held forth as follows:

"*I* knows all about it. *My* father told *me* as how that *his* father told *he*, that when the great earthquake come to pass in this here place in 1692, he warn't weaned; in which regard, his mother, babby in arms, takes and stows herself away in church just as the houses begins to topple. People thinks, in these parts, that the churches is safe, never mind what's a-happening outside. But this time it was no go, you see; 'cause just after she and the young 'un gets inside quite safe, down goes the town, church and all, right into the sea. Well, this, you know, begins to look rather serious! but luck's all in this world, and, somehow or the t'other, the babby was saved. You may laugh, if you like. Why, if what I am a-telling of you warn't true, how could I be here? I should like to know that, 'specially as that poor, tender, innocent babby was my old grandfather. Now, my bo's, I'm quite sure that our killick* is hooked under the *dientical* church-porch which it was the place my great-grandmother goes into. And that's the reason we can't get her out of the ground. What do you grin at, you lubbers? In course, I means the killick, and not my great-grandmother. You may heave at her as long as you like, but she'll never come up no more.†"

Shortly after, the "Lump," or dock-yard lighter, came alongside, and seized hold of the brig's chain with its iron claws.

* Anchor.

† This singular and almost incredible oral testimony corroborates, in a striking manner, the written accounts of the great earthquake at Port Royal, and would seem to be warranted by the known veracity and steadiness of the old sailor, a man of great age.

Still, for a considerable time, the anchor remained immovable; and the belief of all on board in the positive assertion of the old tar was confirmed. The anchor must have got foul of the church, there could be no doubt of it. Horrible sacrilege! But whether the church was most in danger, or the killick, was a matter of speculation, which probably gave rise to a warm controversy.

At last, the anchor gradually yielded to the vast power of the mooring lighter, and came slowly up to the bows.

A singular spectacle now presented itself. Three large anchors were entwined, as it were, in each other's embraces. This, at any rate, looked friendly. One of them was partly fused as if from the action of fire.

So singular a discovery caused much interest and speculation at the time. The old archives of the dock-yard were industriously inspected; but nothing was ascertained worthy of note from any credible authority. A story, nevertheless, became current that the anchors were part of the remnant of a prize captured by Benbow, and accidentally burnt.

As the sea-breeze had now set in furiously, the departure of the vessel was put off till the following day. When, however, the morning dawned, and the expected land-wind failed to arrive, the brig, anxious to get away, shipped her sweeps (eighteen long oars, five men to each), and pulled merrily through the southern passage.

Perched high on her wares, Dolly Johnson, the famous bumboat woman, accompanied the vessel, being towed alongside. This black Amazon gloried in possession of a canoe forty feet long, and barely two wide. Ranged round her were calabashes filled with eggs, yams, fried fish, and tropical vegetables, including pines, avocado-pears, and ochres.

"Tank heben, my sweet son," exclaimed Dolly to the midshipman of the watch, "no nasty doctor" (a particular sea-breeze so called) "come dis morning to mash up poor nigger 'omen canoe."

"Have a care Dolly, my dear," replied the youngster, "have a care; the doctor is coming down sharp. Remember the nigger song:

> 'O Miss Rosee, hab a care of de Jumbo,
> Him prickee de conscience like jigger in um bumbo.'"

"What for you speak like dat to me, bucra?" interrogated Dolly. "You robber, teaf, and hangman too."

Now, although poor Dolly was very irate at the youngster's banter, she had her weather-eye wide open, and was probably conscious of a certain change in the air caused by the approaching sea-breeze. This premonition of the coming wind is not perceptible except by the natives, or by those who have long resided in the West Indies. The author was much surprised at an instance of this kind while sitting after breakfast one morning and conversing with an invalid lady who had lived many years in tropical islands. In the midst of the discourse, she suddenly started from the sofa, and exclaimed:

"Ha, it is coming!"

"And pray," answered her companion, "*what* may be coming?"

"Why, the sea-breeze, to be sure; can't you feel it?"

"Feel it!" echoed he; "why, the thermometer is above 100. My clothes cling to my frame as if they would stifle me. I seem to sit in an oven. Depend on it, there is not the slightest symptom of the trade-wind."

In a few minutes, however, the refreshing rush of pure air was evident enough: there was no mistaking it.

To return to the brig:—every one on board was, in a short time, aware of the proximity of the breeze, symptoms of which grew stronger and stronger every minute.

"Let go de tow-rope, you cussed nigger!" exclaimed Dolly to a negro who was assisting her in navigating the canoe, and who was only a shade or two less black than herself. "Don't you see de man-o'-war bucra makee de sail!"

This was true enough; all hands in the brig were employed in preparing to spread the canvas. In a few minutes, the sails were loosed and set, and the yards braced sharp up on port tack. Before poor Dolly's boat could be cleared from the ship's side, the breeze, in a heavy squall, struck the vessel. So strong and sudden was the wind, that, in spite of letting fly every thing, the brig heeled so much that the lee-port sills were under water.

Impelled by the sudden gale, the vessel dashed madly onward. Alas for poor Dolly! Her "cussed nigger," an infirm old man, had failed to loose the long and narrow canoe from the brig's side. It was, indeed, a frightful thing to see this cockle-shell dragged through the water with such dangerous speed; and to aggravate the peril, the canoe had been fastened to the lowest of the gangway side-steps, now under water from the vessel's inclination. Aid from the ship was, for the moment impossible; and it appeared inevitable that the unlucky negress would be towed under water. At this critical moment, Dolly sprang forward, knocked her lubberly nigger off his seat, and severed the distended tow-rope with a single cut of her knife. This saved them both.

The last thing seen of them, as the vessel bore rapidly away along the coast of Jamaica for her destination, was Dolly with one hand steering her canoe, now under a snug lug-sail, and heartily thrashing her "cussed nigger" with the other.

On went the brig, studding-sails low and aloft. Gradually, the wind felt lighter as she approached the American continent, and at length, when just in sight of the high land of Porto Bello, subsided to a mere whisper. This lull was succeeded by rain which, during twelve hours, poured down without intermission.

Apparently, the deluge had returned, so overwhelming were the torrents. Even the boats at the davits, with plugs withdrawn, were overflowing. A light air at length drew the brig along the land, and she anchored at Chagres.

The whole country, where it could be seen, was covered with a dense forest of most luxuriant foliage; but the view was often concealed by opaque vapors which clung closely to the earth. Even a vertical sun was not powerful enough to clear away this dismal pall. Still, in spite of such repulsive appearances, there was something indescribably grand in that vast solitude. The current of the Chagre river rushing into the sea, formed a narrow line of yellow, which, like a serpent, trailed its hideous and ill-omened length, writhing with numerous intervolutions to the east or west along the coast, as guided and controlled by the tides and currents.

From the excessive dampness caused by almost perpetual rains, and the fact of the isothermal line of equatorial heat passing very near this place, the principle of vegetation is perhaps more powerfully developed here than in any other part of the globe. The vessel was now in the zone of the constant precipitation of rain. Large bushes (twelve feet high) of the sensitive tribe began to manifest consciousness of an advancing footstep, though at five yards' distance. When closely approached, they closed their leaves entirely without actual contact.

Perhaps some explanation of the continuous rains prevailing in this place may be found in the remarkable fact of certain intervals that occur in the chain of the Cordilleras or Andes, where low and level land interrupts the usual mountain ridge—the "back bone," as it has been called of America.

No person who studies physical geography can help being deeply interested by the singular conformation of the land at this precise spot. It is as if nature had anticipated the wants of human beings, and fashioned mother earth to meet the requirements of an advanced age. At any rate, the singular adaptation of ground about the Isthmus of Darien for a canal or railroad to the Pacific Ocean is a great and remarkable fact.

In contrast, as it were, to the prodigious quantity of rain that falls here, a singular phenomenon happens in the height of the rainy season, of which it is impossible to offer any satisfactory explanation. About the 20th of June, the rain suddenly ceases, and the sun shines out during five or six days with dazzling brightness. No instance is known of irregularity in this interruption of the season's course.

The mails having been carefully prepared, a large party of pleasure-seekers, besides the officer in charge, proceeded in the largest boat to examine the country. After a long pull, they arrived at the entrance of the harbor. Passing close to the rocks on the left, on which the Morro, or castle, of Chagres, is built, they were much interested by perceiving numerous guanas (lizards of gigantic dimensions). These hideous reptiles were creeping slowly among the bushes and small trees that clung to the slimy, unwholesome-looking rocks.

On rounding the point, the town of Chagres appeared, and miserably disappointed expectation. It was situated on a cleared space of perhaps one hundred acres, and consisted of a few houses composed of reeds or wood, which presented a scattered and squalid appearance. Having landed, the party was encountered by three soldiers—the custom-house guard. Poor wretches! Blighted by the filthy climate, they were the type of malaria. Their heads were tightly bound with Madras kerchiefs, and they were destitute of shoes or stockings. Instead of the independent and saucy bearing of the revenue guardians of this country, they begged, in whining accents, for tobacco.

As the party proceeded on their expedition, they came upon dense woods of the rankest vegetation. These interminable forests surrounded the plain on which stood the town of Chagres.

Several narrow alleys were cut through the tangled overgrowth, barely sufficient for men on foot to pass in Indian file. The dense jungle, saturated with moisture, cast forth an offensive vapor. With the lightest possible clothing, a serious oppression was experienced, and the weight even of a fowling-piece was a severe labor. Having wandered some hours in pursuit of game, the party was glad to return to the town, being quite exhausted and not having had a single shot.

After some rest, and a substantial luncheon, they proceeded to examine the castle of Chagres. This fortress was built by Spain, after Admiral Vernon's capture of Porto Bello in 1739, and showed evident signs of lavish expense. Before the capture, the fortress was insignificant. The Spaniards relied, as Drake expresses it, "upon the attachment of the natives, the strength of the country, the excessive unhealthiness of the climate, and its abundant fruits being very dangerous to be eaten for breeding of diseases." The great progress of events, however, which wrested these countries from the sway of Spain, entirely destroyed the importance of this stronghold, and the huge and massive fortress was gradually wasting away under the destructive influence of rank and climbing vegetation. What a satire on the extravagances of the old governments of Europe! And now behold the change! By a recent treaty between the great powers of the world, namely, England, France, and America, all this region—the region of the projected communication between the Atlantic and Pacific Oceans—is forever a neutral ground, open to the whole globe. Well may humanity be congratulated on this benign and salutary change in the spirit of the times.

Balboa describes enthusiastically his first view of the South Seas. Departing from Chagres with Indian guides (the Cimmarons), he thus describes the success of his enterprise.

"When," says he, "they pointed out the height from which I might see the other sea, so long looked for, and never seen before of any man coming out of our world, approaching to the top of the mountain, I commanded my men to stay, and went alone to the summit as if to take the first possession thereof; where falling prostrate upon the ground and raising myself again upon my knees, lifting up my eyes and hands toward Heaven, and directing my face toward the new-found South Sea, I poured forth my humble and devout prayers before Almighty God, as a spiritual sacrifice, with thanksgiving that to me was reserved this discovery." When he had said these words, he commanded his men to raise certain heaps of stones, instead of altars, in token of possession.

What a magnificent moment must this have been for the old Spanish adventurer! and with what sublime power and simplicity has he described it.

After a hasty survey of the castle, the party were glad to return to their vessel in the offing. Having been drenched with continual rain, the miserable and scanty accommodations of a small, old-fashioned brig were hailed with delight.

The wonderful improvement in the airiness of ships, and in the conveniences and comforts allotted, in the modern system of naval architecture, to seamen of all grades, is very conducive to discipline and health. For this essential advantage, the Royal Navy is undoubtedly indebted, in a great measure to Sir William Symonds.

CHAPTER II.

Want of Ventilation in the Brig—Myriads of Insects—Force of Habit—A living Snow-storm—Navy Bay—A Mangrove Swamp—Corallines and Stinging Coral—Cocoa-nut Trees—Effect on the Ship's Company of the excessive Rains—Violent Thunder-storm—Fishing Party—A dense Jungle—Adventures of a solitary Midshipman in a tropical Forest—Myriad Army of Ants—The Gekko—Huge Snake—An Alarm—Fugitive Apes—A wild Feast—The Nautilus—Return to Chagres for the Mails—A Spanish Lady and her Daughter as Passengers—The Lady's Canoe and Crew—Projected Theft and its Detection—The Yellow Fever on Board—Prepare for a Trip to Halifax—Effect on the Crew of Change of Climate—Approach to the stormy Region of the Gulf-stream—a Hurricane-squall—A Night Storm—Jollity in the Midshipmen's Berth.

THE brig, whose cruise we have been contemplating, was so confined below, being barely five feet between decks, that the air was extremely vitiated. This will cause no astonishment when it is considered that one hundred and twenty-five human beings were stowed away in her. No possible means of ventilation could be adopted except by hatchways. So oppressive an atmosphere brought into life myriads of insects. The beams overhead and bulkheads were infested by a layer of cockroaches, interspersed, by way of variety, with various other creeping abominations. If a glass containing liquid of any kind, was left but for a moment, the surface was thickly coated with struggling vermin. A favorite amusement in the Mids.' berth, was to pour some rum in a soup-plate, set it on fire, and pass it slowly along the beams and deck overhead. In a short time, these passes were rewarded with a rich harvest of cockroaches. So loathsome did this appear to strangers, who had never before seen any approach to a resemblance of one of the Egyptian plagues, that scarcely a single visitor could be persuaded to remain on board. The Mids., however, were so accustomed to their insect-guests, that, as expressed by one of the party, "We should feel quite lost without them."

Such is the force of habit and the love of *company*.

The following morning, still in pouring rain, the vessel weighed and proceeded to Navy Bay, there to await the return mail from the Pacific for Jamaica and England. A light air filled the sails, and, for two hours, the sun shone forth with piercing rays. The distance we had to run, about fifteen miles, was achieved in three hours. During the whole of this passage, the air was densely crowded with white butterflies, driven out to sea by the land wind. It was impossible to estimate their number, as neither one extremity nor the other of this living snow storm could be traced. So remarkable a swarm of insects gives force to the assertion of a celebrated naturalist who says that "if Nature had not formed numerous and powerful checks to this insect, its increase, in three years, would fill the world."

Navy Bay, now the site of busy preparation for the Darien Railroad, was then unblest by the works of man. From Chagres on the east, to Porto Bello on the west, not a single human habitation could be seen.

The vessel had anchored a short distance within the eastern arm of the Bay, in close vicinity to a mangrove swamp. These singular aquatic forests exhibit an apparent anomaly in nature. The tree of which they are composed, grows to the height of twenty-five or thirty feet, and flourishes chiefly on the margin of rivers close to the sea, salt water being necessary for its nourishment. Many lateral branches project to a considerable length from all sides of the trunk. These are thickly covered with leaves of dark green. At a certain length, the weight of the branch causes it to bend downward, when, attracted by the water, a number of flexible shoots droop down, submerge themselves, and take root in the mud. Then, rising again, they, in their turn, throw out ramifications, and thus extend the forest.

The interlacings of these shoots and branches form a coarse net-work under water, of wonderful strength and durability. The roots are covered with myriads of the family of crustacea and mollusca. These again attract numerous fish to prey upon them, forming altogether a reticulated marine-bower of surpassing interest and animation.

It is scarcely possible to behold such tangled, exuberant, and ever re-producing vegetation as this, without thinking of Milton's noble description of that multifarious tree, which

"In Malabar or Decan spreads her arms
Branching so broad and long, that in the ground
The bended *twigs take root*, and *daughters* grow
About the *mother*-tree, a pillar'd shade
High over-arch'd, and *echoing walks* between:
There oft the *Indian* herdsman, shunning heat,
Shelters in *cool*, and tends his pasturing herds
At *loop-holes cut* through thickest *shade*.*

---

* Nothing escapes the notice of wise poets. Milton could never have seen the Indian fig-tree; but he found an account of it in a botanical book, and then gave it perennial vitality in his great epic. In his notes to "Comus," Wharton, referring to the above passage from "Paradise Lost," tells us that the particulars which Milton has immortalized in his glorious versification, are derived from "Gerard's Herbal" (edit. 1633). "The ends of the branches," says Gerard, speaking of the arched Indian fig-tree, "hang downe and touch the ground, where they *take roote* and growe in such sort that those *twigs* become great trees: and these being grown up unto the like greatnesse, doe cast their branches or twiggy tendrels into the earth, where they likewise take hold and roote; by means whereof it cometh to passe, that of one tree is made a great wood or desert of trees, which the *Indians* do use for *coverture* against the *extreme heate of the sun.* Some likewise use them for pleasure, cutting downe by a direct line a long

Corallines, in large bunches like flowers, and of fantastic shape, flourished in the vicinity. These corals were extracted from the bottom by lowering a swab, the long tails of which became entangled among the delicate branches, and brought them up in triumph. The specimens thus procured, contained several species of the stinging coral, which furnished much *amusement* to the uninitiated by the sharp pain inflicted by them when applied to the tongue. Thus, it would appear that even pain is better than nothing. A sensation *must* be had, cost what it may.

Beyond this swamp, or forest, a fringe of lofty and majestic cocoa-nut trees, bending under their luscious burden, extended to the east. Large boat-loads of the fragrant nuts were brought off, as a supposed antiseptic, for the benefit of the crew. The use of them, however, was prejudicial, instead of salutary; and the health of the men was not improved until they got clear of the West Indies.

The excessive rains and dampness of the climate, and the consequent inability on the part of officers to give active occupation to the crew, had a sensible and deteriorating effect on the ship's company. It was generally remarked that irritability of temper was manifested even by those who had been noted for equanimity. In fact, cheerfulness had vanished under the influence of lassitude caused by this filthy climate. In place of the usual jollity in a man-of-war, a kind of superstitious lethargy appeared to

walke, or as it were a vault, through the *thickest* part, from which also they *cut* certaine *loop-holes* or windowes in some places, to the end to receive thereby the fresh *coole* aire that entreth thereat, as also for light that they may *see their cattell* that *feed* thereby, &c. From which vault or close *walke* doth rebound an admirable *echo* or answering voice. The first, or *mother*, of this wood, is hard to be known from the *children*."—It will be seen from this quotation that the great poet has availed himself of all the prominent words of the old herbalist; but then how skillfully has he epitomized the description, and given to it the graces of resonant verse.

have obtruded itself. This feeling was much aggravated by two days' incessant down-pour. The hoods over the hatchways although well calculated to keep out water, were equally successful in excluding air.

The whole of a particular day had been passed in idleness and sleep below. It can therefore be no matter of surprise that at 11 o'clock, P.M., a sudden and violent thunder-storm should find all hands wide awake, although sweltering in their hammocks and vainly courting sleep. During about fifty minutes, the terrific roaring of thunder shook the vessel to her centre. Vivid and forked lightning pierced the very seams of the decks. In the momentary lulls—lulls of most painful silence—suppressed groans, as if of terror or remorse, were slightly audible. Conscience plays strange tricks with us all. Sometimes it may happen that a bad man, owing to an exquisitely healthy *physique*, may possess a false *good* conscience—a kind of aurora borealis, which is but a mockery of the genuine dawn. While, on the other hand, certain it is, that bodily disturbance, such, for example, as an attack of dyspepsia, will produce a false *bad* conscience, and we are induced to mistake for a weight on the mind, that which in reality is nothing more than a weight on the stomach.

In this latter predicament let us hope the ship's company were placed: one half of them suffering under the malady of the climate, were nervously affected, and the symptoms spread like an epidemic among the rest. For the first time in their lives, the blue-jackets felt sentimental, remorseful, and afraid.

As the bells struck eight, or midnight, the last distant rumbling of the thunder died away, and was succeeded by an intense calm. Suddenly a shrill, strange scream smote the silence; it was repeated again and again; and louder and more frantic grew the outcries, until the din was drowned by all hands rushing up to ascertain the cause, when it was discovered that a favor-

K

ite cat in her nocturnal rounds had fallen overboard. There she was clinging to the ship's side, and holding on with her claws stuck in between the upper sheet of the copper sheathing and the wood-work. On lowering the bight of a rope, the poor animal immediately put her fore-legs in, and was hauled safely on board.

This little incident broke the spell.

Parties were occasionally sent up the bay to explore, or to procure fish and game. On one of these excursions, they proceeded to the head of the bay, where a small rivulet tempted them to land and haul the seine, or net. So great was the quantity of fish taken, that it was considered enough to supply the entire ship's company. A large fire was then kindled, and while some remained to prepare a savory meal, others, well armed, advanced into the interior, taking advantage of the rivulet's bed, which afforded the only practicable path through the dense jungle.

After penetrating some distance, our adventurers felt their curiosity excited by the prostrate trunk of a large tree. This gigantic denizen of the forest had fallen across the bed of the rivulet, forming a complete bridge. The part of the trunk where it had been severed, appeared as though gnawed by some animal, marks of teeth being visible all round the base.

Attracted by this singular circumstance, the party stopped awhile to speculate on it. Some went so far as to assert that it had been purposely felled by the instinct of wild animals, to assist them in crossing the stream. Others ridiculed this opinion, and declared that the marks of teeth were caused by herds of peccary, a kind of fierce, small pig, prevalent hereabouts in large droves, and which are in the habit of whetting their teeth against wooden substances, in order to be ready for any chance encounter that might turn up.

After an animated discussion, the party went on in quest of adventures. One of them, however, a Mid., feeling exhausted by the intense heat, determined to remain and await the return of his companions. Sitting on as dry and comfortable a seat as could be procured, he deposited his gun close beside him, and lighted a cigar.

Having enjoyed a few whiffs, he began to ruminate on the strange scene before him. Surrounded by an intertangled tropical forest, the sun's rays were completely concealed from his view. Close to his feet, his attention was attracted by a narrow ribbon of vivid green, which wound along the earth beneath the thick undergrowth. Examining this green ribbon attentively, he thought he perceived a slight movement in it; and, on a closer survey, he discovered it to be a train of large ants, each bearing upright in its forceps a portion of green leaf.

"Where the deuce does this road lead?" exclaimed he. "May I be hanged, without a drop of grog, if I don't explore this populous district!"

Picking up his gun, and drawing his case-knife to cut away the tendrils and claspers of the numerous climbing plants which impeded his path, he followed the curious "ant-road." This, however, was no joke. Sometimes, crawling on all fours, he became so entangled by the supplejack withies, that he could hardly clear one arm to free the other with his knife. Again, when the absence of underwood allowed a little more space, he was obstructed by the vast and prostrate trunk of a tree of countless age. With a spring and a chuckle, he was resolved to surmount this obstruction; but his meditated triumph was baffled. The tree, though looking sound as when it flourished in its prime, was decomposed, and its treacherous appearance proved a trap into which our middy sank to his arm-pits in a cloud of choking dust. Hitherto, every thing appeared to be what it was *not*: it was a place of grim delusions—a valley of shadows.

In spite of these bewildering discouragements, he persevered three hundred yards farther. Being now quite worn out by the severe labor, he sat down beside the ant-track. To his astonishment, the myriad army had not yet passed. On they came in one seemingly interminable stream; all with similar burdens, and all traveling in one direction. The portions of leaf they carried varied in size, from a pea to nearly half-a-crown. The disburdened ants, returning in the opposite direction, wound their way, so as not to incommode their laden brethren.

Just as he was preparing to return, our adventurer suddenly heard a sound so sharp and clear and close, that he interpreted it into a strange warning. A green lizard, about a foot long, was creeping on a branch within three feet of his head. With a prolonged hiss, it repeated, at short intervals, a sound resembling the words "Gekko! gekko!" It then protruded its forked tongue with sudden darts. Little did our careless Mid. know his danger; but he was fully acquainted with it some years after, when reading the work of that eminent naturalist, Count de la Cepède. "Of all the oviparous quadrupeds," says that author, "the gekko, so named from its cry, contains the deadliest poison. In this lizard, whose species is but too prolific, a corrosive liquor is exalted to such a degree as to carry corruption and death to all animals into which the active humor may penetrate. It is about a foot long; its skin is of a pale sea-green, covered with red spots. The eyes are very large, starting out of the head with long and narrow eye-balls. Its teeth are so sharp as to make an impression on steel. Each of its four legs has crooked claws, armed at the end with nails. The creature is almost entirely covered with warts, more or less prominent. Its bite is certain death, unless the part is cut away or burned."

"Hideous monster!" exclaimed our Mid.; "cut your lucky, or look out for squalls."

"Gekko! gekko! gekko!" iterated the lizard, as if in reply, and drawing himself stealthily toward the Mid.

"Incarnation of the Devil!" vociferated the latter, "put that in your pipe and smoke it."

As he spoke, he pulled the trigger of his gun, and blew the reptile to pieces.

The noise of the gun was followed by a sudden motion in the bushes. Through the curtain of smoke which clung heavily round, he perceived to his horror, a huge and slimy snake gliding past within arm's length.

"Only let me get safe out of this beastly wood!" ejaculated he. "If that infernal varmint had only caught me while hung up in the tangle! O dear! I mustn't think of that. I am sure, though, if he had swallowed me, I should have given him the stomach-ache. There's some comfort in the *lex talionis*."

With cocked gun, he carefully retraced his steps; and, after a while, was delighted to find himself once more beside the bridged rivulet. Taking a long draught of the tepid water, he began anxiously to expect the return of his companions. The brooding silence, nursed rather than disturbed by the streamlet and the gentle buzz of insects and lizards, was harshly broken by the sound of a rather distant shot. Another, and then another. Loud shouts now followed in quick succession, as of men in wild excitement.

As the sounds were evidently approaching, our Middy crouched down, with gun prepared for any game that might be driven past. Suddenly his ears caught a noise as of the light crackling of wood. A moment more, and a shaggy gray head peered out from the jungle, and a large ape leaped with nimble bounds, over the bridge. Our Mid. was so startled by this apparition, that he had not time to fire. Two more apes quickly followed the first, and bounded over. The last of the three stopped short when across, turned round with threatening gestures, and appeared inclined, in spite of the leveled gun, to return and attack the midshipman. His finger was on the trigger, and the barrel was aimed at the brute's heart. He was in the act of firing. What, then, could cause him to lower his gun, burst into a loud laugh, and exelaim, "Go to the devil, you stupid old female simia ?"

The explanation is simple and natural enough. A little baby ape had popped its queer, tiny visage over its mother's shoulders, and magically softened our reefer's nature. The shots now sounded close at hand, and evidently changed the ape's intentions. She turned and fled; the little one, looking round and gibbering with anger, shook its puny fist in impotent rage.

The party now returned to the beach, and feasted sumptuously on fish, armadillos (some of which the sportsmen had shot), and fragrant bowls of cocoa-nut milk.

Close to the beach where the ground was more open, one of the ant-roads was followed several hundred yards in opposite directions. No success attended this exploration; but the same animated and busy scene met the eye at every part of the route. Shortness of time, and the difficulty of following the course, prevented the length of these singular roads being ascertained.

The shores of the bay were strewed with a species of nautilus. Of these, the men picked up dozens, and took them on board to their shipmates, as playthings might be carried home to children, after a short absence.

"I say, Billy, my bo," exclaimed a great-whiskered Jack to his chum, on getting afloat, "here's a hankercher choke full of Portigee men-of-war for you."

"Portigee men-of-war be d—d," replied his friend. "What's the use o' they? You can't eat 'em."

After a stay of ten days, the vessel sailed back to Chagres for the return mail to Jamaica and England. Great was the delight of all hands when the flag, hoisted at the castle, gave notice that the mails had arrived. Boats were immediately dispatched, and were shortly seen returning, accompanied by a considerable freight. Two passengers—a Spanish lady and her daughter—came off in a canoe. Their anxiety to get forward to St. Juan de Cuba, *viâ* Jamaica, was so great, that the captain, out of compassion (to say nothing of gallantry), consented to take them, any delay in such a climate as Chagres being equivalent to a death warrant. The lady's canoe was well ballasted with bags of pesos (dollars). She did not appear in the least embarrassed by the absolute nudity of her crew, composed of six blacks. In some degree resembling the American backwoodsman, whose summer-costume consisted of a shirt-collar and a pair of spurs, the only articles of *dress* worn by the negro canoe-men were a kind of amulet or charm hanging from their necks, which they appeared to regard with the most profound veneration, and a case-knife slung round their middles. On one of the seamen attempting to touch an amulet, he was repelled with fierce indignation and horror by the miserable owner.

In spite of the extreme heat, these black men were shivering with cold, though large drops, like hot rain, rolled off their bare skins. Still they shivered and cowered, and seemed thankful for the smallest shelter, especially if near the galley fire. So relative is the feeling of heat and cold.

The vessel being prepared to sail immediately on receipt of the mails and freight, some youngsters were amusing themselves in the tops; and, while thus occupied, their attention was excited by the singular canoe alongside, and still more singular cargo. In the bottom of the canoe they perceived, fore and aft, a row of grass bags containing dollars. A suspicious movement of one of the blacks caught the keen gaze of a youngster in the top, who lying flat down, projected his eyes over the top rim, and took note of all that passed. During this scrutiny, he saw one of the black fellows, while pretending to fumble at the side of the canoe, gently pull out a small plug, causing a jet of water to run into her. This manœuvre the negro concealed by his leg. In a short time the bags of treasure were covered by water.

"What game are the rascals up to now?" thought our sharp-sighted youngster in the top.

Immediately after, another negro unslung his case-knife from his waist, affecting very industriously to pare his toe-nails; but in performing this natural operation, which created no suspicion in the vessel, he took care slily to rip open one of the dollar bags. Closing his knife, he began to work the bag with his feet, now nearly submerged. As the canoe rolled, the "detective eyes" aloft caught a momentary glimpse of bright new dollars, which were gently oozing out of their place of confinement.

With a bounce of delight, our Mid. flew down the rigging, and, touching his hat to the first lieutenant, explained what had happened. The process of hoisting in the treasure was instantly suspended; the niggers were bundled up on deck, and half a dozen active fellows sent into the canoe to bail her out. A hundred eager eyes, now directed from every position that commanded a view of the scene, were speedily gratified by the sight of a thick layer of sparkling dollars. Several of the bags were already tapped, and, had not a good look-out been kept from aloft, a large sum would have been abstracted.

Immediately after this, the vessel weighed, and proceeded on her trip to Jamaica. In consequence of the equatorial current being adverse, vessels making this voyage are compelled to hug the mainland of Central America, until a position is attained, about Carthagena, sufficiently far to the eastward to make the trade-wind favorable for crossing the Carribean Sea. This is a long and tedious part of the voyage, as light airs and calms are prevalent on the coast of the mainland.

Soon after leaving Chagres, the yellow fever, in a mild form, appeared on board, and attacked fresh victims every day. The moment, however, a departure was made from this pestiferous coast the disease readily yielded to medical treatment. Out of one hundred and twenty-five men of whom the crew was composed, eighty were laid up at one time. The Spanish lady still had excellent health ; and, with her daughter, enjoyed numerous "cigarros papillos." But, on her landing at Port Royal, she was seized with the fever in its most malignant form, and was carried off by it within two days of her landing. Every man of the crew speedily recovered.

Great was the delight of all hands at receiving orders to prepare for a trip to Halifax, and the vessel was speedily on her way there, *viâ* Bermuda. The change of climate had a marvelous effect upon the health of the crew. On entering the Atlantic through the Caycos passage, old and obstinate blains on the legs and feet, healed up as if by magic, and the crew felt braced and lively by so agreeable a change of climate. Calling at Bermuda to deliver dispatches, the vessel once more put her head to the northward.

About ten, A.M., the yards were braced up to a strong breeze from the west, and the ship darted forward like a hound slipped from its leash. The whole day was fine and invigorating, not betraying the slightest symptom of the heavy gale which was soon to menace us. At the usual quarters in the evening, the top-sails were double-reefed, and all made snug for a good night's run. Just as this evolution was finished, a vessel was viewed ahead, and speedily made out to be the packet for Bermuda, now overdue ten days.

While the two vessels were in the act of exchanging numbers, one of our Mids. was sent below to examine the barometer. Returning on deck with his report to the captain, he said he thought the instrument must be out of order, as the quicksilver had fallen so much. This report induced the captain to descend, and carefully note both barometer and simpiesometer. To his great surprise he found they had each sunk considerably. Coupling this disturbance of the quicksilver with the locality we were now approaching, namely, the stormy region of the gulf-stream, it became necessary to keep a sharp look-out. Accordingly, our careful and prudent skipper immediately turned the hands up to shorten sail. Top-gallant yards and masts were quickly got on deck, topsails close reefed, and mainsail furled.

Still all looked bright and clear. At this time, half-past six, P.M., the packet brig was two miles to windward, staggering under a heavy press of canvas, *her* course being due south, *ours* due north, the wind west, or fair for both. Numerous were the gibes and sneers at the captain's "timidity," as it was called. In truth, the contrast was so marked between the canvas carried by the two vessels, that, to those without responsibility, undue caution seemed to be observed.

"Look at that little hooker," exclaimed one, "how she flies! Why, she'll be at Bermuda to-morrow morning."

These words attracted the author's attention, and he looked long and steadfastly at the small vessel. His was the last eye that ever beheld her. A haze crept over the scene: the watch was called, and the men off duty went below.

Suddenly, a sharp, clear voice was heard ringing through the ship:

"All hands trim sails! Man the weather braces! Square away the yards!"

Not one moment too soon was this mandate obeyed. A hurricane-squall had overtaken us from the south, right astern. The vessel heeled violently over; the lee-hammock nettings were under water, and appeared to be flying-to against the helm. The precautions before taken had now their reward; for, in a few minutes, every sail was safely furled, except close-reefed topsails.

"What a pace she is going!" exclaimed the officer of the watch. "Heave the log."

The Mid. of the watch, in spite ot the thorough drenching he got in executing this order, made his report smilingly, and with an air of triumph:

"Twelve and six, Sir."

From that time to this, the packet-brig has never been heard of. The squall that came up astern of our vessel took her aback! Thus perished the poor "Recruit." This rough lesson was not thrown away; the experience gained by it has saved several lives.

As the evening wore on, dark and slate-colored clouds rose in all directions. The air became sensibly colder, and a continuation of violent squalls swept furiously over the vessel. Still the water remained quite warm, forming a striking contrast to the coldness of the atmosphere.

"We are in for a night of it, I am quite sure of that," observed the lieutenant of the first watch, as he came on deck to relieve the other officer. "It is awfully dark and black and dense. Just wait a minute for my eyes to get used to it, before I relieve you."

To the party on deck, the appearance of the vessel was very impressive. Flying furiously through the water, the yard-arms, and boom-ends sometimes dipped in the creamy and sparkling foam. On these occasions the rolling of the vessel was fearful, and the hammock-nettings plunged to such an extent, that whole volumes of water rushed inboard. Before these could wholly escape by the opened ports, they dashed, torrent-like, across the decks, clearing away every thing which was not firmly lashed and secured. Still the ship flew onward with perilous speed. Notwithstanding this rapid dart through the waves, a huge sea would, every now-and-then, overtake us in a threatening manner close to the stern, striking it with gigantic force, deluging the decks fore and aft, and causing the brig to quake and tremble as if with arrant fear. Still, on she went with headlong speed, striving to outrun her watery pursuers.

Let us now descend into the midshipmen's berth. Within this miserable hole were crammed ten juvenile human beings.

Regardless of the furious war of elements above, these thoughtless lads were eager for the arrival of their messmate from the deck. He had promised them a long yarn. In anticipation of this treat the table was spread with a dirty canvas cloth. A bottle of rum peeped invitingly from the corner of a beaufet, and each inhabitant of this dismal den tightly clasped his glass—a necessary precaution, as the excessive motion of the vessel tossed every unsecured article violently about.

"Now then," said one of the youngsters, "hurrah for a long yarn!"

As he spoke, the berth-door was opened, and the mate walked in. Casting his wet coat and boots on the steerage deck, he waited the roll of the ship. Adroitly taking advantage of the proper moment, he vaulted over the table, and seated himself against the after bulk-head. Filling a stiff "sou'-wester," he lifted the brimming glass to his lips.

"Here's luck, my lads," said he; "luck to us all! And now you shall have the discourse I promised."

CHAPTER III.

THE GUNNERY-MATE'S YARN.

"WELL, my lads," continued the mate, "I am not much of a hand at a yarn; but if you like to hear something new about matters connected with gunnery, I shall have great pleasure in communicating to you a few curious facts.

"It is impossible to deny that, of late years, our navy has improved more in the science and practice of gunnery, than in any other branch of the service. But I think there is one kind of projectiles, namely Congreve rockets, which are not sufficiently appreciated. I was more confirmed in this opinion on reading a report of the Select Committee of the House of Commons, on the Steam Navy. The result of this report is that mercantile steam-ships, of the size and strength necessary for the reception of such guns as are in use in the royal navy, would be a most valuable auxiliary force for the national defense.

"Now it is quite clear that none of the 1110 registered British merchant-steamers, mentioned in the report, under four hundred tons, are capable of carrying such guns as would render them available in naval warfare. There remain, therefore, one hundred and seventy-three steamers above that size. Deduct at least twenty per cent., for old and useless vesssels, and barely one hundred and forty are left. In case of war most of these vessels would run their passages as usual, fighting their way. The coasts of England would consequently still remain under the guardianship of the war-vessels. Now, it is quite certain that this latter force would be utterly insufficient to protect all the harbors on the coast of England. I have considered this subject well, and believe that a position of perfect safety may be achieved by arming the smaller vessels of the steam mercantile marine with Congreve rockets.

"These projectiles, and the arrangement of their fittings, are in a very different state from what they were in the late war. At Walcheren, the officers who managed the rocket department had their clothes burnt from their persons by the back-fire. This incident, coupled with the unwillingness of many naval officers of high rank to admit their efficiency, has created a prejudice against their use.

"When Lord Collingwood was first offered the use of Congreve rockets by the Admiralty of the day, his answer was characterized more by prejudice than by reason; he decried the new invention, contemptuously calling them 'useless sky-rockets.' Even at the present day very few officers are acquainted with their power, or have sufficient experience in their management, to make them effective. A very glaring case happened lately in the royal navy. A steam-vessel, fitted with rocket tubes, was being prepared for action. The men, not understanding the use of the little bag of bursting-powder intended to fill the shell at the end of the rocket, employed it in priming the rocket; consequently, when the fuse was applied, a loud explosion ensued, bursting the tube, knocking down the sapient gunners instead of the enemy, and blowing the rocket overboard. This lubberly occurrence was loudly trumpeted forth as an instance of the danger and uncertainty of Congreve rockets.

"Having given you an instance of prejudice in former, and of absolute ignorance in later times, I will now call your attention to the most remarkable instances of the efficiency of the missiles in question, as recently exhibited. First, the destruction of the Chinese Admiral's junk by a rocket fired from the 'Nemesis;' and, secondly, the havoc inflicted by the rocket-battery at San Lorenzo, in the Parana. The latter application of rockets was considered by Sir Charles Hotham as mainly conducive to the safe passage of the convoy past the batteries. He characterized it in his official dispatch, as of 'essential service.' I consider these as the most effective employments of the Congreve rocket that have ever taken place.

"That great military authority, Marmont, Duc de Raguse, speaks in high terms of these projectiles. In his work entitled 'Esprit des Institutions Militaires,' he thus expresses himself: 'I think the Congreve rocket is destined to effect, in the field and in infantry contests, an alteration as extensive as that which in naval warfare and coast defense may be expected from hollow shot, and the Paixhan guns. The first campaign in which Austria may be engaged, is likely to exhibit an extensive use of the rocket.'

"Now, my lads, I am of opinion that the Marshal, though undoubtedly a man well versed in the science of war, did not perceive, with a nautical eye, the most important service to be derived from rockets. Before I enlarge on this, let us overhaul the table of the mercantile marine. This is necessary, as my argument is mainly founded on the statistics exhibited in it. This table embraces only such steam-vessels as the parliamentary committee considers incapable of carrying guns sufficiently heavy to act in offensive warfare. It will be well to bear this in mind.

PORT.	No.	TONNAGE.
London	243	35,460
Boston	1	79
Bridgewater	1	66
Bristol	27	3,015
Caernarvon	1	176
Carried Forward	273	38,796

Port.	No.	Tonnage.
Brought Forward	273	38,796
Cardiff	7	532
Carlisle	2	434
Chepstow	3	191
Chester	6	705
Clay	1	50
Dartmouth	1	25
Dover	2	195
Falmouth	1	81
Feversham	1	28
Gainsborough	2	184
Gloucester	3	295
Goole	5	457
Grimsby	1	81
Hartlepool	3	183
Hull	21	3,070
Harwich	1	294
Ipswich	4	344
Lancaster	3	465
Liverpool	69	10,493
Lynn	3	438
Llanelly	2	206
Maryport	1	54
Newcastle	163	9,124
Newport	2	160
Plymouth	5	568
Poole	1	130
Portsmouth	4	290
Preston	9	1,260
Pwllhelly	1	115
Ramsgate	5	1,150
Rochester	4	296
Runcorn	1	143
St. Ives	4	1,000
Southampton	25	4,432
Shields	27	1,576
Stockton	25	1,744
Sunderland	28	1,541
Carried Forward	719	81,130

Port.	No.	Tonnage.
Brought Forward	719	81,130
Swansea	11	1,141
Weymouth	1	120
Whitby	1	80
Whitehaven	3	587
Wisbeach	4	270
Yarmouth	10	1,169
Aberdeen	7	1,017
Alloa	3	398
Anstruther	2	208
Ayr	1	95
Campbeltoun	2	462
Dundee	7	680
Glasgow	65	10,952
Grangemouth	3	157
Greenock	4	702
Inverness	1	51
Irvine	1	134
Kirkaldy	2	298
Kirkwall	1	182
Leith	18	2,644
Montrose	1	140
Perth	1	49
Port Glasgow	6	787
Belfast	5	620
Cork	13	1,852
Dublin	27	6,593
Dundalk	1	309
Londonderry	3	846
Newry	1	350
Sligo	1	74
Waterford	9	2,614
Wexford	1	362
Drogheda	2	382
Total	937	117,455
Deduct twenty per cent.	187	23,491
Remains	750	93,954

"We have here a list of seven hundred and fifty steamers, of all sizes up to four hundred tons, which, in the Parliamentary Report, are condemned as useless. The tonnage amounts to about ninety-four thousand tons, and the vessels are distributed in the very places required, that is to say, at the ports all round the coasts of Great Britain.

"This force, properly fitted, can be made so formidable, that I advisedly assert, it will be more than a match for the largest fleets the world could muster to attack this country."

"Draw it mild, old chap," interposed a Mid., "that's rather a tough 'un!"

"Well," replied the mate, "it looks so, I confess, at first sight; but just hear what I have to say. Suppose, then, we take one of these little steamers, and estimate the effect, if armed according to my ideas. Say, at a venture, 'Waterman, No. 1,' a vessel which, together with her class, is well known on the Thames above bridge. She is one hundred and five feet long, and thirteen feet five inches beam. Place in her, fore and aft amidship, as many of the new circular pivot rocket-tubes as she will carry. As the newly-invented rockets are projected without sticks or poles, a distance of six feet apart would be ample for the battery. This vessel, therefore, one hundred and five feet long, could carry seventeen tubes, leaving three feet to spare. Should these tubes be skillfully and quickly handled, five discharges from each can be made in one minute, being eighty-five in that very short space of time, or four hundred and twenty-five in five minutes!

"Two men could manage the tube on deck easily. The great difficulty would be a sufficient supply of ammunition, which, however, might be obviated by a man stationed below to each tube, and employed thrusting up rockets, through a round hole in the deck, as fast as wanted. By these means one of the little river-boats could fire at a greater rate than the largest ship in the world.

"I may have underrated the space (six feet) required by the rocket-tubes. At any rate, half the number could be easily placed; and even this great diminution would still give us the vast amount of forty-two and a half a minute. This, however, is an exaggerated reduction. I merely wish to be within the mark.

"Suppose, then, with 'Waterman, No. 1,' thus armed, I could manage to get under a line-of-battle ship's stern, at night or in a fog. What would be the consequence? why, before she could be clear for action—men dressed and all—say five minutes, I should have raked her with four hundred and twenty-five discharges. As I should take good care to be within a few yards, the chances are that every shot would tell. What sort of plight would she be in then? Four hundred and twenty-five shots in one vessel, is more than has yet been received, without destruction, by any ship.

"With a man-of-war screw-steamer, one hundred and eight feet long, you may fairly say the effect would be still greater. Let us compare a vessel of this description with a crack steamer of the present day. The first ship of this kind that I can call to mind as being in admirable order and discipline—in fact, the beau-ideal of what a steamer ought to be—is the 'Devastation,' lately commanded by Captain Henry. She is one hundred and eighty feet long, carries two eighty-four and four thirty-two pounder guns, and can fight four guns on the broadside.

"Let us now suppose this almost perfect steamer to meet our rocket-screw. We will imagine them to commence firing at the same moment. The 'Devastation' would fire her four broadside guns at the rate of one broadside in two minutes. This would give, at the end of six minutes, twelve shots. Now let us see what the rocket screw would have done in the same time. She mounts, we will say, twenty-eight rocket-tubes, taking rather less room than one to six feet. Multiply twenty-eight by five, the number of discharges from each tube in a minute, and six minutes will give the aggregate of eight hundred and forty rockets in the hull of her antagonist. Pray how would poor 'Devastation' feel after this dose ?"

"Hold hard, old chap!" interrupted a youngster. "Your circular tubes would become red-hot after a few discharges."

"Of course they would," replied the mate. "But there would be plenty of water to cool them, wouldn't there, spoony? Of one thing the Ordnance Department must be careful; and that is, to have the tubes made entirely, of metal. Should any wood, or other inflammable substance be present, it will of course burn like tinder after a dozen discharges.* When I commanded a rocket battery, I found, after about a dozen discharges, that the tubes were red-hot. Some stupid gunners had welded one of the tubes with spun yarn, which burned so furiously that the tube was disabled for several minutes. This might have been a serious matter, as I was then covering a large convoy of merchant-vessels with only six tubes, firing at the rate of forty a minute."

"What an awful fire, to be sure!" exclaimed the youngster. "What effect had it on the enemy?"

"The effect," answered the mate, "was prodigious. The enemy appeared quite paralyzed. And well he might, with such a deadly shower."

"I wonder," observed the assistant surgeon, "why the Admiralty has not tried this scheme."

"It is not for want of knowledge," replied the mate. "I was so impressed with its importance, that I was simple enough to put it on paper, and forward it to head-quarters, marked 'Private and Confidential.'"

* We are informed that an experimental metal tube is stowed away in the "Excellent." Some squabble between the Admiralty and the patentee preventing this useful invention being properly tested.

"Never call *me* a spoony again, after that," said the youngster who had previously ventured a remark or two. "But pray what answer did you receive?"

"Why, none at all," answered the mate; "although I fished out that every thing was being prepared exactly as I had suggested."

"You don't really mean to say," inquired the youngster, "that you never received any answer, gentle or simple?"

"None at all, I assure you," iterated the mate. "I suppose the Ordnance will get the credit of it when it comes out, or somebody else."

"Well," remarked the assistant surgeon, "I am no judge of these matters; but your account appears so plausible, that I am convinced it should be tried."

"And if it succeeds," suggested the youngster, "you ought immediately to be promoted, and appointed to a screw-steamer to carry out your plan. Pray may I ask," continued he, "what prospects have you in the service?"

"Why," replied the mate, "I have little or no interest, and therefore do not expect any other fate than to remain on half-pay ashore during the remainder of my life."

"What a dreadful existence for an active fellow like you!" exclaimed the assistant surgeon. "Your mind will prey upon itself. You will either take to literary pursuits, or go mad."

"Neither," returned the mate. "I have ample means. If the service, my great ambition, should be closed against me, I shall take my children to the Colonies, or, what I consider a much better field for activity, capital, and intelligence, the United States of America, that great country, so famous for its common sense and liberality of opinion."

"I can not help saying," observed the assistant surgeon, "that as a family man myself, I quite agree in your view of the matter. If, with your advantages of money and connection, with a high character as a naval officer united to an ardent love of your profession—if you, I say, see no prospect in the navy, but a miserable half-pay, and a realization of the result of 'hope deferred,' what, on earth, will be the prospect of your children fifteen years hence? Go, my friend, go, by all means, to America or the Colonies. In either of those lands, you will have a much better chance of happiness for yourself and family."

The gale now roared with increased fury. The hatchways being battened down, the atmosphere of our berth was not only oppressive but nauseous to a loathsome degree. Still the jolly party there crammed together, were as light-hearted and reckless as if they had continued in the stagnant calm of Port Royal harbor. "Every man to his glass!" was the universal shout "Steward! bring in more grog and biscuits. We will have the remainder of the rocket-yarn, if we founder in the midst of it."

At this moment, a loud and confused sound was heard on deck, followed by the trampling of feet. "Never mind that *bobbery!*" exclaimed a voice. "I know what it is; I always predicted it. The main topsail is blown clean out of the boltropes."

This prophetic announcement was immediately confirmed, accompanied by the additional intelligence that both quarterboats were washed away.

"Now, then, old fellow," said the youngster, "fire away! Let us hear the end of your yarn."

"Willingly," replied the mate. "Let us 'hark back' to our subject. Were we, according to the system I have mentioned, to avail ourselves of the little steamers so summarily dismissed by the report, what would be the result? Sufficiently startling to convince the most sanguine and powerful enemy that his utmost efforts to invade this country would be worse than idle. It is considerably under the mark to take six inches length for every ton of measurement. Ninety-four thousand tons of steam-shipping would therefore be equal to a space of steamer's deck forty-seven thousand feet long. This length, divided by six, will give the number of rocket-tubes capable of being mounted, that is, nearly eight thousand rockets, equal to a fire of forty thousand discharges a minute.

"Let us take, for example, the twenty-four vessels of the Waterman and Citizen Companies, and arm them in the manner above stated. What fleet would be safe against their attack either at sea or in harbor? Who that has been at night-quarters in a line-of-battle ship has not felt the disadvantage of being exposed to the fire of any thing not boxed up, as it were, and confined in its movements? What gallant admiral, with the best organized fleet in the world under his command, could sleep soundly, if he knew these twenty-four little steamers were prowling about within five hundred miles? What harbor in Europe would be safe? what dockyard or arsenal? What precaution could keep any port clear of some part of this hornet's nest of stingers? The most vigilant look-out might be overcome by a squall, a passing mist, or a fog.

"As for blockading an enemy's port, such as the old war-officers are so fond of yarning about, that would be preposterous. No blockading fleet of any force, more particularly sailing vessels, could lie in safety within twelve hours' run of any port whence these steamers could emerge during the night. No doubt *all* the rocket steamers would not escape; a well-directed shot would be sufficient to destroy any one of them. Let me ask, however, if the naval officers of England would not gladly run the chance. Why, for such a service as this, the greatest desire and anxiety would be manifested. Conceive the delight of getting alongside a huge three-decker at anchor. The very idea of a small and miserable mite, a London-bridge 'Cricket,' a wafter of halfpenny passengers, grappling on equal terms, and any chance of success with a huge leviathan of one hundred and twenty guns, would stimulate the imagination of any lover of enterprise.

"Now, my hearties, I will just call your attention to the prodigious power which regularly prepared men-of-war screw steamers would have, if built for this purpose. I feel so convinced on this subject, that if I had command of one of these vessels, I would not hesitate to attack any ship that swims. Not, mind you, as Nelson attacked the French fleet at Trafalgar, for, in the present day, that method of assault would be fatal.

"To conclude, my lads, the management of the navy must be thoroughly remodeled. We must have a permanent Board of Admiralty; some common-sense arrangement, which will at once, and forever, put an end to parliamentary pitchforking into promotion and emolument. This abuse has hitherto been the greatest bane of the royal navy. If these old customs are not modified, if new tactics are not thoroughly examined and tried, if we do not keep pace with the rapid march of the times in the present age, we shall, in the event of another great war, &c., &c., &c. Now let us turn in; I have the morning watch."

This closed the sitting, and all the mess scrambled into hammocks.

During the whole night the brig made good progress to the northward. This favorable run continued during three days; at the end of which time we were, by reckoning, on the tail of one of the lesser banks of Newfoundland. The gale had moderated so considerably, that the usual promenaders of the quarter-deck (the idlers) were enjoying their favorite exercise, which had been so long interrupted.

On approaching the coast of Nova Scotia, dense fogs prevailed. These, together with the impossibility of taking observations, caused great uncertainty as to the vessel's position. She was now, by dead reckoning, close to the land, in forty fathoms water. As it is usual in these blinding fogs to signalize the shore by means of cannon, a thirty-two-pounder was fired. All hands were now on the alert, every man listening attentively for an answer. The brig was lying-to in a light air, and the sea was as smooth as glass. During a brief interval, the only sound that met our ears was the fall of large drops of moisture, condensed on the shrouds and rigging. After a few minutes of earnest attention, a distant boom was heard in reply.

"That's the shore gun!" was the universal exclamation.

"Let them have another!" ejaculated the captain.

The gun was once more loaded and run out, and again opened its hoarse throat to its mate ashore. This was replied to immediately. Being now tolerably certain of the brig's position, the order was given, "Hands make sail! Topmen aloft, and loose top-gallant sails! Overhaul the gear of courses! Brace up the main yard!"

In a moment the brig was sliding through the thick shroud of fog in the direction indicated by the answering gun from the land.

"How oppressive, thick, and heavy, is this fog!" exclaimed the surgeon. "To make use of a Mid's. expression, you might cut it with a hatchet."

"It is so, indeed," observed the purser. "Why, one can not make out the people on the forecastle."

The brig seemed to grope its way onward like a blind man. As, however, the roaring of the port gun (increasing in strength) indicated our approach to the iron-bound coast of Nova Scotia, we felt confident in our course, though external objects were thickly vailed from sight. Louder and louder grew the reports, till, at length, one explosion, sounding almost overhead, caused a sensible vibration in the brig.

Suddenly, as if by magic, the whole scene changed, as the bowsprit and forecastle emerged from the bank of fog, and drew out into bright and clear sunshine. In a moment more the vessel was clear, as if in a new world. It is impossible to describe the enchantment of this sudden and unexpected change. Astern, like a huge and dingy cliff, loomed the fog bank which had so long enveloped the brig. Even the breeze appeared to sympathize with the exhilaration of the crew, and freshen considerably.

Our vessel now darted forward with great speed, quickly gained the entrance to Halifax harbor, and was soon comfortably anchored off the dockyard of that port.

HOW TO GOVERN A MIDSHIPMAN'S MESS.

CHAPTER I.

Blockading Squadron off Alexandria—The Egyptian Fleet—A longed-for "Scrimmage"—Disappointment—Commotion in the Midshipmen's Berth—Attack on the Caterer—Turbulent Discussion—Signal to Quarters—Radical Meeting—The Caterer Deposed—Anarchy—Alexandria and Pompey's Pillar—Monopolizing System of the Pasha—Her Majesty's Ship "Medea"—A Steamer a-fire—Explosion of a Shell—Disastrous Consequences—The Syrian Gale—Casualties.

Beautiful to behold was the English blockading squadron off Alexandria in November ,1840. During several weeks six huge two-deckers "patrolled" before the entrance of this classic port. The weather was settled and delightful—the sea as smooth as a sylvan lake.

The Egyptian fleet, outnumbering our blockading ships threefold, apparently made every preparation to come out and force the blockade—a manifestation which sometimes proceeded so far that their royals were set and head-yards braced for casting. This looked as if the enemy were really in earnest, and caused most intense anxiety on our part for the fulfillment of what was thus threatened. Snuffing-up with delight the gentle breeze blowing directly out of port, we hugged closely and in compact line of battle, the hostile shores bristling with batteries.

Thousands of eyes from the blockading ships were directed toward the enemy's movements. In that magnificent squadron there was not one man who would not joyfully have given a year's pay to insure the longed-for "scrimmage." But it was not to be: Mehemet Ali had too great a regard for the safety of his ill-gotten fleet; and all his threatening preparations ended in "moonshine."

Our expectation of a brush with the Egyptians being thus disappointed, an unusual portion of ill-humor prevailed afloat; and, as if no additional cause for grumbling should be lacked, our fresh provisions were exhausted by the prolongation of the blockade. We had, consequently, a dreary prospect of "short commons and *ennui*."

In this state of things, not much surprise was felt at hearing that the midshipmen's berth in the —— had been the scene of a violent commotion on the part of the "young gentlemen," who were aghast on finding one day nothing to cover their ample table but four scanty dishes of salt horse. Midshipmen are not, in general, the most patient or reasonable of human beings; and, on this occasion, the anger of the youngsters in question was unbounded, and could scarcely find adequate vent, although the maledictions leveled against the caterer (who unfortunately for himself, was a civilian) were exceedingly ingenious in their variety, including some choice specimens of novel vituperation, in the contrivance of which sailors surpass every class of men on earth.

When downright hunger is the subject of debate, the suggestions of reason are faint indeed. The unfortunate caterer tried to justify his administration by pleading necessity, and by urging every other argument dictated by good sense and prudence, and warranted by truth. All was of no avail: borne down by the clamor of the middies, he took refuge in the sick-bay, followed by a general shout of "Down with the doctor's mate!" No starving caterer! Hurrah for a radical mess! Republics for-ever!"

Having thus compelled the flight of Æsculapius the younger, a very turbulent discussion took place in the gun-room. Many orators rose at once—different schemes were simultaneously proposed—all were speakers and no hearers—every one declaimed with peculiar nautical eloquence, but no one would listen; and the hubbub and the din were bewildering:

> "Forthwith a hideous gabble rises loud
> Among the speakers; each to other calls,
> Not understood; till hoarse, and all in rage,
> As mock'd, they storm."
>
> MILTON.

Suddenly, however, the well-known signal to quarters was heard. This, in an instant, stilled the tumult. There was a quick rush to the door; all strove and scuffled to get rapidly to their stations in different parts of the vessel; and, in an incredibly short time, the ship, a huge eighty, was cleared as if for action. Her magnificent lower deck showed to great advantage a formidable row of sixty-eight and thirty-two pound guns, manned by a crew in a perfect state of discipline. Well might an Englishman be proud of that ship, and of her efficiency. She was a counterpart in order and discipline of nearly every one of the Mediterranean fleet, which, at that time, consisted of seventeen sail of the line. Never before had England so well-equipped and efficient a fleet at sea.

After quarters, a meeting of the radical portion of mates and Mids. was held on the fore part of the main-deck, to take into consideration what measures should be adopted toward a reform of the mess. As a preliminary, it was put to the vote that "the doctor's mate be deposed."

This was carried by acclamation; but so wide was the difference of opinion touching the other proposed resolutions, that none of them were approved, and not even a successor was named to the former caterer. Nothing, therefore, could ensue but perfect independence and liberty, delightfully evidenced the next time the mess sat down to dinner, when potatoes, books, junks of salt horse, &c., did duty as missiles, and were hurled across the table from the hand of one to the head of another, as a pleasant and graceful fancy might dictate. Every member of the company seemed resolved, by exhibiting his individual proficiency, to justify the old injunction—"Go to sea and learn manners."

All this was vastly agreeable for a time, until it was discovered that the viands were frequently waylaid on their road to the gun-room dinner-table; and then it was suspected that "radical institutions," however specious in their origin, might possibly not promote the comfort of communities, and that disorder, however fascinating in itself, was not altogether free from inconveniences. Be this as it may, it is certain that the poor republican middies were half starved, and that their democratic leaders grew proportionately plump.

We shall see by-and-by that the old march from rebellion to despotism was repeated in the instance before us. At present, however, other matters claim our attention.

One morning the squadron in line of battle was standing to the northward. Longing eyes were fixed on the classic city of Alexandria, about five miles under the lee. Pompey's Pillar (improperly thus called), defying the wear of ages, attracted the curiosity and admiration of officers and men. The next conspicous object which excited the attention of the numerous lookers-on in the squadron was the Schuna, or range of warehouses for the reception of the surplus produce of Egypt.

According to the Pasha's monopolizing system, the entire growth of the country comes into his hands at prices fixed by himself, and the grower is not permitted to resort to other markets. Not only does this restriction apply to the commodities of Egypt, but to those of adjacent countries wherever the Pasha's influence extends embracing the coffee of Mocha, the gums and drugs of Arabia, the tobacco of Syria, feathers from the interior, elephants' teeth, &c.; all of which are purchased for *him* in the first instance.

Thus did the wily Mehemet Ali combine the tyranny of the ancient time with the commercial spirit of the present day.

With the admirable spy-glasses in the —— the most minute objects could be perceived on the enemy's batteries. An English line-of-battle ship is better supplied with these instruments than the shore-going reader can imagine. The most costly glasses are "plenty as blackberries." The author possessed at that time a capital Dollond, which was supposed to be absolute perfection, and yet this glass having recently undergone the process of "illuminating" by Mr. Knight of Southampton, has been improved thirty-three per cent. A knowledge of this is of obvious importance to naval officers.

To seaward, and about five miles to windward, was her Majesty's steam-ship "Medea" under easy sail *without steam.* Slowly and majestically did our huge leviathans of the deep pursue their course in such close and compact order, that to an uninitiated observer they would appear in dangerous proximity. The mate of the —— forecastle, perched upon the Jacob's ladder of the fore-rigging, noted the wide difference in the sailing qualities of the squadron, and hugged himself, with a sailor's glee, in the conviction that the ——, with only her three topsails, could easily preserve her station, while the vast machine ahead, with double the sail on her, could hardly keep her hinder parts clear.

Suddenly the order was given, "after-guard and mizen-top men, trim sails! Square the cross-jack yard!"

The yards were instantly squared—the giant ship felt the check and gradually increased the distance (somewhat too short) from the vessel ahead. The mate's triumphant smile at this clear proof of his pet ship's speed was changed by the boatswain exclaiming "Mr. ——, there's summut to do now, I'll bet my seven-bell tot. Look at the flagship's buntin' a-going up. I'm blest, but the steamer's a-fire!"

This was too true. On glancing to windward, smoke appeared issuing from the steamer, though her boilers were not in use. Simultaneously the answering pennants of all the ships were running up to the commodore's signal, "Boats to proceed to assistance of ship in distress!"

The ponderous yards were instantly squared, and the two-deckers which before appeared calm, silent, and almost sluggish, were now, as if by magic transformed into the most intense activity. In a few minutes, the barge and pinnance of the —— were suspended high in air: a succession of loud splashes announced the reception by Mother Ocean of these boats and the two cutters; and, a moment after, thirty or forty other boats belonging to the squadron were pulling as if for life, in the direction of the steamer. A double stimulus actuated the crews: not only did they desire to outrun the boats belonging to their own ships, but were tenfold more desirous to get ahead of the boats of others.

The mate (to whom allusion has already been made) being in the barge, and having seen every thing to rights in his boat, turned round to look at the ships. They were now under a cloud of canvas, striving, by beating to windward, to approach the unfortunate steamer. His delight, and that of the boat's crew, was extreme, to see their ship gradually draw away from and distance the rest, as though they were at anchor.

As they approached the steamer, all sorts of conjectures were hazarded. It certainly appeared very strange that both ensign and pennant were flying, as if nothing had happened. At length she was reached, boarded, and the cause discovered.

It appeared that a gunner's mate or bombardier had been screwing, or unscrewing, the cap of a shell-fuse; the composition had ignited, and the shell, of course, exploded. As, at the moment, it was quite impossible to know what effect this might have on the magazine, the signal of distress had been made. A better idea of the effect of these destructive projectiles can not be given than in describing the scene at this moment below the deck of the "Medea."

The shell had burst on the lower deck, just above the shell-room, killing the unfortunate bombardier who had meddled with the fuse-cap. The explosion had thrown down all the bulkheads from the captain's cabin to the boilers; several planks in the upper-deck were forced up; and a large mass of the shell, apparently two pounds in weight, had half buried itself in an upper-deck beam. Some of the poor victim's brains were scattered against an officer's book-shelves, and several men were wounded. One extraordinary escape deserves notice. An officer was driven up the skylight, and found himself on deck unhurt.

The vessel was now surrounded by boats, and the decks were crowded with officers, all congratulating the "Medeas" on their extraordinary and providential escape.

The above, however, was not the only instance of fool-hardy carelessness in the squadron. A few days previously, the gunnery-lieutenant of one of the line-of-battle ships had occupied himself during church-time in doing the self-same thing on the orlop-deck, exactly under the spot where the mass of the ship's company were assembled for divine worship—an unconscious Guy Fawkes. It makes one shudder to think of the dreadful carnage which must have ensued had an ignition similar to that on board the steamer taken place. And, by a curious coincidence, on the arrival in England of a report of the "Medea's" disaster, another poor man was killed in trying the same experiment. Precautions are now adopted to prevent accidents of the like nature.

Soon after the above occurrence we had a taste of the celebrated Syrian gale, which lasted several days. The motion produced by it was no trifle. It has been the lot of the present writer to make acquaintance with heavy gales and furious seas in all parts of the globe. He has been in a cutter near Cape Horn; in a small yacht in the Pentland Firth, the Sunburg Roost, and the Race of Alderney; but the worst tossing he ever remembers was in this very gale, and in this large two-decker. As a specimen of the extreme violence of the motion, a lee-lurch submerged the muzzle of a forecastle gun, and, at the same time, jerked the carriage up off the deck. At the precise time this movement occurred, a seaman fell from the weather-side, slid rapidly down, and was entrapped (on the weather-roll of the ship) by the gun-carriage falling down upon his legs: his thigh was broken. Perhaps this excessive violence of motion may be partly accounted for by the fact that, a few minutes prior to the above accident, the close-reefed main-topsail was blown clean out of the bolt-ropes; the main-staysail shared the same fate in setting; consequently the ship for a time was without any sail whatever.

CHAPTER II.

Bay of Marmorice—Rebellion in the Midshipmen's Mess—Election of a new Caterer—Vote by Ballot—The successful Candidate—His despotic Views—Committee of Appeal—A *Coup d'état*—Struggle for Authority—The Dictator's Triumph—A Discussion—Plot to Maintain "Order"—Its Success—Eradication of a bad Habit—The Irish Mate and the Omelet—Stale Eggs—Paddy doubly Fined—Eventual Prosperity of the Mess.

As soon as the gale moderated, we bore up for the Bay of Marmorice, much to the satisfaction of the mates and middies, who looked forward with delight to what they called "a full-bellied place." In a few days the squadron was snugly moored in the above magnificent harbor of Asia Minor; but, to the infinite annoyance of the hungry expectants, the first day passed without the savory additions they looked for. This again raised in the mess the spirit of rebellion, which was only dormant, not dead. Loud and angry were the complaints; but when the second and third days passed with like scarcity, the empty, and therefore furious stomachs broke out again into open and violent revolution.

Peremptory calls were now made for universal suffrage, and vote by ballot, to elect a caterer who would administer to popular wants. But even in the prosecution of their own designs the agitators made so desperate a tumult, that, for half an hour nothing could be heard. The old difficulty in effecting a change of things was therefore renewed.

At length, to the disgust of the universal-suffrage men, the franchise was limited to those who had been two years at sea,

Though at first denounced as an illiberal restriction, this was ultimately confirmed, especially as, by a compromise between the parties, the ballot was ordained as the mode of voting.

The election immediately took place, and the elder members of the mess pledged themselves to accept the office, if chosen. On examining the ballot-box, it appeared that the majority of votes had fallen on an old mate of some sagacity, who at once perceived that to keep thirty riotous messmates of all ages in any degree of order, it was necessary to possess extraordinary authority; the former amount of privilege was clearly not sufficient. Cromwell had more irresponsible power than Charles whom he deposed for imputed tyranny. Why, then, should not our old mate strive to imitate Cromwell's example?

"Well gentlemen," said the newly-elected ruler, "you have, it seems, elected me caterer of the mess."

"To be sure we have," was responded, with loud cheers.

"You know," continued the old mate, "that you are a very difficult set to keep in order."

"Yes, yes, we know that," replied the young gentlemen; "but we want a good mess. Our constitution has been perverted. Reform! reform!"

"Well, then," pursued the mate, looking as if his brain were full of schemes for the general good, "if I am to be caterer, I must have extra powers."

"By all means," was universally responded. "Any powers you like, as long as we have lots of grub."

"Well, but I must be despotic," urged the mate. "I must exercise the privilege of levying fines whenever, and for whatever I please. My word must be law, against which there can be no appeal."

"We consent that it shall be so," replied the middies. "Do you stipulate for any thing else?"

"No," answered the mate; "and to show you my liberality,

I will grant you a tribunal, to be elected by myself, to which you may appeal against my decisions whenever you may hold them to be unjust."

"Hurrah, hurrah! the new caterer forever!" was vociferated by the assembly.

"Gentlemen," continued the mate, "I name as the Committee of Appeal, Brown, Barry, Jones, and Robinson; myself president."

"Bravo!" was shouted. "Can't be better."

"The committee, however," added the mate, "must not be called together for nothing. If any one appeal to it, a bottle of champagne will be drunk, and either the appealer or the mess must pay for it, as the committee may decide."

This, being considered a violent stretch of absolutism, excited the first symptoms of dissent. Much confusion prevailed in the meeting, amidst which arose exclamations of "Oh, ah! You are carrying things, you know, with *rather* too high a hand! 'Twon't do. We shall be worse off than ever. So much for a *protector!*"

The caterer saw that the time had arrived when it became necessary he should strike a decided blow; his newly-assumed authority was at stake; it must perish, or be enforced by a *coup d'état.* He resolved, therefore, to take the first opportunity that might present itself of bringing things to an issue. This was speedily afforded by one of the youngsters, nick-named "Cheeky," shying his cap at another across the table.

"Mr. Cheeky;" said the caterer, rising, and looking very solemnly. "I commence the duties of my office, by fining you one shilling for shying your cap at Mr. Kilderbee's head." (*Immense uproar, laughter, and cheers.*)

"I'll see you hanged," said the offender, "before I pay any fine. I appeal to the committee."

"Bring a bottle of champagne!" exclaimed the caterer. "Gentlemen of the committee, you hear the appeal. Please to arrange yourselves round this end of the table." Then, addressing the steward, he added, "Holmes, produce the glasses."

A dead silence prevailed. The "young gentlemen" perceived that the reform for which they had clamored was carried beyond what they had bargained for. The bottle and glasses were brought, and the whole mess assembled round the "board," wondering what would come next.

Filling up the five glasses for the committee, the old mate looked smilingly round. He well knew the great struggle for authority had commenced. Should he, on this occasion be successfully opposed, the mess would once more, and forever, be disorganized.

"Gentlemen," said he, "I drink this wine at somebody's expense, not my own, to a just decision of the committee—to a good and vigorous government of the mess, and to abundance of savory dishes for us all." (*Great cheering.*) Then turning to the committee, "Gentlemen," pursued he, "you have been present at the whole scene. Is Mr. Cheeky fined justly or not?"

"We approve! we approve!" simultaneously shouted the committee.

"Then, Mr. Cheeky," persisted the caterer, "you are not only fined one shilling, but are amerced also in the cost of this champagne. Holmes, put the wine down to Mr. Cheeky's account."

This sentence excited uproarious applause, accompanied by derisive cries, such as, "Halloa, Mr. Cheeky, how does the wine taste?" "Cheeky and champagne!"

The victim lifted up his voice in indignant remonstrance; but it was speedily drowned by the shouts and screams of the whole mess, and the old mate, under the plea of maintaining "order," safely achieved the first step on the road to despotism.

The news of so "strong a government" in the midshipmen's mess, flew like wildfire through the ship. The champagne-punishment received abundance of comments, and the unlucky offender was greeted wherever he went with mock commiseration and ironical questions.

Meanwhile, the infliction, which not only covered the transgressor with ridicule, but invaded his pocket, produced a marvelous effect. The old mate now took care that the table should be well spread. Some degree of regularity was soon attained, and, the first time for weeks, the mess-table could boast of decency and decorum.

The members of the committee had been wisely chosen; they were the *élite* of the mess, and determined to uphold the caterer. There was something that prodigiously tickled their fancies in legislating to the taste of champagne; they had seen, moreover, the beneficial effects of the initial measure of the new authority.

At first the old mate took especial care to bring forward only glaring cases, and to pounce exclusively on those who had little or no influence aboard.

Brown and the caterer were walking the deck one night, when their conversation turned on the reformed government of the mess.

"I do not think," said the former, "that you will be able to carry out your plans with the committee."

"Why not?" demanded the old mate.

"Because, when I was in the *Rodney*," replied Brown, "old Parker sent for several of the seniors of the mess and tried to form them into a committee. But it did not answer. If, therefore, such a body failed under the auspices of so mighty a man as the captain of a line-of-battle ship, how can yours hope to succeed?"

"I'll tell you," replied the mate; "old Parker, although a very 'cute hand, did not take the right steps. He ought to have chosen *one person*, such as yourself, and then desired *him* to form a committee. If *five men* are told to do any thing, nothing will be done. A committee is helpless without a head. I wish to have a 'board' merely to back my authority—nothing more."

"Nevertheless," responded Brown, "I think you will fail."

"You may depend on it I shall not fail," replied the mate, "and for two good reasons; first, that I shall carry on my measures with perfect good temper; and secondly, that the majority are for *order*, a word which, according to their definition, means lashings of good beef-steaks with a yellow selvage to them."

Though the mess rapidly improved, our caterer perceived that rocks were in the way, to steer clear of which required skillful management. A principal obstacle was the high tone of some of the senior and stronger of the mess, who now began to consider themselves privileged. As yet, the old mate had not thought it advisable to bring *them* to book; but as such a course would soon become absolutely necessary on account of the growing dissatisfaction of the weaker members, and in order to promote the "public good," he determined in future to pay no respect to persons.

One evening a large smoking-party had assembled on the port side of the main deck forward; the chief topic of discourse was "Cheeky" and the champagne-forfeiture. Our old mate listened to the observations, and set his wits to work to gain his end.

Among the most jocose of the company, was Barry, a tall, Herculean mate, good-tempered and popular, but extremely fond of having his own way. He was, moreover, invested with the dignity of a committee-man. This was the instrument our wily caterer determined to get hold of to consolidate permanently his power in the mess.

The party having separated, our two friends were left alone; and the caterer soon discovered, that though Barry was favorable to the new order of things, he was not aware of the dangers ahead. Having advised him of these, the old mate said suddenly,

"The only way, Barry, to keep our big fellows in any order is to fine you heavily."

"Fine *me?*" echoed Barry. "Come, I like that. What am I to be fined for?"

"Why," replied his companion, "you are the biggest and strongest in the mess, and nearly the senior. If I fine you, and you pay without a murmur, no one will dare resist."

"Not a bad idea," returned Barry. "But it depends, you know, on the amount. What sum do you propose?"

"A mere nothing," was responded; "only a dollar and a bottle of champagne."

"The devil!" ejaculated Barry. "Do you call that nothing? Why, it will cost eight shillings and eightpence."

"Never mind," said the old mate; "I'll deduct it from your mess-money at the end of the month, and charge it in the accounts as secret-service money."

"Ha, ha! capital. I'll do it, by Jove!" declared Barry.

"Very well," rejoined the old mate; "but mind you don't laugh when I charge you, as I mean to do, in the middle of dinner to-morrow."

"What offense shall I commit?" demanded Barry.

"Let me see," responded the caterer. "I have it. There is a bad habit among us of leaving cocked-hat boxes, dirks, and swords, kicking about the mess-table. Leave one of your boxes there to-morrow. I will do the rest."

The following day a hat-box appeared on the table, just as the mess were sitting down to dinner.

"Gentlemen," said the caterer, "this nuisance has become intolerable. You all must see the necessity of abating it: an example shall be made. The owner of this box shall pay the piper, and no mistake. I care not who he is. He's fined a dollar. To whom does this box belong?"

After some hesitation, Barry, in a low voice replied:

"I believe it's mine."

"Oh, ah!" was the general cry. "*He* won't pay! he's too big!" "Yes, he shall!" "No, he shan't! "Shame, shame!" "Down with all tyranny!" "Oh! that infernal caterer!"

When, however, Barry rose to reply, the utmost silence prevailed. Every one was anxious to see what he would do, and all were ready to take the cue from him.

"Gentlemen," said he "I acknowledge my error. I bow to the judgment of the caterer."

Such a reply from a man of his known influence and personal prowess, excited astonishment, heightened by the caterer saying:

"Sir, as you are a member of the committee I fine you, in addition to the dollar, a bottle of champagne."

This little trick had a great effect, and assisted materially in reducing the mess to order.

Our caterer had to eradicate another bad habit into which the strong members of the mess had fallen, namely, of sending the servants on trivial errands, such as "How is the wind?" "What sail have we set?" and so forth. Too glad to make this an excuse for absenting themselves from the duty of the mess, the servants, in attempting to justify their fault would say:

"Why, Sir, we were ordered to go: we dared not refuse—we must obey orders from our superior."

Such excuses were unanswerable: but it was impossible not to see that the general business of the mess was retarded by so idle a practice, and that it interfered with the comfortable preparation of the meals. The steward complained bitterly, and declared the work could not be done while the time of the servants was so invaded.

The old mate was rather puzzled at first in attempting to devise remedial measures; but at length he determined how to act. Calling all the servants together, he informed them that, although they were bound to obey the orders of their superior officers, yet, as caterer, and having command of the mess-funds, he would stop a shilling out of their private pay every time they absented themselves on any pretense whatever; and that whoever informed against them should have half the fine, and go ashore in the beef-boat to market to spend the gratuity.

A few minutes after this regulation was made, a huge Irish mate cried out:

"Holmes, run up the galley and make me an omelet."

"Please, Sir," said Holmes, "if I goes to the galley I shall be fined one shilling."

"Obey orders," retorted Paddy. "Go directly."

Away started Holmes to the galley with half-a-dozen eggs. In a second, one of the boys rushed into the gun-room and informed against him.

"Steward," said the caterer, "Let Tom go ashore to-morrow morning with you in the market-boat. Here, boy, is your sixpence."

Poor Holmes was immoderately laughed at by the other servants, and was persuaded to tell the Irish mate how he had been mulct. Paddy was bound in honor to repay him. This getting wind caused many jeers at the Hibernian's expense.

"Why, Paddy," said one, "I could get a message taken from Cumberland Gate, Hyde Park, to the Bank for a shilling."

"Oh, Paddy, my boy!" exclaimed another, "twopence a piece for eggs is dear carriage to the galley."

"I say, Paddy," observed a third, "I could ride ten miles in a buss with a *bushel* of eggs for a shilling."

"Go to blazes with you all!" vociferated Paddy; "I wish the eggs were rotten and down your cursed throats."

Either out of devilment, or by chance, the eggs were very stale indeed. When, therefore, they appeared smoking hot in the shape of an omelet, the bad odor was so evident that all hands were obliged to hold all noses. This speedily attracted a host of Paddy's uproarious messmates, who, delighted that his wish was partly fulfilled, hovered about him like gnats, and stung him with unwelcome jests. His patience at last became quite exhausted; and, with an unpronounceable Irish oath, he flung the tainted morsel in their faces. This made them frantic with joy. Uttering screams of delight, they immediately demanded that he should be fined a dollar.

As this was but fair, the old mate, who had all the time been *egging* on the tormentors, and was, moreover, enjoying the success of his *ruse*, issued his edict as was in that case made and provided.

Still burning with rage, the Irishman swore by all the powers he wouldn't pay a farthing more than the shilling, and concluded by appealing to the committee; which, meeting on the following day, confirmed the fine; so that poor Paddy was compelled to pay the dollar, and also to supply a bottle of champagne as the price of his appeal.

The old mate's dictatorship was now thoroughly confirmed; and the mess in a short time was not only in admirable order, but became very rich.

WILD SPORTS OF THE FALKLANDS.

CHAPTER I.

Occupation of the Falklands—Report of the Commissioners for 1846—Royal Indenture—Population—Captain Sulivan's Expedition—Government Aid—Facilities offered to Mariners by the Falklands—Climate of the Islands—Anson's erroneous Statements—Tussock-grass—Prodigious Increase of Cattle—Robberies on the Cattle-stations—Method of preventing this Pillage—Frauds on Underwriters—Marvelous Abundance of wild Horses—Port Stanley.

As the spring-tide of emigration appears to have set strongly toward the colonial possessions of Great Britain, it may not, perhaps, be superfluous, by way of introduction to the following sketches, to give a brief summary of prominent circumstances connected with the Falkland Islands since they were first occupied by an English governor (Lieutenant Moody), whose appointment took place in 1842, to which year the birth of the colony may be assigned. Soon after the governor's arrival, the intended site of the principal town was changed from Port Louis, at the head of Berkeley Sound, to Port Stanley, as a more convenient spot at which passing ships might call, when in need of repair or victualing.

For some time, however, the infant colony languished for want of maternal care: the government expenditure on its behalf barely sufficed to keep life within it. Still, though the islands were not so fortunate as to excite interest in England, it was far otherwise on the adjacent coasts of South America. The English merchants residing in the latter country, actuated by the keen foresight and enterprise of their nation, wisely turned their attention toward the only spot of land, within thousands of miles, that hoisted the British standard; and one of these merchant-princes immediately took steps to make an agreement with government to purchase a large extent of territory in the Falklands.

The following condensed extract from the report of the Colonial Land and Emigration Commissioners for 1846, will give the material parts of the agreement. It is a curious and interesting document.

"1st. Indenture, made the 16th day of March, 1846, between her most gracious Majesty Queen Victoria, of the one part, and Samuel Fisher Lafone, of Montevideo in South America, merchant, of the other part. Her Majesty Queen Victoria sells to Lafone that part of East Falkland lying south of the isthmus in Choiseul Sound. Also the islands in Choiseul Sound, and all other islands adjacent to the coast purchased; also Beauchene Island; also one town allotment of half an acre, and one suburban allotment of twenty-five acres in the principal town.

"2d. For six years and six months from this date, Lafone to have absolute dominion over all wild cattle, horses, sheep, goats, and swine on East Falkland.

"3d. For the above advantages, Lafone is to pay her said Majesty, Queen Victoria, £60,000 by installments in the following manner: £10,000 within ten days (since paid); £5000 on the 1st of January, 1851; £5000 on each succeeding 1st of January, until the whole shall be paid in full.

"4th. Technical reservations of lands for government purposes, such as arsenals, ports, bridges, &c.

"5th. That Lafone is to deliver to the governor yearly in good health the following stock: in 1847, 500 cows, 5 bulls, 4000 sheep, 40 rams, 20 horses. In 1848, 1000 cows, 10 bulls, 5000 sheep, 50 rams, 20 horses, 50 mares, 5 stallions, 30 sows, and 10 boars. In 1849, 1500 cows, 15 bulls, 5000 sheep, 50 rams, 50 mares. In 1850, 6000 sheep, 60 rams. The sheep to be all white ewes, good breed (not merinos), common and hardy, similar to those in the colony. The stock to be delivered at such good and safe ports as the governor may direct." *

In 1848, when a new governor was appointed, sixty houses had been erected at Port Stanley, besides the establishment of Mr. Lafone in the southern peninsula, and a small farm of sheep and cattle, belonging to Mr. Whittington, at the old settlement of Port Louis. The entire population numbered from three hundred to four hundred souls.

Toward the end of 1848, Captain Sulivan, R.N., deeply impressed with the great advantages to be derived from a sheep and cattle grazing-farm in the Falklands, determined, as the chance of employment was small indeed, to form a company for the above purpose on a large scale.

In a great country like ours, an enterprise of so prominent a nature as the one in question is seized on with avidity, particularly by those who happen to have a large family of sons. The needful arrangements were therefore speedily completed, and a vessel of three hundred and seventy-five tons (the "Australia") was chartered to take out stock and materials necessary to set the venture "well afloat."

As the author is very much interested in the success of this enterprise, he is anxious to correct an error into which he fell some years ago, in reference to the seal-fishing of these islands, when, writing about the Volunteer Rocks off Berkeley Sound in the South Sea Rocks slightly to the southward of the former, he stated that they are superior, in number of fur seal and ex-

* This arrangement has been considerably modified by government.

tent of surface, to the island of Lobos in the Rio de la Plata, for which is paid a yearly rent of eighty thousand dollars. In making this statement he was much mistaken, and regrets having fallen into an exaggeration.

Since the departure of Captain Sulivan's expedition, government has taken up the "Nautilus," a vessel of two hundred tons, to convey the necessary materials for repairing ships at the Falklands. This is, indeed, very much required, especially since the "golden dreams" from California have set all the rest of the world dreaming of mines of gold, which, says quaint old Burton, "is of all others a most delicious object. A sweet light, a goodly lustre hath gold, and we had rather see it than the sun. Intolerable pains we take for it. Long journeys, heavy burdens, all are made light and easy by it. The sight of gold refresheth our spirits and ravisheth our hearts. *It will make a man run to the Antipodes.*"

Even before the existence of the Californian mania, the average number of vessels passing the Falklands both ways was five per diem. Most of these ships sighted the islands to verify their chronometers; and it is not too much to say, that if captains of vessels were generally acquainted with the facilities offered by the Falklands, such as the abundance and marvelous cheapness of provisions, the admirable havens—more like basins than harbors—the great facility of entrance and departure, and, though last not least, the ports being perfectly free, full ninety per cent. of the above-named vessels would call there, to carry out a proper system of economy on the long-voyage trade.

With regard to the climate of the Falklands, it is a singular fact that this archipelago has always been characterized as barren, desolate, and tempestuous. Nothing can be more erroneous. The misrepresentations in "Anson's Voyages" have probably strengthened, if not created, the general prejudice; but there can be little doubt that this navigator's passage round Cape Horn manifested more zeal than judgment, particularly in keeping his squadron together, rather than appointing a rendezvous in the Pacific. It is notorious that his vessels were badly found and fitted ; his crew was not only weak, but the majority untrained ; and, to complete the list of evils, the very worst time of year was, by defective arrangement, forced upon them for rounding this prominent southern headland.

Where so many elements of disaster exist, it is not surprising that misfortune should occur. The Falklands being in the vicinity, came in for a share of the misrepresentation which still retains a hold on the public mind. Captain Sulivan was employed seven years in minutely examining and surveying these islands. He was accompanied by his family, who not only enjoyed uninterrupted good health, but considered the climate better, on the whole, than Cornwall or Devonshire.

Voyagers frequently form erroneous impressions of climate from the temporary nature of their sojourn. This is remarkably exemplified in the journal of Darwin, who is generally an accurate author. He says—" The climate of the Falklands may be compared to that which is experienced at the height of between one and two thousand feet on the mountains of North Wales, having, however, less sunshine and less frost, but more wind and rain." After this assertion had been proved to be totally incorrect, and after the evidence of Captain Sulivan's letters, it is surprising that in the second edition of " A Naturalist's Voyage," the author should have made the following remark :

" From accounts published since our voyage, and more especially from several interesting letters from Captain Sulivan, R.N., employed on the survey, it appears that we took an exaggerated view of the badness of the climate of these islands. But when I reflect on the almost universal covering of peat" (query, what has that to do with climate ?) " and on the fact, of wheat seldom ripening there" (incorrect), "I can hardly believe the climate in summer is so fine and dry as it has lately been represented."

Now the truth is, that the temperature of the Falklands is very similar to that of Devon or Cornwall, with this difference, that it is rather milder, much drier in summer, but very windy.

The evaporation is excessive ; so much so that, in this particular, it exceeds the Cape de Verds. This is, indeed, an extraordinary fact, especially when the latitude of the latter region is considered. So extreme a dryness of air may hereafter be turned to excellent account in the manufacture of salt ; and should this anticipation turn out to be practically correct, a valuable article of commerce will be added to the productions of the Falklands. South America is now principally supplied from Cheshire in England, and the Cape de Verds ; the length of the voyage in both instances being much against a cheap and certain supply.

The Falklands are remarkably accessible to pedestrians ;* and the earth is clothed with a variety of nourishing grasses, which are as sweet as the delicate parts of the foliage of Indian corn.

It is not at all surprising, therefore, that the animals should grow to a great size, nor that their meat should prove to be of a very delicate flavor.

The tussock † is a gigantic species of grass, frequently growing to the height of ten feet, and, where abundant, not only capable of sheltering, but absolutely concealing, herds of cattle or horses. Tussock is called "the glory of the Falklands." An instance is mentioned in Ross's voyage of two American seamen (deserters), who lived solely on the core of this grass for fourteen months ; and, when reclaimed from their wild wanderings, were plump, healthy, and in excellent spirits ! Cattle and horses are ravenously fond of tussock ; so much so, that the author has a vivid remembrance of the wild cattle eating the dry thatch, composed

* See "Fitzroy," p. 247.

† See "Ross's Voyage," p. 269.

of this material, from a small cabin he had erected as an armorer's forge. This was seen by him with a spy-glass from the deck of the "Arrow," when the beasts were descried, reared on their hind legs, easily pulling down what the crew with so much trouble had completed.

In 1839, the cattle were computed to be about thirty thousand head. Their increase since that time must have been immense, as they are now estimated at two hundred thousand. The only way to account for this prodigious multiplication is, that since the former period, whalers and other marauders have been kept off from some of the stations, by the settlement and occupation of the islands. It is, however, to be regretted that in the remote parts great depredations are still committed on the cattle.

This is beginning to be felt as a serious drawback to the outlay of capital. Pebble Island, for instance, and the islands adjacent, are admirably adapted for cattle-stations. Unfortunately, however, this is the very locality now resorted to by marauders for stealthily obtaining beef, not merely for present supply, but for committing so wholesale a destruction as will enable them to salt down sufficient for a long cruise. It is pretty well known that in numerous vessels from England, America, and other places, a stock of salt is taken out for the purpose of curing a supply of provisions at the expense of these islands.

The only way to prevent this pillage, which years of impunity have seemed to sanction, would be by stationing on the spot one or two small vessels—for example, two cutters, rigged as ketches, under a commander: these, constantly moving about, would not only scare away the light-fingered gentry, but a portion of the crews would be eminently useful in erecting buildings for government purposes, cultivating gardens, and making preparations for colonization, either penal or otherwise. The expense would be little or nothing: say, one commander, one lieutenant, two second masters, twenty able seamen, twenty marines, and sixteen others

—in all, sixty. These officers and men could easily navigate one ketch of one hundred and twenty tons and another of sixty, and be a complete protection to the whole islands.

It is believed that these islands are frequently made use of by fraudulent persons much in the same manner as the Bahama banks are in the West Indian seas; that is to say, ships are purposely lost there to defraud underwriters. Many instances are known of vessels being "cast away" in the most unaccountable manner. In several instances ships thus *lost* in some of the basin-like harbors, have been sold for a "mere song," recovered at little expense, and are still bearing rich freights across the seas! The very fact of a naval officer being on the spot would prevent such disgraceful proceedings, and save thousands yearly.

The undeservedly bad name borne by the Falklands, tempts fraudulent adventurers; but were people in general well-informed as to the admirable and safe ports in these islands, the utmost surprise would be expressed at ships being lost there. As it is, the unprincipled master has a certainty of a *safe* and comfortable wreck; preserves his life and as many private stores as he may think necessary; loudly trumpets forth the dangerous nature of the islands; and thus disarms and silences suspicion. From the astonishing increase of trade round the Horn, the author ventures to predict that the underwriters in England will be thoroughly fleeced in insuring vessels to the Falklands, and that the islands will be innocently accused of being the cause; but he asserts advisedly that no well-found, well-managed ship need be lost on the Falklands.

As a corroboration of the apparently marvelous increase of animals alluded to above, the following is quoted from the narrative of a voyage by Lopez in 1586, published in the third volume of "Hakluyt's Voyages and Travels:"

"Of all the men Don Pedro left behind him, there were but two hundred left alive, who, in the ship's boats, went higher up the river; leaving in the place called Buenos Ayres their mares and horses. But it is a wonder to see, that of thirty mares and seven horses, which the Spaniards left there, the increase in forty years was so great, that the country twenty leagues up is full of horses; whereby a man can conjecture the goodness of the pasture and the fruitfulness of the soil."

The following sketches are extracted from a diary kept by the author while surveying the Falklands in 1838 and 1839. On the site of the present town, Port Stanley, he shot five wild geese at one discharge. Before that time the harbor was unsurveyed, and consequently unknown; and the whole population, exclusive of the officers and men surveying, consisted of about one dozen persons!

CHAPTER II.

Inclement Gale of Wind—Dreary Situation—Adventure on a Tussock-islet —A Conflagration—Narrow Escape—An exploring Excursion—Abundance of Game—A huge Bull—A *Ruse*—Desolate Scene—Attack on two wild Bulls—The Combat—Herds of wild Cattle—Outlying Bulls.

THE barometer fell so fast, that the surveying party did not think it prudent to leave the vessel which was moored in Pleasant Harbor. Every preparation was made for a heavy gale; as we knew, by experience, that the weather-glass is a faithful monitor. At noon we began to feel the breeze; and by two P.M. we had as hard a gale of wind, accompanied by as fierce and powerful squalls, with numerous flakes of snow, as I ever experienced.

Our situation was desolate in the extreme: to leeward, a range of rocky hills, covered with snow; the harbor itself (a branch of Port Fitzroy), lashed by the furious gale into one sheet of foam; and to windward, a small islet covered with tussock, the long leaves of which, bending and bowing as in despair, added to the dreariness of the prospect. The entrance to the harbor and the head of the bay were hidden from our view by large flakes of snow driving furiously past us.

To deepen the effect of this dismal picture we were conscious of being 104° of latitude from Old England; and that, in case of need, we were several hundred miles away from the nearest assistance. In spite of all this, we felt perfectly comfortable and jolly, and cared not one farthing for the gale, as we had not only full reliance on our own resources, but abundance of "creature comforts," to say nothing of the appearance of our spritsail-yard, which was not merely decorated, but positively loaded with game of all kinds.

Toward night, as usual, the gale abated. The next morning, after divisions, it being Sunday, divine service was performed—a ceremony omitted only on one occasion while Captain Sulivan and myself were aboard the vessel, when, during a very heavy gale of wind, we were battened down. After the ship's company had dined, some of the crew were allowed to land for a walk; but as no fire-arms were permitted to be carried on the Sabbath, it was customary to put the men on an islet, in order to avoid any danger from the wild animals which infested the mainland.

On the day in question, about twenty were landed on the little tussock-isle close to which we lay; and as certain of the officers (myself among the number) wished to go, we all went together, and soon began to amuse ourselves in the best way we could. These tussock-beds are very singular places; they have been undisturbed for ages, and by the perpetual decay and renewal of the flags the whole place where they grow is covered with large lumps of vegetable matter as inflammable as tinder. The long thin leaves interlock above, and form, here and there, little cloisters from five to twenty yards long in some places. The paths thus formed are trodden perfectly smooth by the numerous penguins, whose holes branch off in every direction.

As we were looking about us, one of our party suddenly observed that he smelt smoke. Though such a remark on an uninhabited island was of a nature to excite surprise, no one seemed to heed it till, in a few minutes, thick reeky volumes began to roll over our heads when it struck me that some of our careless vagabonds had set fire to the weather-side.

Off we started for very life, though we had only about two hundred yards to go. The ground was excessively difficult, as some of the lumps were five feet high, and the flags on the summits many feet above our heads. The crackling of the flames was plainly heard, as if close to us, and we were nearly suffocated by the dense smoke.

At length, after a desperate struggle, in which several shoes and caps were lost, we gained the beach, rushed into the boat, and pushed off. We were barely in time; for the next instant the little bank over which we had scampered was a mass of bright flame.

Not a moment was lost in sending a boat round to the weather-side (the leeward being impracticable, on account of heat and smoke) to look for the rest of our men, about whom we were, of course, very anxious. The thoughtless fellows were found sitting quietly on the beach smoking their pipes, and looking with vacant pleasure on their work, not dreaming that some of their shipmates might, as the Americans say, have been "used up" by it.

The next morning, anxious to see the effects of the fire, I landed early, and having examined the ashes, ascertained that a very great number of birds had been destroyed by the conflagration. The island consists of about three hundred acres, of which, I am convinced, there are not a dozen square yards without a nest of some kind of bird containing four or five eggs or young birds. In the portion of land wherein the fire raged, the young birds were roasted alive, besides a few seals, whose remains we found pretty well singed. The authors of this wholesale destruction said it was quite pitiable to see the larger birds, such as geese, caranchos, &c., flying round the flames that were consuming their young, and screaming with horror. Now and then one of them would fall in; either suffocated by the smoke or scorched by the heat.

A day or two subsequently, Captain Sulivan and myself landed with our guns on an exploring excursion. After about an hour's walk round a chain of ponds, during which we jointly bagged upward of forty teal, we saw, on turning the corner of a gully, a huge bull half hidden among the bushes, as if fast asleep. Dropping on our knees, we crawled back some distance, for the purpose of changing our small shot for ball. Having thrown down our game and shooting-jackets, we stealthily advanced on all-fours, and crept up to a small bank within fifteen yards of the brute's great head, which lay fully exposed to us; then, resting our guns, we both fired our left barrels at a concerted signal, reserving the right.

The beast did not move; and, to our mortification, we found, on a nearer approach, that we had valiantly been attacking a dead animal. It was some consolation, however, to discover that our two bullet-holes were touching each other in the centre of his brain.

Knowing full well that we might reckon on a speedy detection of our exploit, and, consequently, on being well laughed at, we determined to ward off the expected ridicule by turning the tables on our shipmates; accordingly, going on board with joyful countenances, we said (which was true enough) that we had shot a bull through the brain, and that he had not stirred afterward.

On hearing this a party was formed, and saws, knives, and other butchering instruments were taken, for the purpose of cutting up the spoil, toward which, after receiving the necessary directions, they started in high glee; while we sat down to dinner chuckling at our *ruse*, which, if it did not ultimately deceive our companions, had the desired effect in diverting the laughter from ourselves.

When we had completed the survey of Pleasant Harbor, we took the vessel some miles further up. As we advanced toward the head of the harbor, the beauties of the place opened on us. Sometimes the passage was so narrow that one might have thrown his hat ashore on either side; and anon it spread out to a broad sheet of water. The whole scene was so desolate and dumb that, in giving the word of command, as the different windings made it necessary to shift the yards, my own voice

M*

startled me. The water-fowl, noiselessly parting on each side of our bow as the vessel came up to them, did not appear alarmed, but stared at us with grave astonishment.

At eight o'clock we came to and moored in a large sheet of water, about ten miles from the harbor's mouth.

While enjoying my cigar on deck, and deriving pleasure from the soft, serene air of evening, I perceived two bulls grazing close to the shore just ahead of the vessel. The surveyors, who were engaged below laying down their work, immediately stopped business and came up. Having only one day's beef on board, we determined to attack the bulls; and, in a few minutes, four of us were pulling for the shore with well-loaded guns. Our proceedings had got wind on the lower deck, and all hands crowded up the rigging to see the battle.

We landed under the bank in such a position as not to be seen by our prey, who were quietly grazing all the time. Stealthily, like Indians, we climbed the bank, and jumped over the brow full before them. They immediately turned tail and fled. Captain Sulivan fired at the nearest brute as he turned, and, though at the distance of fifty yards, we could clearly hear the sound of the ball striking him, which it did about six inches behind the heart.

This was a staggering blow, but did not prevent his running away. La Porte (our dog) was immediately slipped, caught the bull about three hundred yards inland, and flew at his flank, which caused him to face about and attack the dog. Time was thus given me to get within fifteen yards of the spot, when, lowering his head, the brute charged me. My right-hand barrel, however, damped his ardor, and he turned half round as if to fly. My second bullet now went clean through his body a few inches above the heart, and, for a moment, brought him on his knees. While I drew my knife in order to hamstring him, he suddenly rallied and appeared to collect what strength was left him for one last desperate effort—always the most dangerous.

At this moment a shipmate came up and presented his gun, but the vile Brummagem snapped without going off, and we should have been in rather an awkward predicament, had not Captain Sulivan, with his remaining barrel, within five yards, laid the bull dead at his feet, the bullet passing through the centre of his brain, and coming out at the back of his head. The moment he fell, we were greeted by three loud cheers from the people at our mast-head, and, in a few minutes, had thirty stout fellows with us.

After disemboweling our prey, we attached a strong line to his horns, and, with a sailor-song from thirty hoarse throats, dragged him down to the water's edge, towed him off, and hoisted him in with a runner and tackle, not liking to trust his great weight to the yard.

As the survey detained us here several days, we had a good opportunity of exploring the immediate vicinity. Not a day passed without our seeing herds of cattle grazing around. To attack these would not be so dangerous an adventure as to encounter the outlying bulls, which, in number, are disproportionate to the cows. This, no doubt, has arisen from the great slaughter for food of the latter, whose flesh is preferable to that of the male—a slaughter committed by ships of all nations some few years ago, before the Falklands were under the English flag. I generally remarked that the outlyers were covered with gashes, received probably, in many a hard battle ; and that they labored under the disadvantage of not having their horns pointed upward whereas the bashaws, who lived in female society, had remarkable advantages in that weapon of offense.

This may be a wise ordination of nature, to prevent the great number of males from injuring the breed, which would certainly ensue were not some of the bulls turned out of the herd and kept at a distance by their more favored brethren.

CHAPTER III.

Endeavor to carry out an Admiralty Order—Wild and sequestered Lake—Majestic Swans and innumerable other Birds—Their familiar Confidence—Flock of Teal—Flutter and Confusion among the Water-fowl—Skeletons of Quadrupeds—Author attacked by wild Bulls—Refuge on the Summit of a Rock—Blockaded by the Beasts—Escape—Combat with a Seal—A surveying Party—Dangerous Conflict—Bulls in Chase—A wild Banquet.

Having seen that every thing was in order in our little vessel, I thought a good opportunity was before me to carry out one of the orders given by the Admiralty to my commanding officer, namely, to form little gardens in any convenient spot in the Falkland Islands. I therefore determined to seek out a locality adapted to so well-intentioned a purpose.

At half-past ten in the forenoon, I manned my barge with four boys, and pulled along the shore, frequently landing as a favorable place seemed to present itself, each of which, however, on examination, proved impracticable. At length we arrived at a little creek, about forty yards wide, running inland. Up this we went, following the windings of the stream about a mile, when they terminated in a small rivulet running from a lake situated at a short distance.

Leaving the boat in charge of three of my young crew, I landed with the fourth boy, and walked to the wild and sequestered mere, which presented a sight to charm the eye of a sportsman. The extent of the water—barely two acres—was thickly dotted with birds. Two majestic swans, with ebony necks issuing from snowy bodies, floated, with an air of haughty patronage, among innumerable geese, ducks, teal, and divers; but, to my great amazement, the feathered crowd, instead of appearing the least alarmed and skurrying off, drew toward us: unlike their *civilized* brethren, they were ignorant of the treachery of man.

I sat down on the brink of the lake, wondering whether, on my return, I should be able to convince people of the truth, of that which I then beheld. Except the swans, the whole assembly of fowl approached gradually until some hundreds were within twenty yards of me. A chorus then arose from them, as if with one accord they inquired my business there, and sought to know in a friendly way why I disturbed their privacy.

I may here remark, that the sounds they utter in a wild state, are totally different from their notes when domesticated, and I should not have recognized the species by the ear alone. The entire congregation appeared to be so tame and unsuspecting, that, reluctant to make my presence shunned by dealing death among them, I contented myself (although my double-barrel, loaded with No. 6, was lying across my knees), with taking the seal-club from my boy's hand, and shying it among the birds.

This had an effect contrary to what I expected; for, instead of being alarmed, they gathered, as if with curiosity, round the missile, and pecked at it. Never was so glorious an opportunity of making an immortal shot! But again my humanity struggled with my love of sport: I could not kill the poor confiding creatures, who placed themselves within my grasp.

At this moment a more legitimate opportunity offered: a flock of teal flew over my head from another place. Mechanically my gun jumped to my shoulder, and before I was aware of it, both barrels had done their work; five birds fell from the discharge of the first, and four from that of the second. For a few minutes, the flutter and confusion that followed on the lake was indescribable; but quiet was soon restored, except that every now and then were heard little bursts of rapid chattering, as if excited by wonder.

Bagging my teal, I resumed my quest of a site for a garden, passing more than once the skeleton of a wild bull or cow—rather grim land-marks in a wild solitude. One of these strongly excited my attention. It lay in a pass over a small boggy rivulet at the bottom of a deep ravine. Here the poor brute must have stuck in trying to cross: the surrounding earth was torn up, and the vegetation destroyed as if by hoofs and horns. I was inclined to suspect that this might have been done by wild cattle, in horror at the terrible death of their fellow, who must have perished of starvation: his head was stretched out as in the act of bellowing.

While "moralizing this spectacle," I quite forgot the purpose for which I landed; and was only roused from my brown study, and warned of my distance from the boat, by the sudden trumpeting of wild bulls. I felt convinced we were chased.

Hoping to get back in a direct line, we ascended the side of the ravine, and made for a hill, on the summit of which was a little rock which, luckily for us, was scalable. On gaining the base of this position, impregnable to quadrupeds, I climbed up, closely followed by my boy, who had hardly got a footing on the top, when we descried five huge brutes who closed in our little fortress, and declared war by furiously tearing up the ground.

With all convenient speed I drew from my gun the charges of small shot, and loaded with ball; but, not expecting a fight, I had only four bullets; and considering those not quite sufficient to physic five full-grown bulls, I determined to lay them by for a last resource, and await the chapter of accidents; knowing full well that, should we not return by a certain time, a party would be sent to our assistance, who would soon deliver us by raising the siege.

To beguile the time I struck a light for my cigar, and reclining at my ease, expected the brutes would take themselves off. But no such thing: they did not even graze, but watched the rock as a cat would watch a mouse-trap. I could not help laughing to see my little companion every now and then lift up his head, reconnoitre the enemy, and extend his fingers from his nose according to the elegant method now in vogue of "taking a sight."

We remained thus blockaded about three hours, when suddenly came on a furious squall of snow and sleet, which completely enveloped us all in the clouds. This being too good an opportunity to be lost, we swiftly and silently evacuated our position, and ran at least a mile without stopping; after which a rough walk of an hour and a half brought us down to the boat. I resolved that, in future land excursions I would carry more bullets.

In the afternoon of the following day, I again landed, having our purser for my companion. While rounding an angle in the island, I saw, spread out fast asleep, a hair seal of about seven feet in length. Being anxious to observe the movements of one of these creatures, I halted, and quietly watched him. My friend had also seen the animal from another point of view, and, being armed with a boarding-pike, had stealthily approached him. The assailant, brandishing his weapon, had so earnest an expression of countenance, and seemed inspired by so knightly a determination (as though a new St. George was about to attack a new dragon), that I could not refrain from bursting into a loud laugh.

This roused the seal, who, slowly raising his head, gazed round about with sleepy eyes. The next moment the purser's pike was stuck with right good-will into the beast's hind-quarters, on which he scuttled into the water, followed by his persecutor, who, in his excitement, tumbled after him (repeating his digs) into the water, whence, what with my excessive laughter, and the thick kelp, I had some difficulty in extracting him.

Thus ended our exploration for the day. In the thoroughly soaked condition of my friend, a speedy return to the ship was necessary.

As, about this period, we had not much experience in combating wild cattle, we deemed two persons with guns quite sufficient to attack one beast. When, however, we had gained a little more knowledge, we became cautious and generally took with us three or four men well armed. Our first irrational valor arose from ambition of the honor of vanquishing a bull single-handed—an exploit attempted by Captain Sulivan and myself; after which, being satisfied with our experiment, we were in no hurry to repeat it.

One morning early the surveying party landed, and were soon lost in the windings of the creeks. About two hours after their departure I ascended with my spy-glass, to our mast-head, for the purpose of getting a better view, and could see the party on a distant hill building a mark. In a short time I observed them pointing their glass very earnestly in the direction of a particular spot, much nearer the vessel, toward which, having finished the mark, and put a pole on its summit, they started at a rapid pace. I conjectured that the object of their anxiety must be a herd of cattle.

Immediately arming myself with my usual weapons, I pressed into the service my dog La Porte, together with a brave boy of the name of Popham, who afterward always carried my second gun, and who never once flinched from putting it into my hand at the proper moment. Knowing, from the nature of the ground, that I should stand a much better chance of getting near the animals than was possessed by the surveyors, who must cross one or two creeks and approach their prey from an open plain, I landed, and marched in a direct line to the place denoted.

After progressing about two miles, we observed, just over the crest of a hillock, a black ridge or eminence, like a bush or small rock, which suddenly started into life, developing a huge head and a pair of horns. It was a bull, grazing; and a magnificent creature he appeared to be.

These wild fellows are very different from their species in a tame state. I can not more fitly describe them than by saying they have a *terrible* aspect; so much so, that some of our men, and one officer, although as brave and careless of their personal safety as any could be, were never able to get over their dread of the gorgon-like visages of these beasts, which operated so powerfully on one or two occasions, as to prevent the individuals in question from venturing on the main land. This peculiar terror on the part of men of high courage, must, I imagine, have arisen from early impressions made in childhood, similar to the dread some persons have of being alone in a dark place.

While considering how best we might attack the brute, a herd of about forty or fifty was suddenly exposed to our view. Starting La Porte at them, and enjoining my brave young companion to keep close to me, we ran full speed toward the animals, the whole of which seemed panic-stricken, and scoured off. One bull took a direction across my path, at a distance of about fifty yards. I leveled my rifle at his fore shoulder, and heard (immediately after its sharp crack) the dull sound of the bullet striking him. This enraged the animal, when turning his head at me, on he came at speed, with tail high above his back.

In a moment I had changed guns, and, with my left knee on the ground, waited his approach. La Porte did all a dog could do to divert his course; but on me the bull had fixed his eye, and nothing could shake his purpose. I must confess I felt as if I should have been much safer any where else; but it was too late to think of that.

The animal was within twenty yards when my first barrel opened on him. The ball entered his forehead, but not sufficiently deep to cause instantaneous death, or even to disable him for the moment. Regardless of pain, he still galloped forward, when, at ten yards, my remaining barrel pierced his left eye.

Mad, and half blinded, he now swerved from me and rushed headlong on my boy, whom, without attempting to toss, he knocked down, trampled on, and passed over. Before he could turn, La Porte had him by the nose, and for a few seconds held him; but he soon threw the dog off, and came upon us streaming with blood. During the next two or three minutes we exerted every nerve and muscle to keep clear of his repeated though weakened charges, and only succeeded by La Porte's powerful assistance who, when we were nearly caught, sprang upon him like a tiger.

At length the bull appeared to stagger slightly, and the dog pinned him. Drawing my hunting-knife—which, by-the-by, I could shave with—I ran up, and was in the act of hamstringing him, when once more he threw off the dog and bounded at me. While making the third bound (and when I fancied I could feel his hot breath, he was so close), the tendon having been severed, the remaining cartilages of the leg gave way, and, with a loud bellow, he was stretched on the earth. The next moment my knife was sticking in his heart.

After a little time we cut his throat and examined his wounds, each of which was mortal. He was of the low-quartered breed, but young. One of the surveying party, who afterward came up, pronounced him to be only three years old.

We now collected our hats, guns, &c., which had been scattered around, and were beginning to compose ourselves, when, to our infinite discomfort, two more bulls appeared over the rising ground, with tails up (a sign of mischief), and making direct for us. My first impulse was to load, and be prepared to receive our pursuers; but in the heat of the last battle I had dropped my powder-flask. Nothing therefore remained wherewith to defend ourselves but our knives, which we clutched desperately, taking up a position behind the carcass of our former antagonist.

The brutes advanced furiously; flight would have been impossible; we deemed our case hopeless. At the moment when the bulls were within two hundred yards of us, we were unexpectedly cheered by a loud shout, and, with delight inappreciable by any one who has not been in a similar predicament, we saw all the surveyors hastening to our assistance, some with guns, others with boats' stretchers, and one with a very suspicious instrument, which looked marvelously like a theodolite-stand.

This timely diversion had the desired effect. The bulls stopped short, and our allies giving a shout, turned tail and fled.

We now cut up the carcass of the bull I had slain, carried the joints down to the boat and then proceeded to prepare lunch. Four men were employed to collect "*diddledee;*"* one was sent with my rifle to procure a couple of geese, and another was busied in lighting a fire. In a very short time a heap of wood was fiercely blazing, and a couple of geese lying beside it.

Our cookery was not very elaborate: the man whom we deputed to officiate cut off the heads of the birds, pulled out the long wing-feathers, and rolling up the bodies in a heap of "diddledee," committed them to the flames. In about twenty minutes the geese were thoroughly roasted, and unceremoniously kicked out of the fire. Thus *dressed,* they looked exactly like two balls of cinder: this dirty appearance, however, vanished on skinning them, when they were as white as, and seemed much more delicate than their tame brethren with all the sophisticated treatment of a scientific cook. The insides were not disturbed during the process of roasting, or rather burning, in order to prevent the juices of the flesh from being dried up.

* A small shrub, of so inflammable a nature that it will burn fiercely even when soaked in water. The above name is given to it by the sailors.

These birds, together with a few beefsteaks from the beast just killed, made (considering we were in the wilderness) a most sumptuous luncheon, salt and biscuit being always carried with us. After our repast we lighted our cigars, and being still further animated by a potent glass of grog,

> "Fought all our battles o'er again,
> And thrice we routed all our foes, and thrice we slew the slain."

I am sure we enjoyed our entertainment in these primeval solitudes with greater zest than could have been felt in nine-tenths of the sumptuous pic-nics at Richmond or elsewhere—always excepting the irresistible charms of ladies' eyes, of which, alas! we were destitute.

After spending a reasonable time in this wild pleasure, I returned to the vessel, and the surveyors resumed their work.

CHAPTER IV.

Traces of wild Pigs—An Attack on the Swine—Its Failure—A Sea-lion——A Man missing—Search for him—Discovery—Cause of his Disappearance—Necessary Precaution in wandering about uninhabited Lands—Shooting Excursion—Exploit of the Dog, La Porte—Wild Lake—Ascent of Mount Pleasant—Nervous Work—Fixing the Theodolite-stand—Extensive but barren Bird's-eye View—Freezing Temperature—Concerted Signals—Singular Effects—A huge Eagle on the Mountain Peak—Fierceness of the wild Cattle—Gales, with Snow and Sleet—Practice with the Broadsword—Mysterious Incident—Termination of our Survey and Wild Sports.

A FEW evenings after this, having surveyed the upper part of the harbor, we dropped down toward the entrance and moored abreast of a long, narrow tussock-islet. On examining this the next day, we discovered traces of pigs; and an officer having caught sight of one wandering along the beach "at his own sweet will" (an enjoyment seldom permitted to pigs), punished the vagabond by knocking him over in fine style at a distance of sixty yards, with no better weapon than a short ship's musket.

This exploit set us all agog for pork—a delicacy which we esteemed the more, as relieving us from the *toujours bœuf.* Being thus haunted with delectable visions of griskins, sparo-ribs, chines, black-puddings, sausages, &c., we planned, in our enthusiasm, an attack on the swine.

To secure such a culinary luxury was an affair of serious importance, and we set about it seriously in the following manner; viz., first, a man with a boat's flag stuck on a boat-hook marched down the centre of the tussock; and though he himself was invisible in consequence of the great height of the leaves, his banner flaunted gayly above, and was plainly visible to all. Every now and then he sounded a little hunting-horn, which was responded to by hearty cheers from six men on either side, who, inspired by love of pig-meat, and armed with boarding-pikes, were so spread out as to take up nearly the whole breadth of the island, thrashing and hallooing with all their might. About two hundred yards in advance stood myself, rifle in hand, backed by my boy with another gun; and on each side of me, at about eighty yards, were two of our best shots.

"The deuce is in it," thought I, exultingly, "if we shan't revel in pork now, both fresh and to pickle."

It was an invigorating anticipation. On came the beaters with shouts of expected triumph. They were formed, like the Spanish Armada, in a half-moon, the horns rather in advance; but, also like that redoubtable armament; our present enterprise ended in a ludicrous failure. The pigs were so stupid (poor wild, benighted creatures!) that they would not come to be killed and cooked. Our exquisite generalship was thrown away; we bagged only one little boar, and even that exploit was owing not to human but to canine agency. La Porte had seized the straggler firmly by the back, and held him there, squeaking terribly, till we came up and captured him alive.

But though we could not achieve a success adequate to our gallant preparation and array of force, we consoled ourselves in the reflection that we had "done more—deserved it."

During our pig-hunt we were tantalized every moment by a clownish penguin, which would first pop out his head to survey us, and then stalk by with grave and silent contempt. He evidently saw that the swine would outwit us, and participated in the triumph of the quadrupeds.

At length a desperate rustling gave notice that something large was at hand; and immediately after, to our infinite disappointment, for we had calculated on the advent of a good fat hog, out waddled a sea-lion. The beast's huge logger-head was hardly visible, when it formed a target for our guns, of all which the contents crashed into his skull nearly at the same moment. Down he dropped immediately, and only showed that life remained by writhing for a few minutes.

On one of our excursions ashore, the following singular circumstance occurred. I have read in medical and other works instances of a similar nature, but never witnessed one. We had breakfasted early and hastily one morning, in order to have a long day before us, and at seven o'clock landed for beef. Having walked three hours, we wounded and, after a running skirmish of two miles, killed a fine cow. This was very fatiguing work. We then rested a short time, and began to retrace our steps toward the shore, in doing which we shot a calf, thus adding considerably to our load.

As I had only five persons with me, I did not take the usual precautions for keeping my party together; and, on stopping to rest, I found that a portly marine was missing. Taking the least tired of my men, I went back some distance to look for the absentee, and having paced two weary miles, was nearly giving up the search, when we observed a flock of caranchos poised nearly motionless in the air.

My companion shrewdly judged that the birds were balancing themselves over our lost one; and, on going up to the place, I found his suspicions correct. The marine was lying on his face as if fast asleep, while a couple of caranchos sat watching him within two feet of his head.

Thinking this was only a lazy fit, and being tired and angry, I brought the whole weight of my rifle down on a well-covered part of his frame, causing, to my surprise, only a deep groan; and we ascertained that the fat lout had lost all power of movement, and could not even lift his arm. We were, therefore, under the necessity of carrying his heavy body back to our party, who were then at least six miles from the beach.

On our arrival there, we tried to recover him; but, as he did not appear to mend, we were obliged by turns to carry him the whole way—and weary work it was. We did not get in sight of the vessel till past seven o'clock in the evening. The people on board, feeling rather alarmed at our protracted absence, luckily kept a good look out, and a boat was on shore nearly as soon as we arrived on the beach.

Having seen the patient, our doctor said that nothing but food would restore him; an opinion borne out by the fact, inasmuch as the man was as well as ever after a good meal. His total prostration up to this time forcibly impressed me, as he was a young and powerfully built man. I afterward learned that this was not a very uncommon case, when violent and long-continued exercise was combined with an empty stomach. Had the man been left all night in the wilderness, he would, in all probability, have died.

As it was, we lost, through the marine's illness, our calf and the prime parts of the cow which we intended to carry on board.

When first we arrived at the Falklands, I used almost to laugh at one of the orders given by Captain Sulivan, that no one belonging to the vessel should be allowed to go on shore without a companion; an order which I understand was rigidly enforced by Captain Fitzroy, while in command of the "Beagle," which was only once broken, and then ended fatally. I am now convinced that it is a very necessary precaution, and, if strictly acted on in all uninhabited or unknown countries, would be the means of saving many valuable lives. Two or three instances have lately occurred of persons going out to shoot in health and spirits, and being found dead the following morning. Exhaustion and exposure to the weather have, in most cases, produced these melancholy results; but with common prudence and a companion there is little or nothing to fear, especially if one is well-armed—a practice which I earnestly recommend to all persons who are desirous to return home with a whole skin.

As I was a passable shot, and an untiring pedestrian, I was invited by Captain Sulivan to accompany him to the top of Mount Pleasant, a hill about eight miles distant from our anchorage. The morning of November 30th being beautiful and calm, we determined to set out, and accordingly started after an early breakfast, having two men with us to carry our instruments, &c. For the first half-mile we amused ourselves very well with shooting snipe and other birds; but we were speedily warned by the bellowings all round us that we should keep more on our guard, which we instantly obeyed, by loading our guns with ball and keeping close together.

Thus prepared, we advanced about a mile farther, when four bulls drew out of a herd and manifested symptoms of resenting our invasion of their territory. Not liking the look of the enemy, we slunk back a short distance, and made a *dètour* of nearly two miles to get clear. La Porte, however, suddenly dashed away, and for nearly twenty minutes was lost to us—much to our vexation, as he was a most puissant ally. Our pleasure, therefore, was proportionately great when we perceived him driving toward us a little calf, *baa-ing* most pitiably.

The moment he was near enough, La Porte seized the animal's nose, and held it until we came up. Our first impulse was to let the poor thing go; but the dog, in his anxiety to secure his prey, had broken the upper jaw, and we therefore put an end to the creature's sufferings by killing it, marking the spot, that we might pick it up on our return.

After this, we marched on through the wilderness, still in battle array, and dispersed a small herd, out of which the dog captured another calf, but which, being uninjured, we let go again.

At length, we came to the bank of a large lake, whose wide, unruffled gleam, quietly reflecting the sky, made the solitude look more solitary. Through this sheet of water we in vain attempted to wade, and were finally compelled to walk round its shore—a great addition to the fatigue of our journey, which, though in a straight line not more than eight miles, amounted, by these necessary deviations, to thirteen or fourteen, and principally among long, soft, springy grass, eighteen inches high.

About one o'clock at noon, we reached the base of the mount, and sat down beside a streamlet winding along the bottom. After recovering a little from our fatigue, we commenced our ascent, and crossed once or twice a long line of those stones mentioned with much surprise by every traveler in this region. Some were so large that we could not have got on them without the help of a ladder. But what struck me most was, that when half-way up, we could hear, on listening intently, a stream rapidly running, and by the deadened noise, evidently some feet below the surface. Half an hour's more toil brought us to the top of the mount; but here our progress was arrested by a perpendicular wall of rock running to the height of nearly three hundred feet.

After a long search, we found a practicable breach. Leaving our guns and other heavy articles behind, we scrambled up as well as we could—no easy matter, from the nature of the rock and the incumbrance of the theodolite-stand, which we intended to erect so as to take a round of angles from the very summit.

With difficulty we gained the apex, but so sharp was it that we could not fix the stand, and were obliged, cross-legged, to drag ourselves over a short ridge to a better place. This was rather nervous work, for my left leg hung over the perpendicular wall as completely at right angles with the surface of the earth as if the side had been built with a plumb-line.

On this narrow altitude we had room to fix the stand, preparatory to making the "observations." A perfect bird's-eye view was now beheld of nearly the whole of the southern part of the east island from the range of Wickham Heights. The prospect was grand on account of its extent, though I could not have imagined any thing so apparently barren and comfortless; the grass seemed every where brown and parched, and innumerable lakes of all forms and sizes gave, with their wan gleam, a melancholy effect to the view. I tried several times without success, to count the cattle in sight; but, after repeated attempts, gave up the endeavor. The temperature was bitterly cold, although a dead calm; and large icicles were hanging in various fantastic shapes from all the overhanging points of rock.

Before leaving the vessel, we had made arrangements with Mr. Bodie (the master) that we should announce our arrival on the summit of the rock by lighting a fire, the smoke of which would direct him to let fall the topsail, and fire a gun exactly five minutes after (to a second). By this sound we expected to get the distance. Collecting what material we could for ignition, and having settled ourselves in comfortable positions to watch with our Dollonds, the word was given to light the fire.

In a moment, a small column of smoke slowly ascended. (We afterward heard that the effect, as seen from the vessel, was beautiful; the vapor being visible to the naked eye, and ascending like a tiny thread from the very peak of the mountain to a great height, until dissipated by the upper currents of air.) No sooner was this seen, than it was responded to by a dozen diminutive objects, descried through our glasses, climbing up the rigging like ants. A moment after, a small speck of white became visible, which announced to us the fall of the topsail. As the second-hand of Captain Sulivan's chronometer reached the five minutes, a thin puff of smoke appeared to spurt out of the vessel's side. All was now attention to catch the sound; but we were too far off.

During the time we remained up here, not a single noise disturbed the death-like silence, neither was the solitude invaded by any other living object than ourselves, excepting that a huge eagle alighted to plume himself on a pinnacle within twelve yards of the theodolite.

After descending with some trouble, we picked up our guns, &c., and commenced our return. The homeward journey was a painful one; as our two men, not being accustomed to such long walks, were knocked up, and the wild cattle, as though they knew we were fatigued, were bolder and fiercer than in the morning. One beast chased us to the edge of a morass, in which we were glad to take refuge. Finding from the nature of the ground that he could not get at us, he worked himself up into a state of madness, which was not at all allayed by a couple of ounces of lead which we sent into his body.

Not wishing to be benighted, we hastened on, and having found the calf we had killed in the morning, got safely on board at seven o'clock to a capital dinner, of which the only fault was a total absence of vegetables.

A succession of heavy southwest gales, with snow and sleet, put a stop, during five days, to all out-of-door work. In the evenings we were much at a loss how to find amusement, as all the books in the ship had been read and re-read dozens of times. I hardly know how we should have diverted the *tædium vitæ*, had I not, before leaving England, luckily provided myself with several single-sticks and hilts from my esteemed friend Mr. H. Angelo, of whom I am proud to acknowledge myself a pupil; and whose skill in the art of offense and defense in the use of the broadsword is above that of any other professor I ever met with. Our people took great delight in this exercise; and, by imparting the knowledge I had acquired under Mr. Angelo, I so trained my men, that I flatter myself few of Her Majesty's ships could have turned out a crew equal to the "Arrow's" ship's company in expertness with that thoroughly English weapon, the broadsword.

We were now beset by a succession of heavy gales. I landed only once, and that was abreast the vessel for an hour or two. With the assistance of the crew, I managed to haul our little dingy over a small bank, and launch her again in a fresh-water lake, where in a very short time we bagged upward of sixty teal, and double the number of various other birds, not mentioned in the game-list.

On Sunday, the 10th of December, the gale had increased prodigiously. It was well for the little ship, which rode to three anchors, that the holding-ground and our ground-tackle were so good ; for, with all our precautions, and though nothing was left to hold wind, but the bare lower masts and hull, we were in momentary fear of going adrift. We could hardly hear the church service performed, even on the lower deck, with the hatches down, so loud was the roaring of the gale.

About sunset, as usual, the wind gradually sank to a hoarse murmur, and at midnight we had fine weather once more, the stars shining as brilliantly as if within the tropics. Such sudden alterations form one of the marked peculiarities of the Falklands.

The next morning, some time after the surveyors had departed, I was much surprised by observing a large column of smoke rising several miles to the southward. This, naturally enough, caused great excitement among us, as we knew our party had gone in an opposite direction. So strange an incident in an uninhabited island brought to my recollection Robinson Crusoe's discovery of the foot-print of a man on the desolate sea-shore. All manner of conjectures were hazarded, and truly some of them were wild enough.

The next morning, as soon as I could spare them, I sent off four steady fellows, well armed ; but nothing could they discover save the remains of a fire, a few singed feathers, and a very old-fashioned rusty hatchet without a handle. Imagining some ship-wrecked mariners might be near, we fired a blue-light as soon as it was dark, and then a sky-rocket, but without any result. Who could the adventurers have been?

Two days more were sufficient to finish the Choiseul Sound; and early on the following morning we sent both our boats sounding down toward the entrance. At two o'clock we followed them in the vessel. About twelve miles from the mouth of the sound we perceived a splendid little harbor on the northern shore, where we anchored for the night, intending to leave the next morning; but unsettled and tempestuous weather detained us several days, which, though a grievous infliction to us at the time, was pleasant in its results, as we had a most gallant and satisfactory campaign in our Wild Sports in this part of the Falklands.

SUPPLEMENT TO THE FALKLANDS.

It is not to this day known if our government was informed of Spain having purchased the French settlement made by de Bougainville. However this may be, we find in the year 1769, that England had a frigate and sloop at the Falklands. Captain Hunt of the "Tamar" frigate, being on a cruise in the neighborhood, fell in with a schooner belonging to the Spanish settlement of Port Solidad. Captain Hunt, in pursuance of his orders, warned this schooner off the coast, which, he asserted, belonged to his Britannic Majesty. The schooner immediately departed; but, in the course of a few days, returned with a Spanish officer, with letters and a present from Don Philip Ruez Puenta, governor of Port Solidad. The letters were couched in terms of the greatest civility. The Don pretended to disbelieve the account he had heard from the captain of the schooner; but attributed Captain Hunt's being in those seas, to chance or distress of weather; and upon that presumption offered him every assistance and kindness in his power; though, if he should be otherwise engaged there, the Don reminded him of the violation of treaties, asserted his master's dominion over that part of the world, charged him hypothetically with insulting the Spanish flag, and ordered the officer formally to warn him off the coast, at his peril; at the same time desiring a written answer.

Captain Hunt, in reply, asserted the sole dominion of the King of England, as well by right of discovery, as of settlement, and warned the Spaniard, in his Britannic Majesty's name, and by his orders, forthwith to quit the coast, and, that he should not be inconvenienced thereby, allowed him six months from the date of his letter, to prepare for his departure.

The Spanish officer made a formal protest, as well upon the grounds here mentioned, as upon Captain Hunt's refusing to let him visit the settlement. His threatening to fire into the Spanish schooner, upon her attempting to enter the harbor, exasperated the Don, who also protested against the English captain going to Solidad, which he had proposed in an amicable manner, and declared that it should be considered as an insult.

This produced, about a fortnight subsequently, another letter, another answer, and another protest. In the course of two months after this transaction, two Spanish frigates, of considerable force, with troops on board for the new settlement, arrived at Port Egmont, under pretense of wanting water. The commander-in-chief wrote a letter to Captain Hunt, in which he expressed great astonishment at seeing the English flag flying, and a kind of settlement formed; charged him with a violation of the last peace, and protested against the act in all its parts. He declared, at the same time, that he would abstain from any manner of proceeding, till he had acquainted his Catholic Majesty with this disagreeable affair. Captain Hunt, as before, founded his possession on the claim of right, justifying his conduct by the orders of his sovereign, and again warned the Spaniards, to depart totally from these islands. The Spanish frigates continued eight days at Port Egmont, and were supplied by our people with water. The captains and officers behaved with civility, and declined going on shore, though permission was offered by Captain Hunt.

As these transactions seemed indicative of some such consequences as followed, the English commander deemed it right, as soon as possible, to depart for England with an account of the whole proceeding. On the 3d of June, 1770, he arrived at Plymouth, and immediately sent an express to the Admiralty.

The "Favorite" sloop, Captain Maltby, succeeded the "Tamar," at Port Egmont; and, with the "Swift," Captain Farmer, each of sixteen guns, formed the whole force on that station. This was, however, soon lessened, by the "Swift," being wrecked in the Straits of Magellan, where she had gone to explore: the ship's company, except three, were fortunately saved, but were still liable to perish by that greatest of all calamities, hunger, if the fortitude and bravery of a small part of the crew had not saved the whole. These brave men, in a small open cutter, undertook a voyage of about three weeks, in the most boisterous seas in the world; and, having happily and miraculously arrived at Port Egmont brought the "Favorite" to their relief.

It was not long after this loss, that a Spanish frigate put into Port Egmont under the pretense, that having been fifty-three days from Buenos Ayres, she was in great distress for water. Three days subsequently, four other frigates hove in sight; and it soon appeared that they had been only twenty-six days at sea, and had been separated a short time before in a heavy gale.

The squadron now threw off the mask of deception, and announced that they had arrived at the place of their *destination*. These five frigates carried one hundred and thirty-four pieces of cannon, and had between sixteeen hundred and seventeen hundred men, including soldiers and marines, on board; besides which they brought a complete battering train, and other material, sufficient to attack a regular fortification, instead of a miserable wooden block-house, which had not even a port-hole cut in it, and only four small pieces of cannon, which at that time were sunk in the mud, to defend it.

A Spanish broad pennant was immediately hoisted on the arrival of the four frigates; and as no doubt of their intentions now remained, Captain Farmer ordered most of the officers and men who had belonged to the "Swift" to come on shore for the defense of the settlement, and directed Captain Maltby to bring the "Favorite" close into the cove.

On the first motions of the "Favorite," one of the Spanish frigates sent an officer on board to acquaint Captain Maltby, that if he weighed they would fire into him; he, however, got under sail, regardless of these menaces, and the frigate fired two shots, which fell to leeward of him. Immediately afterward three of the Spaniards weighed and beat to windward in company with the "Favorite." In the mean time Captain Maltby had sent a message to inquire the reason of the shots being fired; the answer to which was, they were intended as signals.

From the first appearance of these vessels, Captain Farmer had been active in clearing the stores, &c., out of the block-house, and in endeavoring to make it as defensible as its nature would permit. The crew dragged up, with much difficulty, four pieces of cannon (which had originally been intended to protect the landing-place) from the mud in which they had sunk, from neglect, and placed them in the block-house, clearing out the platform, and cutting port-holes to make them effective.

In the mean time, both the English captains had written to the Spanish commodore, that, "as he had been furnished with what he required, they requested he would take himself off forthwith, and evacuate the whole coast, neglecting which, they threatened him with the ire of their royal master." At the same time, the Spanish admiral wrote to them, requesting them, in the kindest manner, to remember his great strength, and the powerless, and defenseless situation they were in, and that by quietly going away they would prevent his forcing them, which would obviate any disastrous collision, and thus hinder the possibility of continuing their voyage home.

The Spanish commodore now offered, that if the British commander would quickly, and with good-will, abandon the place, he would land his troops peaceably and quietly, and treat them with all the consideration that the harmony which subsisted between the two sovereigns required; he would, in that case, also allow them to carry away all their effects and stores; and if, from want of time, want of room, or any other cause, any thing should be left behind, he would give a receipt, and leave the matter to be settled by their respective governments. But if, contrary to expectation, they should endeavor to maintain their footing on the islands, he would immediately proceed to the fulfillment of his orders; and in that case threatened them, in the most pompous terms, with an attack by sea and land, and all the consequences of fire and sword. He concluded by an assurance that if a decided and favorable answer was not returned in fifteen minutes, he would commence operations; and talked largely of the spirit and brilliancy with which his land and sea forces would begin the onslaught. At the same time he recommended them to meditate upon the fatal consequences which their obstinacy would bring upon the unoffending British subjects.

To these truly Spanish effusions our officers returned for answer that words were not deeds, and that they could not believe that, in a time of profound peace, and when the greatest harmony subsisted between England and Spain, he would attempt to put his threats into execution. That they did not doubt he was thoroughly convinced that the King, their master, was sufficiently capable to demand satisfaction in all parts of the globe, of any power whatsoever that should offer to insult the British flag; and if the time was limited to one minute instead of fifteen, it should not alter their determined resolution, to defend to the utmost of their power the charge committed to them.

Previously to the attack the Spanish admiral, to show the uselessness of any resistance, requested that some of our officers might be sent to view the number and condition of the troops and artillery that were ready to be landed; which was accordingly complied with the same evening, and found by the British officers as described. Immediately afterward the Spanish frigates warped in close to the block-house.

At night Captain Maltby landed with fifty of the "Favorite's" men, and brought with them two six-pounders, small arms and ammunition. The next morning a part of the Spanish troops disembarked half a mile to the northward of our people; and when they had advanced half way toward the English station the rest of their boats pushed off from the frigate, and pulled in directly for the cove, being covered by the fire of the frigate, which passed over the block-house.

"Our people," states the 'Annual Register,' "fired some shot; but, seeing the impossibility of defending the settlement, and the Spaniards having now broken through all the limits of peace and amity, even to the actual committal of hostilities, so that their conduct was neither capable of being denied, or explained away; our officers, as they had judiciously led them to this explicit avowal, and supported the honor of their own country, as far as the means in their hands would admit of, with the same propriety preferred saving the valuable lives of their people, and leaving the injury to be redressed by their country, to the throwing of them away in an unavailing contest, which afforded neither a possibility of gaining any advantage, or a hope of obtaining honor. They accordingly hung out the flag of truce, and demanded articles of capitulation.

"These articles were concluded between the Captains Farmer and Maltby on the one side, and Don John Ignacio Madariaga, Major-General of the royal navy of his Catholic Majesty, on the other. The substance of them was, that in a certain limited time, but discretionary on the part of the commodore, the English were permitted to depart in the 'Favorite,' and to take with them such part of the stores as they chose, or she could conveniently carry; that an inventory should be made of all the stores, and the remainder deposited in the hands of the Governor of Solidad, who was to become answerable for them; that the English flag was to continue flying on shore and on board the sloop; but that they were to exercise no jurisdiction except with their own people; and that they should be allowed to march off at the time of embarkation, under arms with drums beating and colors flying; but that they were to give the Spanish commander proper notice, that he might appoint an hour for their departure, as they were not otherwise to be armed.

"The restrictions with respect to the time of their departure, were, until the Governor of Solidad or his deputy should arrive to make the inventories, and to take charge of the stores (supposing that they were to arrive within forty days), and until twenty days were elapsed after the sailing of a Spanish frigate, which it is to be supposed the commander intended to send off as an express. But the most degrading of all the circumstances attending this transaction, and particularly a new, and to all appearance wanton insult to the British flag, was that for the better security of this limitation, the 'Favorite,' was deprived of her rudder, which was taken off and kept on shore during the time of their detention.

"As the Spaniards, previous to this expedition, must have been tolerably well informed of the state of our settlement at Port Egmont, nothing can appear more ridiculous than the preparations they made for it. The train of artillery consisted of twenty-seven pieces of cannon, from twenty-four pounders downward; besides four mortars of six inches, four hundred bombs, and all other kinds of ammunition and utensils, proper for carrying on a siege, in proportion.

"The stores which our people left behind, were considerable, both in quantity and value, and the inventories having been properly stated and authenticated, as well as the stipulated time elapsed from the departure of the Spanish frigate, the 'Favorite' was at length suffered to proceed on her way to England, with all our people on board. She accordingly arrived at the Motherbank, near Portsmouth, on the 22d of September, after a voyage of seventy days, by which it appears that she had continued at Port Egmont thirty-four days after the signing of the capitulation."

A war with Spain nearly resulted from these proceedings, as the public mind in England was greatly excited, not so much on account of any supposed value of the Falklands, as by the insolent acts of the Spanish authorities. The celebrated Junius brought his powerful pen to bear on the subject, and hostilities were averted only by Spain relinquishing to Great Britain, in 1771, her claim to the sovereignty of the islands in question, which were now utterly disregarded by all nations. In 1820, the Republic of Buenos Ayres assumed a right to the Falklands, and a colony from that state settled at Port Louis, which increased rapidly, until, owing to a dispute with the Americans, the settlement was destroyed by the latter in 1831. Two years afterward, the British flag was again hoisted at Port Louis and at Port Egmont; and His Majesty's ship 'Tyne' was sent to take charge of the islands for the purpose of keeping permanent possession.

APPENDIX.

HAVING been much interested by the newly-invented plank roads which have conferred great facilities of intercommunication in America, and being of opinion that in certain English localities, particularly in some of our lanes and by-roads, they may be found very serviceable, I have extracted, by way of Appendix, a few particulars connected with the origin, construction, and expense of plank roads, as compared with the formation of other roads. This information is derived from a pamphlet by W. Kingsford, Esq., Civil Engineer of the Hudson River Railroad, printed in Philadelphia but not known in this country.

"Within the last three years, the plank road system has become a part of the economy of the State of New-York. Special enactments have been made to meet the circumstance, and hence in the western part of the State private enterprise has been abundantly enlisted in this species of improvement. So satisfactory have been the results, that the neighboring and more remote southern States, have commenced to inquire what are the benefits which plank roads extend; and it would seem that this improved mode of communication is likely to become generally introduced.

"Very little has hitherto been said upon the subject, and the writer has thought that it would not be unacceptable to many, to enter upon an inquiry as to the mode of construction and the probable cost of plank roads, and their advantages and disadvantages, considered in connection with the old roadway—bringing forward statements of the results which are admitted to have proceeded immediately from the introduction of plank roads. It must, however, be allowed, that hitherto, with the advantages which are direct, and recognized by all, some demerits have been found. These, the writer believes he will be able to establish to have grown up from vicious principles of construction, and can be guarded against, and in the greater part averted by prudence and care.

"HISTORY.

"The first plank road laid down in this continent was on the road leading east from Toronto, during the government of Sir Francis Bond Head, in Upper Canada, in 1835–36. And the fact is recorded in the Report of the Commissioners of the Younge Street road, dated 29th January, 1837. It was laid down experimentally, with twelve-feet plank, without any principle of construction, beyond laying the plank on sleepers. The circumstance is thus commented upon:

"'The trustees, having examined the piece of planked road made last year, and finding that it answered a much better purpose than could have been anticipated, both with regard to the ease of traveling, and the very trifling expense attending the keeping the same in repair, came to the determination of proceeding with it; they accordingly contracted with the proprietor of the steam saw-mill to plank one mile, which was completed in a very short time, for the sum of £525 (2100 dollars), exclusive of forming the channels, and laying on a coat of loam, or sand, to prevent the wear by horses' calks and friction of the wheels. They beg further to state the road has given more general satisfaction to the country, and as it is evident from the experience they have already had, that the cost attending it is very little more than one-fourth of a stone road; and the expense of keeping a Macadamized road in repair being greater than was anticipated, they have altogether abandoned the idea of Macadamizing, and have contracted for continuing the plank road early next season.'

"There is no certainty as to the originator of the experiment. It is, however, generally believed to have been Mr. Darcy Boulton.

"During the following year, troubles broke out in Canada, and all public works were stopped, until the arrival of Mr. Thomson (afterward Lord Sydenham), when an impetus was given to the whole country. The Hon. Mr. Hamilton Killaly was appointed President of the Board of Works, and under his direction plank roads became one of the improvements of the day. They were introduced with great success in Upper Canada. In Lower Canada, Colonel the Hon. George Cathcart* was the means of

* The late Governor of the Tower of London, and one of the most distinguished cavalry officers of the day. Colonel Cathcart was at Waterloo, as aid-de-camp of the Duke of Wellington; and was formerly Colonel of the King's Dragoon Guards. He is one of the many instances of military men bringing to civil life a high order of intellect, which service seems to have quickened. And like his great master, he thinks no detail too insignificant, no labor too great. The Chambly and Longueil road was constructed principally after his instructions.

the first plank road being laid down between Longueil and Chambly, in 1841.

"As yet, nothing had been done in this State toward bettering the lines of communication, and it was reserved for the city of Syracuse to be the first to set other localities an example. In 1837, the Salina and Central Square road was laid down under the direction of the Hon. Mr. Geddes and Mr. S. Alvord, who are entitled to the credit of having introduced the plank road system in the United States, and of having contributed most of the improvements on the *modus operandi* observed in Canada.

"One can not help contrasting the difference in the progress the system has made in Canada and in the State of New-York.

"In the former, where, dating from the arrival of Lord Sydenham, plank roads have been known ten years.

	Miles.
Government have constructed	192
And private enterprise about (this total is assumed, as no statement has been published)	250
Total miles	442

In the State of New York, where the system has been introduced about four years, upward of two thousand one hundred and six miles have been registered, and are constructed, or are in the course of construction, at an average cost of 1833 dollars per mile.

"COMPARISON WITH OTHER ROADS.

"The road which must be considered principally in connection with plank roads is the Macadam road. And if it can be shown that the cost of a plank road is infinitely less—that it is easier for the horse to draw upon—and that such a road costs less for repairs, and is more durable than a Macadam road—the proposition of superiority may be considered proven.

"The question of draught is the one first to be considered. Experiment has determined the load which a horse is capable of drawing on the plank road to be so weighty, that one almost hesitates to set it down from fear of the accusation of exaggeration. On the Salina and Central Road, a few weeks back, for a wager, a team * brought in, without any extraordinary strain, six tons of iron from Brewerton, a distance of twelve miles, to Syra-

* Where this expression is made use of, it means two horses

cuse. One and a half cords of green beech is a common load, which is equivalent to 90 cwt.$=4\frac{1}{2}$ tons. And there is so little resistance on a properly constructed road, that an average team can travel with this load from thirty to thirty-five miles, day after day, at the rate of from three to four miles an hour. Indeed, the farmer does not seem to make any calculations of the weight taken. He loads his wagon as best he can, and the only care is not to exceed the quantity which it will carry; whether the team can draw the load, is not a consideration—for those who travel on plank roads affirm that the only danger is that the wagon can not bear the load, not that the horse can not draw it.

"A good instance of what can be accomplished may be related of the Western Road, which commences at Albany. A farmer who had a large timbered farm, having sold the wood, carted it to the side of the plank road, and piled it. His contract was to take the wood into Albany, a distance of eleven miles, at 1·50 dollars per cord for hauling. With a single team his load consisted of a cord and a half, and having engaged to transport plaster for a miller, at 75 cents the ton, he loaded his wagon for the return trip, which was weighed in the usual manner for the adjustment of the carrying account. The ordinary load was three tons. The trips backward and forward were easily made in a day. Thus his receipts were

	Dollars.
Cartage $1\frac{1}{2}$ cord of hard wood, at 1·50 dollars..........	2·25
3 tons of plaster, at 75 cents	2·25
	4·50
Payment of tolls, 11 miles each way, 22 at ·01$\frac{1}{2}$ dollars..	33
Return per diem	4·17

"That great loads can be drawn on Macadam roads (or metal roads, as they are often called in America) can not be called in question, but at the same time it is to be remarked that, on the first construction at least, the resistance to the tractive power will be greater than on the smooth, even, compact surface of the plank. A period must even intervene before the metal becomes solid: and those who have at all watched how metal roads are influenced, admit the necessity of constant repairs. In and about large towns the main Macadamized avenues have annually to be covered with an entire coat of metal, and the road, to be kept in order, has constantly to be watched from the day the stone is first placed upon it.

"Thus, independently of the difference of surface of the best metal road and of the ordinary plank road, constant repairs increase the resistance. When newly laid, the resistance for heavy trains on the latter has been calculated variously at 1 in 98, and at 1 in 70, while that of the stone road in perfect condition is named at 1 in 67. But while the plank road for at least two years after it has been laid down retains an equality of surface, the stone road is never in such order that so low a ratio of resistance can be received. In ordinary condition, the resistance of 1 in 25 is received. Taking a mean of the two, we may call the average resistance of the Macadam road 1 in 46.

"To recapitulate, we have the two resistances.

"On the plank road 1 in 70.

"On the Macadam road 1 in 46.

"Nor can it be said that this comparison is much exaggerated. Even those who differ from it supply data but little less favorable. The comparison even continues as both roads are worn. On the Macadam road the *detritus*, which in dry weather finds vent in dust, in wet weather exercises considerable resistance, so that whatever inequalities exist are felt in all weathers. Whereas on the plank road, in dry weather, the cavities which are worn are traversed imperceptibly by the tire, for they are closed up by the indurated sand and earth deposited on the surface. But in wet weather it is not so—the sand softened by water offers no resistance to the tire, which sinks down to the worn plank. And as in pine roads the surface is generally worn with regularity, although inferior to a new road, there is nothing strikingly objectionable in it, after it has been somewhat worn.

"Some comparison can therefore be made between a Macadam road and a plank road in that state. In dry weather the planks, being protected by the sand placed over them, present a hard regular surface; while on the Macadam road whatever is bad is felt by the traveler without counterbalancing influences. Nor in wet weather is the plank much deteriorated. For so long as the planks are firmly fixed and do not spring, there is little increased friction; but with regard to Macadamized roads, independently of ruts and holes, the resistance is increased by the pulverized stone, formed by the water into an adhesive matter; so much so, that a word has been appropriated to denote this state. Thus, to speak of 'heavy roads' is to convey a clear and definite meaning. It is therefore apparent that, in pursuing the inquiry to what extent the tractive power is impeded on each class of road, in the different stages of newly laid and out of repair, the superior advantages of the plank road become fully established.

"Some attempt has been made to draw comparisons between the time a horse will last on a Macadam and on a plank road. It has been asserted that horses traveling mostly or occasionally over plank roads are ruined before their time. But it will be found that this opinion rests altogether upon what is observed to occur, either when the plank surface is badly constructed, or where the power of the animal is mismanaged. If, for instance, the stringers are laid without care, the percolations of the water increase the defect, and any weight passing over the road is succeeded by a rebound, varying with the velocity of the passage; and it is this rebound or elasticity which operates perniciously on the horse. It is only necessary for a man to run some little distance on a causeway having this defect, and he will feel at once the difference between a well and ill-constructed road.

"Mismanagement is a principal and frequent cause of deterioration of the horse's vitality and endurance. Owing to the trifling resistance encountered on a plank road, and the consequent ease with which a great weight is drawn, drivers, without noting the rate at which they travel, press their horses beyond their strength. The axiom has long been received that it is speed, not weight, which destroys the horse. 'It is the pace that kills.' The argument against the plank road derived from this observation, and making its inference from the very excellence of the road, is palpably vicious. On the Albany road two gentlemen in a hired buggy with an ordinary hack, went a distance of twelve miles out, and returned. This was in the month of April last, at the breaking up of the winter, when the other roads were nearly impassable. The distance between two gates, five miles, was performed at the usual natural gait, without the animal being in the least kept up to his work, in twenty-three minutes going, and twenty-seven minutes returning. On their return to Albany, the horse evinced no signs of fatigue.

"In reality, there is nothing to warrant the inference that the horse is a sufferer on a well-made plank road. On the contrary, it may be said, without contradiction, that the horse, when not pressed beyond his strength, can work longer and be always in better condition on a plank road than on any road whatsoever.

"Sufficient data are at hand to form a proximate ratio of the superior advantages of the plank road.

"The preponderance in favor of the plank road, as compared with a common country road, may be stated as ranging from $2\frac{1}{2}$ to 1, to 6 to 1—varying with the season and the locality. The former ratio may be considered to denote the average comparison, at the commencement of the bad season, on gravelly soils—the latter, where the road passes through heavy sand. Farmers take a cord and a half of green wood, in place of half and three-quarters of a cord; 80 bushels of rye, and 100 bushels of oats, when, formerly, they carried 40 and 50 bushels; 200 plank in the place of 80 to 90. This is done at the rate of four miles an hour; whereas, three miles an hour, when the road was in tolerable order, was considered rapid traveling with a team.

A manufacturer of Utica formerly transported from the railroad to his establishment—a distance of seven miles—ten bales of cotton per day, with two teams, which made, each, but one daily trip; but on the recently constructed plank road, one team performs the journey twice, delivering fifteen bales daily. The average weight of a bale of cotton is 5 cwt.; therefore, one team is now equal to the work of 75 cwt., while on the old road it was equal only to 25 cwt. These loads must be considered fair average burdens, without the energies of the horse being unfairly taxed. On a level, Macadam English road, writers agree that the extreme weight of draught for a single horse, in perfect condition, is 3100 lbs.—and that 'to place on more becomes a cruelty,' which would give the maximum power of traction to a team of 6200 lbs. That such is inferior to the amount which has been carried on a plank road, without distressing the horses, the incident of six tons taken on the Salina road is a proof.

While, therefore, we take 3 to 3½ tons as a medium load on a plank road, we may assume 2 tons to be fair draught on the Macadam road—the same time to be made by each.

"These calculations would give a ratio of 3 to 2 in favor of the plank road. Mr. Gillespie, in his work on roads, rates the difference at twice as much.

"COMPARATIVE COST OF THE TWO ROADS.

"The next inquiry is the comparative cost of plank and Macadam roads. This, of course, will vary with localities. Known results in one region will assist in forming estimates for another.

"It is stated in the Report of the Commissioners of Board of Works of Canada, for the year ending 1848, that the average cost of the fifty-six miles of Macadamized road under the jurisdiction of the Montreal Turnpike Trustees, was 3462 dollars per mile. Two miles were laid by way of experiment, costing 3233 dollars per mile—the lowest price at which any Macadam road was made—the greatest cost being 4888 dollars. But on this road, extending seven miles from Montreal to Lachine, there was heavy cutting on two hills. The repairs for the last eight years have been, annually, 200 dollars a mile—about $\frac{2}{35}$ of the original cost. At Quebec, the average cost of thirty-one miles, was 3600 dollars per mile; the repairs amounting per mile, annually, to 165 dollars—$\frac{2}{45}$ of the whole cost. On the Port Hope road, the repairs per mile were 300 dollars; on the road from Toronto to Springfield, 511 dollars; but this road is described as worn out in many places. Therefore, the cost of a Macadamized road may be safely assumed at 3400 dollars per mile, with the necessity of an annual expenditure of about 130 dollars per mile.

"The cost of a plank road depends on contingencies, but may be stated, with tolerable accuracy, to range from 1200 dollars to 2000 dollars per mile, where there is no extraordinary item of expenditure, and according as the road may be built of hard wood—maple or hemlock.

"For the sake of establishing a comparison, a medium cost, 1750 dollars per mile, is assumed.

"The repairs which a plank road will need for the first two years ought to be trifling. To a great extent, at this early period, they depend upon the mode in which the road has been constructed. If it has been well kept up and well drained, and the sleepers have been carefully laid, there is little fear of the road settling, nor will any of the plank become loose. Even on roads built before experience had pointed out a good mode of construction, the repairs were not a heavy charge. The Chambly and Longueil road, Canada-East, was laid down in 1841, with white pine, which generally lasted about four years. It has since been renewed, and the road has been more carefully constructed; and there is a reasonable expectation that it will last seven years. The ordinary annual repairs have been $7\frac{1}{2}$ dollars a mile. It is not possible to give the exact traffic, as the tolls for sixteen miles are farmed out for 5220 dollars per annum. It can not be considered, by any means, that this road is too favorable a criterion, for it was among the first built on the continent.

"WHAT PLANK ROADS DO FOR THE FARMER.

"The farmer has what he never had before, a good road every day in the year, the same in all seasons. Formerly, the spring and fall were periods when the avenues to the neighboring city were closed to him. On the plank road, he can select for his journey days when he can not work on the farm, taking with greater ease, in half the time, three times what he formerly could carry; and while residing close to the road, he sees his neighbor, living five miles off, bringing two wagons to the planks, and then transferring the contents into the larger, and moving off with it—he can load his single vehicle with the full amount it can carry, and proceed onward without delay. His woodlands acquire, intrinsically, a value which they had not before, for he can cart sufficiently in one load to pay him for the expense of carting and cutting, allowing a fair value for his timber. His farm increases in value from 10 to 50 per cent, and commands a sale from the fact that the produce never lacks a market, and has a more regular and higher net value. By the current price, he knows what he can count upon. His grain is worth what all grain fetches in the next market, deducting the cost of cartage to take it there, which he can calculate to a cent, and deliver when he needs money. The adjoining tannery (and the probability is that there is one within twenty miles) will buy his bark. His cord wood can be carried the same distance. He sells, for remunerating prices, his perishable produce, such as vegetables and fruit, pumpkins, corn-stalks, and fall apples, which brought him previously a very small sum, as the only market was in the small villages where there was little demand for them.

"The wear and tear to his horse, harness, and vehicle is reduced at least one-half. The tolls not only pay themselves in this saving, but even leave a surplus in the pocket of the farmer, which would otherwise have been spent on repairs. Horse-shoes last twice the time. Instead of frequent new shoes, it is only necessary to have the old ones periodically renewed. The very labor of cleaning the horse comes into calculation; one farmer assuring the writer that in very bad weather, setting aside all question of increase of load and saving of time, he would sooner pay the tolls than have to rub down his horses in the state they used to be after travel on the old road.

"The price of cartage having generally been reduced where plank roads have been laid down, it becomes an inquiry, whether it is at the cost of the teamster. Some instances are given in a former part of this *brochure*, and we will adduce two others, to show that the increase of load carried, and the time made, more than counterbalance any reduction of price.

"On the Taberg and Rome road, there is a furnace, nine miles from Rome, from which furnace to the canal at Rome 1·25 dollars per ton was formerly paid for carting. The load each way was precisely one ton, equal to two tons per day at 1·25 dollars, giving 2·50 dollars for the day's work. Now, the price allowed is 0·75 dollars; but the teamster takes two and a half tons each way, equal to five tons per day, at

	Dollars.
	0·75=3·75
Deducting toll for eighteen miles, say	25
	3·50

Being an increase of one dollar in the daily wages of the teamster.

"The Rome and Turin road passes through a dairy country, and cheese and butter are brought by it to the canal, where they are shipped. Formerly farmers brought 1500 lbs. to the canal, and took two days to go and return: now they cart from forty to fifty cwt. and return the same day. The smallest load carried is thirty-six tubs of butter. A farm, ten miles off from a city, is almost as near as one only a mile from it; the surplus distance being in calculation convertible into time. But at a more extended distance, say one hundred miles, it is worth while examining how the plank road can compete with the railroad. Canals being main links of water communication, do not suggest themselves as a matter of inquiry. But many vegetable products now find their way to market by the railroad; and if it can be established that a farmer, using his own motive power on the plank road, can travel at half the cost, a very essential benefit is established.

"Thus it is evident that the farmer does his own business, to his own satisfaction, with a wagon to make a return trip, bringing back all his family may require from the city; such as a quintal of cod-fish, a chest of tea, a barrel of pork, flour, and assorted articles, cheaper than he could buy them at a country store; together with the experience of his trip, and the information picked up at the inns where he has stopped; and all for exactly half the cost if he had sent by railroad and had his business done by an agent. It is pre-supposed that the farmer can be absent from his farm, without injury to himself.

"On Sunday the farmer can go to church with regularity, which was not always possible in the fall, when the church was one-fourth of a mile from the farm. He can live with more friendliness with his neighbors—for the plank roads have led to an increased intercourse between families. Socially, the farmer becomes a better and a wiser man. He can meet people of his own pursuits more frequently, and converse upon prices current and improved modes of farming. He learns what is new, and what benefits any particular experiment has led to. In case of sickness, relief can be obtained readily, and with dispatch; and if medical skill can save the head of a family or a young wife, the physician can be soon brought to the bedside.

"Indeed, all the advantages which result from a road of superior excellence accrue to the farmer. There is nothing which so much retards improvement as imperfect communications. 'Of all inventions,' says one of the greatest writers* of the day, 'the alphabet and printing-press alone excepted, those inventions which abridge distance have done most for civ-

* Macaulay. History of England, Chap. III.

ilization. Every improvement of the means of locomotion benefits mankind, morally and intellectually, as well as materially; and not only facilitates the interchange of the various productions of nature and art, but tends to remove national and provincial antipathies, and to bind together all the branches of the great human family.'

"If ever such a remark could be directly applied, it is to the sections traversed by plank roads. The family, instead of periodical visits to the neighboring city, are continually passing to and fro. The change, the bustle, the animation, all have their influence. The farmer sees other farms, finds them perhaps better fenced than his own, better cultivated, and better 'cleaned off.' A spirit of emulation is excited in him, and his outbuildings and fences gradually acquire a greater air of neatness. The comforts of the city make the want of them to be painfully felt in his own homestead, and his wife and daughters are awakened to exertion by the contrast. His dress is marked by a greater air of neatness. The same can be said of the female members of the family. Indeed, in all the ramifications of life, the contrast with civilization, brought about by improved communication, causes itself to be felt. In a word, the farmer learns that there is such a thing as progress.

"A gentleman, who was among the first to introduce these roads into the country, remarked to the writer, concerning a road which it is obviously not necessary to name: 'The farms are no longer the same—the proprietors have cleaned them; pulling out the stumps, erecting better fences, and generally improving their property; some even, at their own expense, have run plank roads to their lots, to assist the draught of the horses. The people too are changed, dress better, look better—their manners are better. Their wives and daughters are no longer the same persons. They have improved wonderfully.'

"Such are the results that have in every instance attended the introduction of plank roads.

"WHAT PLANK ROADS DO FOR THE STOCKHOLDER.

"The tolls authorized to be collected in the State of New York, by the Plank Road Law, are not to exceed one cent and a half per mile for a vehicle drawn by two animals; and one half cent per mile for every additional animal; for every vehicle drawn by one animal, three-quarters of a cent per mile, and for each horse and rider, or led horse, half a cent per mile. In the original enactment, the profits of the road were limited to a dividend of ten per cent., and the appropriation of ten per cent. as a sinking fund. But this clause was repealed in 1849; so the above tolls can be levied irrespective of profits.

"There are, however, some non-paying exceptions, such as jurors, witnesses, troops, and travelers attending religious meetings.

"With the above rates, the profits of existing companies have been made, and the best criterion of the character of the stock is to examine what these profits have been.

"Some few companies depart from the rates prescribed, and charge less; taking six and a quarter cents for the five miles. Some companies agree with the farmers to charge the distance per mile they live from the gate. These cases are exceptions to the general rule.

"Among the many roads constructed in the State, some few have been built more as the means of opening up the communication than as an investment. In these, farmers have freely subscribed. But, throughout the State, it can be asserted positively that the stock of no plank road is below par. Nor can any stock be bought, except from individuals who are pressed for money, and, in common with plank-road stock, have to sell other property to obtain it.

"Where the travel is limited, the plank will of itself decay, and need restoration, without a sufficiency of receipts to pay for restoring it. But from such a postulate, no deduction can flow. A road, to be remunerative, must first be required. A good road increases travel; but there must be other causes to create it.

"ON THE FACILITIES OF TRAVEL GIVEN BY PLANK ROADS.

"There is some difficulty in instituting a comparison between a plank road and a railroad. Both have their distinct uses. The railroad is important to the manufacturer, the miner, the metal founder, who have to send their fabrics and their coal and iron a distance from their localities, the means of doing which they have to hire; and the numerous class of travelers who desiring to be carried with dispatch, must seek a public conveyance. The plank road is for an agricultural population, and for the accommodation of those who, having cattle, need not incur the expense of motive power. To lay greater stress on the utility of the one, the circumstances of the comparison must be given.

"To examine the difference of cost, we can refer to the Annual Report of Railroad Statistics for the State of New York, made to the Legislature, 20th February, 1850. We learn in this document, that the whole amount which has been expended on the 1201 miles of railroad in the State, to set them in operation, is 46,604,921 dollars, giving an average per mile of 38,805 dollars for construction and about eight years' repairs. The cost of construction and of eight years' repairs on the plank road may be assumed at 3106 dollars.

"The average pace of railway passenger trains is twenty-three miles an hour, and of freight trains fourteen miles an hour. The fare is about two cents per mile for long distances, and from three to six for short distances.

"On the plank road a stage-horse can travel from eighteen to twenty miles a day, at the rate of seven to nine miles an hour.

"It is, therefore, evident, that traveling at the rate of seven to nine miles per hour, is performed on the plank road at three cents per mile.

"We have then these results:

"The cost of the railroad is at least twelve times as great as that of the plank road.

"That travel for short distances can be done for less on the plank road than on the railroad.

"In average distances, the fare on the plank road is three cents per mile, while on the railroad the fare is from* two to two and a half cents per mile:—nevertheless, in one instance the stage fare has been less than on the railroad.

"Time is the only strong point of view favorable to the railroad, and it is found that the distance can be performed in one-third the time on the railroad of what it can be made on the plank road.

"Whether to gain this advantage such an additional expense ought to be incurred, can not be considered by the writer, abstractedly; but one fact is certain, that in an agricultural country it is manifestly to the greatest benefit of the farmer to have a well-laid causeway on which he can use his own motive power in bringing his produce to market.

"Plank roads are the feeders of railroads and canals, and are not inferior to either in their particular uses. In some instances, indeed generally in manufacturing districts, speed is indispensable. But economy of transport in an agricultural section of country, is the main point. In a former part of this work it was shown that the farmer can successfully compete with a railroad within one hundred miles of the market; therefore, it would seem that the plank road is of more utility to him. And it has this in-

"* It must be recollected that the grades on these roads vary from 250 to 350 feet in a mile, and therefore can not be taken as a minimum price at which travel can be performed. It is possible, if the grades of the roads were reduced to a maximum of 150 in the mile, that the expense of transporting passengers and merchandise would be from one-half to two-thirds the present price."

fluence upon his property, that it raises it considerably in value—a remark which does not apply to the same extent to railroads.

"There are a class of travelers who turn aside from the railroad. The Erie Canal statistics prove this sufficiently. Men of quiet temperament who dislike the bustle and excitement, and not being in great haste to arrive at their destination, take other conveyances.

"That this class will increase when plank roads have been longer established, there is reason to believe.

"CONSTRUCTION.

"Where there is only a single track required, it is not the custom to lay the plank in the centre of the causeway; generally, the left-hand side of the road leading from the city is selected, by which arrangement loaded vehicles coming into the city have the right of way. Running parallel to the planks the road is carefully made, and the name by which it is now known indicates its use. It is called the 'turn off.' Necessarily, it ought to be kept in sufficient repair—since vehicles going in either direction take the plank, and those not having the right of way, abandon it when meeting a vehicle which has.

"For ordinary travel, a single plank track is sufficient—an assertion fully proved by very few roads having a double track. But if the press of business renders a double track necessary, it ought to be laid down in two tracks of eight feet, not in a single track of sixteen feet. The best mode is first to lay down a single track, and if found insufficient in any particular locality, such as the immediate approach to a city, another one can of course, be added.

"The cost of the several roads varies. This is attributable to the difference of the amount paid for surveying, right of way, grading and laying plank—the prices of lumber, and the expense of bridging, &c. The lumber which has been principally used is hemlock and white pine, until within the last few months, when hard wood has somewhat come into use, with a fair expectation of proving more suitable. On the Salina and Syracuse road, beech and maple have been laid, and on the Rochester road some elm—the latter not exceeding twelve inches in width.

"The principal experiments have been made with hemlock, and it has been proved that it is not the best fitted for the purpose. It is loose grained and knotty—consequently, the plank soon wears away, stringing off from friction, leaving hard knots standing erect. Independently of the rugged surface which these knots present, they may be classed among the principal causes which lead to the destruction of the road, for as the shoe of the horse strikes the knot it slips from it, and a cavity is made. White pine, which has been used, has the advantage of being free from knots.

"But it is argued that this wood is liable to decay. All lumber used on a road will undoubtedly decay of itself—even should it remain without any traffic passing over it. Two influences work upon the plank: the damp from below causing mildew, while the upper part is alternately drenched with water, and exposed to the burning heat of the sun. An examination of a plank long in use, is sufficient evidence of this fact. Against some of the influences it is not possible to guard, and they come under the head of wear and tear. But good construction will do much to obviate others.

"In the advertisements for the plank road timber, great care has been taken to specify that the plank has to be sawed out of sound timber, free from wane sap, rottenness, knot holes, and excessive knottiness. Still these precautions are valueless where the timber is naturally imperfect, and in spite of the fears that pine becomes 'dozy,' yellow pine is a durable wood, free from knots, and is, therefore, preferable to hemlock, as it will keep longer sound.

"The most important point in the construction of plank roads is drainage. Without drainage, however well a road may be otherwise laid, it can not remain in good order. And a sufficient ditch should be cut, at least two feet below the crown of road. The road should be well crowned up, so that the water would readily flow from it, with a firm bed made for the stringers. Where the soil has been made, a heavy roller (which can be formed with a portion of the trunk of a large green oak) should be passed over the roadway, till it is perfectly firm, and the sleeper should be imbedded in the soil, till the top is on a level with the earth. The planks then, laid transversely, require to be well mauled, until firmly settled; care being taken to drive each home to the one laid behind it.

"The mode of laying down stringers varies with the soil; and on this point there is some difference of opinion. It is generally conceded, however, that sand does not require so heavy a stringer as clay. On the Salina and Syracuse road, in order to insure thorough and effective drainage, a transverse fall of two inches has been given to the planks. With such a declivity, the load is unequally divided, and the weight falls heavier on the lower, in the proportion of 3100 lbs. to 2900 lbs. in a load of three tons. Independently of this pressure against the lower linch-pin and hub of the wheel, it is urged, that it is advisable to make the lower scantling (or stringer) double that of the upper, in order to guard against the increased pressure on the lower side of the road."

WISCONSIN.

BY DANIEL S. CURTISS, ESQ., OF THE UNITED STATES.

An early copy having been sent to me of Mr. Curtiss's "Western Portraiture," published in America within the last month, I hasten to present my reader with some passages relative to Wisconsin, as confirmatory of the opinions I had previously formed on the subject, and which I have embodied in the present volume.

"From the best authorities, it appears that the earliest visits of white men to the territory that now forms the State of Wisconsin, was in 1654, made by some French traders, from Montreal to Lake Superior. The first white settlement was made in 1665, by Claude Allouez and others, at Lapointe, on an island of the same name, in the western end of that lake; and a few years before the establishment of the settlement at Puans (Green) Bay. According to the authorities quoted by Bancroft, Schoolcraft, and others, those settlements were made in 1665 and 1669; and in 1673, Father J. Marquette, accompanied by Joliet, went up the Nenah (Fox) River, passed the short portage of a mile or two into the Wisconsin River, then descended it to the Mississippi, which they reached in June of that year. The Legislature have named one of the counties, near that portage, Marquette, after that adventurer, one of the first, who ever saw that mighty stream.

"In 1679, La Salle made a voyage up the lakes, in the first vessel ever built above Niagara Falls; he called it the 'Griffon!' and he has claimed to be the first white man who ever saw the Mississippi; but this is disputed, as Bancroft declares that H. de Soto was the first European that discovered the 'Father of Waters,' and crossed it in 1541. The 'Griffon' is said to have been a plain, substantial little schooner, of some sixty tons burden, and carrying five small guns. On the 7th of August, 1679, she sailed from Niagara with thirty-four men, bound for the western lakes, and reached Mackinaw the last of the month; on the 2d of September she sailed again for Green Bay. At that port she was laden with peltries; and on the 18th of the same month, La Salle put her in charge of the pilot and five men, and sent her back again; but they never reached their destination, vessel and crew having perished, which was a severe loss to La Salle, as the vessel and cargo had cost him about 60,000 livres. Still, he and his comrades continued their voyage up the coast of Lake Michigan in canoes to the mouth of Chicago River, where they erected a fort; and shortly afterward Father Hennepin, with others, passed from that river into the O'Plain, then the Illinois, and down that river to the Mississippi.

"Wisconsin constituted a portion of New France, under French authority till 1763, when it was surrendered to Great Britain. In 1783, a settlement was began at Prairie du Chien, by Giard, Autaya, and Dubuque, near the site of the earlier French settlement. In 1819 Governor Cass explored the northern country; during which year the garrisons of Prairie du Chien and St. Peter's were established. In 1823 Major Long explored the same region; and in 1832 an expedition under Schoolcraft passed through the country. In 1836 it was organized under a territorial government, with the title of Wisconsin Territory.

"This was a Territory, under one authority or another, from 1787 to 1847, when it became an independent State of the Union, making the twenty-ninth star in that galaxy of political existences, whose light is seen throughout Christendom, and whose influence is felt wherever the breezes have carried paper and powder. In fertility of soil, comfort of climate, and all other natural facilities of successful agricultural operations, Wisconsin is scarcely behind any of her sister States; and perhaps is surpassed by none in the rapidity with which her population has increased during the last eight or ten years, and their intelligence. In 1840 the population was something over 20,000; in 1845 it was about five times that, say, 115,000; and in 1850 the census shows it to be 305,528.

"I take the following boundary of this State from 'Darby's Gazetteer', of 1845:

"'Wisconsin Territory of the U.S., if taken *in extenso*, is bounded on the N. by the British territories; by Mississippi River, W.; Illinois, S.; and by Lake Michigan, the northwestern part of the State of Michigan, and Lake Superior, E. In latitude it extends from 42° 30′ to 49° N., and in longitude from 10° to 18° 30′ W. of Washington. Measured by the rhombs, the area comes out so near that we may assume 80,000 square miles. This region comprises the northwestern part of the original U.S. domain by the treaty of 1783. From S.E. to N.W. by a diagonal line, the length falls but little short of 600 miles. The breadth is about 160 miles.

"'That portion of Wisconsin, organized and subdivided into counties is bounded E. by Lake Michigan; N.W. by Green Bay, Fox, and Wisconsin rivers; W., or rather S.W., by Mississippi River; and S. by the State of Illinois. In latitude it extends from 42° 30′ to 45° 20′, and in longitude from 10° to 14° 5′ W. of Washington. From the S.W. angle, on Mississippi River, to the N.E. point between Green Bay and Lake Michigan, the length is 280 miles. The breadth varies from near 100 to a mere point;

area about 11,500 square miles. The face of the country is rather waving than either hilly or flat, though both extremes exist. It is a territory in a remarkable manner supplied with navigable streams. Fox River, flowing into Green Bay, and Wisconsin, into Mississippi River, approach each other so near as to leave but a short portage between their channels. The higher branches of Rock River rise in Wisconsin, and flow into the State of Illinois.

"It has a coast of about 200 miles on Lake Michigan, over which flow some small streams, but the shallowness of the water of the lake precludes any harbor admitting vessels of more than very moderate draught. The rivers afford much more extensive navigable facilities than does the lake.

"'The town of Madison, on what is called the Four Lakes, is the capital of the Territory. This town is situated at N. latitude 43° 5′, and longitude 12° 12′ W. of Washington, and almost directly S. of the portage between Wisconsin and Fox rivers; distance about 40 miles, and about 140 miles a little N. of N.W. from Chicago.'

"Something of the climate and winters of Wisconsin may be judged by the following statement of the clearing and opening of the harbor, at Milwaukie, for some ten years past. The freezing up of the harbor, during that time, varied from as early as November 15th, to as late as the 1st of December.

"In the spring it has opened, some years as early the first week in March, and at others not till as late as about the middle of April.

"The township organization system prevails throughout most of Wisconsin, very similar to that in the State of New York; most of the counties have adopted the system.

"No argument is needed to show moneyed men that the West is a more advantageous place to loan their funds than the East—that money can be let at higher interest and oftener turned, and always in active demand on safe securities; for this is all very well known, and is so generally remarked, that it has grown into a proverb. It is because there is much land and little money in the West—the country being new, filled up with recent settlers, who are nearly all engaged in making improvements, which, as yet, yield but small revenue; and real estate rising more rapidly, and money scarcer, proportionately, than at the East; the latter being in greater demand, until larger crops are ready for market. So that those having surplus funds, whether to invest in improvements, or to loan, will readily see that it is to their interest to locate in the West, for the highest profitable operations.

"In Central and Western New York real estate increased in value more rapidly—after the opening of the Erie Canal and some of the railroads, bringing the products with speed and cheapness to market—in proportion, than it did at the East. In like manner, and for the same reasons, will property be enhanced in value in the States west of the lakes, above those on the Atlantic; so ample now are the means of communication between the seaboard and the frontier country.

"In conversation, a short time since, with an extensive grain and flour dealer of a Western State, my attention was called more forcibly to the contrast between the time occupied a few years ago and that required at the present day to take a barrel of flour from Wisconsin or Illinois, and return the necessary merchandise. Then, two to four weeks were occupied, each way; now it only takes some six to ten days; and soon, when the whole line of railroads now commenced shall be completed, only two or three days will be consumed in the passage between New York and Chicago, or Milwaukie. And what is better, decided cheapness, too, is attained in this rapid transit. But that is not all, nor even the greatest advantage, resulting to the western settler by this speedy transportation; his chief benefit gained by it, is the increased price secured to him for his products—a price approximating very close to the prices of New York and Philadelphia.

"All who know any thing about it, understand very well that the prices at the West depend altogether upon the eastern market; and the longer the time which transpires between the sale and the date at which the articles reach that market, the wider must be the margin and fluctuations in the prices, and greater must be the hazards and contingencies, all of which the purchasers are bound to take into the account when buying the western commodities; as prices at the time of his buying are liable to fall at the East, before those products reach their destination. But when the transit is quicker—reduced to two or three days—these chances of decline in prices, and all the risks, are much diminished, and the insurance is less, so that the produce speculator can very safely venture to pay prices much nearer the full eastern value.

"Under these circumstances, western lands must be greatly enhanced in actual value; increased in a ratio decidedly greater than the eastern lands, when taking into the account the respective prices at which both are now held, the former realizing nearly as high profits as the latter, while the cost of producing is vastly in favor of the western farmer—which proves the wisdom of investing in and improving western real estate, while it may be obtained for low prices; as the astonishing progress making in transit facilities is constantly hastening the time of an equilibrium in land value East and West. And when we consider the wonderful productiveness and easy tillage of western soils, even at the same cost per acre, the profit of the capital invested is nearly or quite as great in the one location as the other.

"The river floods, an event of great sublimity, and characteristic of the West, occurring annually, are forcibly described in Mr. Thomson's Letters. Memorable and destructive floods occurred on the Mississippi and Illinois rivers, in 1832 and 1846:

"'Observing some warehouses surrounded with water, from which boats were taking in their freight, we concluded that the owners had hit upon this expedient for the convenience of those engaged in transportation; but we were presently informed that in ordinary stages of the water these warehouses stood high and dry upon the levee, and that what seemed to be the bed of a wide, flowing river, was usually a bottom—the name given to a low tract of land, meadow or timbered, on the margin of a river, and intervening between its channel and the bluffs or high grounds denoting its ancient bed. Some of these warehouses were surrounded with water, to the depth of ten or twelve feet. Indeed I was assured that at one time the water rose fourteen feet in twenty-four hours, and some 3000 sacks of grain, stored in a new warehouse, built quite above the old high-water mark, were destroyed in a single night.

"'As we proceeded down the river we saw on every hand the desolations of the flood. In nearly every river-town the street fronting the river was overflowed, and stores and dwellings were submerged to the depth of ten or twenty feet. In some places large and cultivated farms were entirely under water; the stock, crops, fences, every thing destroyed. The loss falls most severely on the poor woodmen, who occupy log-cabins on the river bottoms, and earn their living by supplying the boats with wood; the whole winter's work of many has been swept away in an hour, while they and their families have been obliged to leave their huts and flee for refuge to the bluffs, at a distance often of several miles. At some points the river is expanded from an average width of half a mile to the breadth of eight to ten miles from bluff to bluff. We saw several cabins and houses, of which the roofs only were above the water. But I have since seen so much greater desolations on the Mississippi, that these seem almost of no account.

"'A western steamboat is at first sight a novelty to one familiar only with eastern models. The boats on the western waters are very slightly built, mere shells of pine, shallow, long, narrow, flat bottomed, open and flaring on all sides, just as represented in Banvard's panorama. There is no cabin either below the deck or upon it.

"'Most of the boats have good cabins and well furnished saloons, both for ladies and gentlemen, beside state-rooms,

"'The engines are placed immediately on the lower deck, two huge furnaces flaming upon you as you enter the boat, and giving you rather uncomfortable hints of a choice between fire and water in making your exit from the world.

"'Huge flaming brands and coals are dropping continually upon the thinnest possible sheathing of sheet-iron, in many places worn through to the plank; heated pipes, on which you can not bear your hand, are in immediate contact with boards as dry as tinder, and perhaps already charred; goods, you know not how inflammable, are strewn promiscuously round the boilers, while huge piles of dry pine-wood, waiting to be consumed, are crowded in the vicinity of the fires. But not every traveler has the habit that I confess to, of prying into every thing about him, and therefore few probably enjoy the peculiar sensation of sailing on the rim of a volcano. However, there is nothing like getting used to it, and I learned to sleep quite soundly.

"'The cabin is up-stairs, and extends nearly the whole length of the deck, over which it is perched upon sundry posts, that seem too frail for a summer's breeze; this is divided into a long, narrow saloon, from stem to stern, and a row of state-rooms on either hand. An apartment for ladies is curtained off at one extremity, while the main saloon is used for meals, conversation, promenading, card-playing, and whatsoever one may list. The kitchen, pantry, bar, &c., are all contiguous to the saloon; with every convenience for life above stairs, so that passengers may spend days in and around this saloon, without knowing any thing of the deck life below. Some of the state-rooms, that open both into the saloon and upon the guard, are very airy and pleasant. If, however, there is any deficiency in regard to neatness and comfort, it is in this department of the boat. We took passage in the 'Prairie State,' one of the best boats on the river. The furniture was neat, and the table excellent, always excepting the preponderance of grease in western cookery. But the ideas of civilization exhibited in the state-rooms reminded me of Dr. Bushnell's discourse on Barbarism as the first danger of the West, a sermon that contained some of the truest of his paradoxes. In a cozy chat with the captain, I found him a clever, polite, and attentive gentleman.

"'The scenery of the Illinois River is rather low and monotonous, but sufficiently picturesque to arrest the eye of a stranger. It savored of the romantic to sail at times through the woods, the water spreading indefinitely among the trees, and in the middle of the stream to bring up at the second story of a house, that seemed to say, 'For freight or passage apply within.'

"Peoria is the most beautiful town on the river. Situated on rising ground, a broad plateau extending back from the bluff, it has escaped the almost universal inundation. Indeed, the river here expands into a broad, deep lake, that embosoms the rising flood. This lake is a most beautiful feature in the natural scenery of the town, and is as useful as it is beautiful, supplying the inhabitants with ample stores of fish, and in winter with an abundance of the purest ice. It is often frozen to such a thickness, that heavy teams and droves of cattle can pass securely over it. A substantial draw-bridge connects the town with the opposite shore. The town is neatly laid out in rectangular blocks, the streets being wide and well graded. A public square has been reserved near the present centre. The place wears quite a New England aspect; its schools and churches are prosperous, and its society is good. Back of the town extends one of the finest rolling prairies in the State; this region already furnishes to Peoria its supplies and much of its business, which is destined to increase as plank roads and like improvements shall bring the producer nearer to the market. I am struck with the sagacity shown in selecting the sites of many of these western towns, of which La Salle and Peoria are examples. May the children of light be equally sagacious in choosing their points of action and influence for Christ!

" 'Traveling on these western waters, throws one into all sorts of society, and affords a fine opportunity for the study of human nature. I found a number of emigrants, Irish and German, on the deck, occupying sundry extempore bunks, and living on their own bread and cheese.

" 'These emigrants have a hard life of it. Poor fare and exposure to the elements, on the open deck of the boat, often engender disease among them, and break up families before they reach their destined home. There should be an active missionary agency on all the rivers of the West. The deck-hands need such an influence, for they have no Sabbath, and are fearfully addicted to profaneness and intemperance. Their manner of life begets a recklessness of death and of all solemn and sacred things. A man overboard, no unusual event on boats nowhere guarded by a rail, or a death by cholera, now becoming frequent, make these men callous rather than thoughtful, and render life and death alike cheap in their estimate.

" 'The freedom of the western character and the independence of the western mind, united with the native love of argumentation in the Anglo-American race, render it easy to engage men in discussion, to while away the listless hours of steamboat traveling.' "

THE END.

Travels and Adventures in Mexico:

In the Course of Journeys of upward of 2500 Miles, performed on Foot. Giving an Account of the Manners and Customs of the People, and the Agricultural and Mineral Resources of that Country. By WILLIAM W. CARPENTER, late of U. S. Army. 12mo, Paper, 60 cents; Muslin, 75 cents.

A Dictionary of Practical Medicine;

Comprising General Pathology, the Nature and Treatment of Diseases, Morbid Structures, &c. By JAMES COPLAND, M.D., F.R.S. Edited, with Additions, by CHARLES A. LEE, M.D. Part XXII. now ready, price 50 cents. In 3 large 8vo vols., Muslin, $5 00 per Vol. Vols. I. and II. now ready.

A Manual of Roman Antiquities.

From the most recent German Works. With a Description of the City of Rome, &c. By CHARLES ANTHON, LL.D. 12mo, Muslin, 87½ cents.

A Manual of Greek Antiquities.

From the best and most recent Sources. By CHARLES ANTHON, LL.D. 12mo, Muslin. (*Nearly ready.*)

Forest Life and Forest Trees:

Comprising Winter Camp-life among the Loggers and Wild-wood Adventure. With Descriptions of Lumbering Operations on the various Rivers of Maine and New Brunswick. By JOHN S. SPRINGER. With numerous Illustrations. 12mo, Paper, 60 cents; Muslin, 75 cents.

Elements of Algebra,

Designed for Beginners. By ELIAS LOOMIS, M.A. 12mo, Sheep, 62½ cents.

Analytical Geometry and Calculus.

By ELIAS LOOMIS, M.A. 8vo, Sheep, $1 50.

Nile Notes of a Howadji.

With Engravings. 12mo, Paper, 75 cents; Muslin, 87½ cents.

The Fifteen Decisive Battles of the World,

From Marathon to Waterloo. By E. S CREASY, M.A. 12mo, Muslin, $1 00

A Latin-English Lexicon,

Founded on the larger Latin-German Lexicon of Dr. WILLIAM FREUND. With Additions and Corrections from the Lexicons of Gesner, Facciolati, Scheller, Georges, &c. By E. A. ANDREWS, LL.D. Royal 8vo, Sheep extra, $5 00.

Lamartine's History of the Restoration

Of Monarchy in France. Being a Sequel to the "History of the Girondists." By ALPHONSE DE LAMARTINE. Vol. I., 12mo, Muslin, 75 cents.

Robinson's New Testament Lexicon.

A Greek and English Lexicon of the New Testament. A new Edition, Revised, and in great part Rewritten. By EDWARD ROBINSON, D.D., LL.D. Royal 8vo, Muslin, $4 50; Sheep, $4 75; half Calf, $5 00.

Buttmann's Greek Grammar,

For the Use of High Schools and Universities. By PHILIP BUTTMANN. Revised and Enlarged by his Son, ALEX. BUTTMANN. Translated from the 18th German Edition, by EDWARD ROBINSON, D.D., LL.D. 8vo, Sheep, $2 00.

The Nile-Boat;

Or, Glimpses of the Land of Egypt. By W. H. BARTLETT. With Engravings on Steel and Illustrations on Wood. 8vo, Muslin, $2 00.

Comte's Philosophy of Mathematics,

Translated from the Cours de Philosophie Positive of AUGUSTE COMTE, by W. M. GILLESPIE, A.M. 8vo, Muslin, $1 25.

History of the United States.

By RICHARD HILDRETH.——*First Series.*—From the First Settlement of the Country to the Adoption of the Federal Constitution. 3 vols. 8vo, Muslin, $6 00; Sheep, $6 75; half Calf, $7 50.——*Second Series.*—From the Adoption of the Federal Constitution to the End of the Sixteenth Congress. 3 vols. 8vo, Muslin, $6 00; Sheep, $6 75; half Calf, $7 50.

Louisiana:

Its Colonial History and Romance By CHARLES GAYARRE. 8vo, Muslin, $2 00.

The Lily and the Bee:

An Apologue of the Crystal Palace. By SAMUEL WARREN, M.D., F.R.S. 16mo, Paper, 30 cents; Muslin, 37½ cents.

The Queens of Scotland,

And English Princesses connected with the Regal Succession of Great Britain. By AGNES STRICKLAND. 6 vols. 12mo, Muslin, $1 00 per Volume. Vols. I. and II. ready.

A New Classical Dictionary

Of Greek and Roman Biography, Mythology, and Geography. For Colleges and Schools. By WM. SMITH, LL.D. Edited, with large Additions, by CHARLES ANTHON, LL.D. Royal 8vo, Sheep extra, $2 50.

The English Language

In its Elements and Forms. With a History of its Origin and Development, and a full Grammar. By WILLIAM C. FOWLER. Designed for Use in Colleges and Schools. 8vo, Muslin, $1 50; Sheep, $1 75.

Harper's N. Y. & Erie R. R. Guide:

Containing a Description of the Scenery, Rivers, Towns, Villages, and most important Works on the Road. Embellished with 136 Engravings on Wood, by Lossing & Barritt, from Original Sketches made expressly for this Work, by WM. M'LEOD. 12mo, Paper, 50 cents; Muslin, 62½ cents.

The English in America.

Rule and Misrule of the English in America. By the Author of "Sam Slick the Clockmaker," "The Letter Bag," "Attaché," "Old Judge," &c. 12mo, Muslin, 75 cents.

The Literature and Literary Men

Of Great Britain and Ireland. By ABRAHAM MILLS, A.M. 2 vols. 8vo, Muslin, $3 50; half Calf, $4 00.

A Greek-English Lexicon,

Based on the German Work of Passow. By HENRY G. LIDDELL, M.A., and RICHARD SCOTT, M.A. With Corrections and Additions, and the Insertion in Alphabetical Order of the Proper Names occurring in the principal Greek Authors, by HENRY DRISLER, M.A. Royal 8vo, Sheep, $5 00.

The Recent Progress of Astronomy,

Especially in the United States. By ELIAS LOOMIS, M.A. New Edition. 12mo, Muslin, $1 00.

Cosmos:

A Sketch of a Physical Description of the Universe. By ALEXANDER VON HUMBOLDT. Translated from the German, by E. C. OTTE. Complete in 3 vols. 12mo, Muslin, $2 55.

Bickersteth's Memoirs.

A Memoir of the late Rev. EDWARD BICKERSTETH, Rector of Watton. By Rev. T. R. BIRKS, M.A. With a Preface, &c., by Rev. STEPHEN H. TYNG, D.D., of New York. 2 vols. 12mo, Muslin, $1 75.

Foster's Christian Purity.

The Nature and Blessedness of Christian Purity. By Rev. R. S. FOSTER. With an Introduction by Bishop JANES. 12mo, Muslin, 75 cents.

Elements of Natural Philosophy.

Designed as a Text-book for Academies, High-Schools, and Colleges. By ALONZO GRAY, A.M. Illustrated by 360 Woodcuts. 12mo, Muslin, 70 cents; Sheep, 75 cents.

Lord Holland's Foreign Reminiscences.

Edited by his Son, HENRY EDWARD LORD HOLLAND. 12mo, Paper, 60 cents; Muslin, 75 cents.

Curran and his Contemporaries.

By CHARLES PHILLIPS, A.B. 12mo, Paper, 75 cents; Muslin, 87½ cents.

The Irish Confederates,

And the Rebellion of 1798. By HENRY M. FIELD. Portraits and a Map. 12mo, Paper, 75 cents; Muslin, 90 cents.

The Harmony of Prophecy;

Or, Scriptural Illustrations of the Apocalypse. By Rev. ALEXANDER KEITH, D.D. 12mo, Muslin, $1 00.

The Bards of the Bible.

By GEORGE GILFILLAN. 12mo, Muslin, 35 cents.

Abbott's Illustrated Histories:

The following Works of the Series are now ready: Josephine, Cleopatra, Madame Roland, Xerxes the Great, Cyrus the Great, Darius the Great, Charles I., Charles II., Hannibal, Julius Cæsar, Alfred the Great, Maria Antoinette, Queen Elizabeth, Alexander the Great, William the Conqueror, Mary Queen of Scots. 16mo, Muslin, with Illuminated Title-pages and numerous Engravings, 60 cents per Volume.

Abbott's Franconia Stories:

Comprising Malleville, Beechnut, Mary Bell, Wallace, Mary Erskine. 16mo, beautifully bound in Muslin, Engraved Title-pages and numerous Illustrations, 50 cents per Volume.

Kings and Queens;

Or, Life in the Palace: consisting of Historical Sketches of Josephine and Maria Louisa, Louis Philippe, Ferdinand of Austria, Nicholas, Isabella II., Leopold, and Victoria. By J. S. C. Abbott. With numerous Illustrations. 12mo, Muslin, $1 00; Muslin, gilt edges, $1 25.

A Summer in Scotland.

By Jacob Abbott. With Engravings. 12mo, Muslin, $1 00

Five Years of a Hunter's Life

In the Far Interior of South Africa. With Notices of the Native Tribes, and Anecdotes of the Chase of the Lion, Elephant, Hippopotamus, Giraffe, Rhinoceros, &c. By R. Gordon Cumming. With Engravings. 2 vols. 12mo, Muslin, $1 75.

Sydney Smith's Moral Philosophy.

An Elementary Treatise on Moral Philosophy, delivered at the Royal Institution in the Years 1804, 1805, and 1806. By the late Rev. Sydney Smith. 12mo, Muslin, $1 00.

Travels in the United States, etc.

During 1849 and 1850. By Lady Emmeline Stuart Wortley. 12mo, Paper, 60 cents; Muslin, 75 cents.

Dealings with the Inquisition;

Or, Papal Rome, her Priests, and her Jesuits. With Important Disclosures. By the Rev. Giacinto Achilli, D.D., late Prior and Visitor of the Dominican Order, &c. 12mo, Muslin, 75 cts.

Leigh Hunt's Autobiography,

With Reminiscences of his Friends and Contemporaries. In 2 vols. 12mo, Muslin, $1 50.

Campbell's Life and Letters.

Life and Letters of Thomas Campbell. Edited by WILLIAM BEATTIE, M.D. With an Introductory Letter, by WASHINGTON IRVING. 2 vols. 12mo, Muslin, $2 00.

Doctor Johnson:

His Religious Life and Death. 12mo, Muslin, $1 00.

Southey's Life and Correspondence.

Edited by his Son, Rev. C. C. SOUTHEY, M.A. Portrait. 8vo, Muslin, $1 75.

Southey's Common-place Book.

Edited by his Son-in-Law, JOHN WOOD WARTER, B.D. 3 vols. 8vo, Paper, $1 00 per Vol.; Muslin, $1 25 per Vol.

History of Greece,

From the Earliest Times to the Destruction of Corinth, B.C. 146; mainly based upon that of Bishop THIRLWALL. By Dr. L. SCHMITZ, F.R.S.E. 12mo, Muslin, $1 00.

History of Rome,

From the Earliest Times to the Death of Commodus, A.D. 192. By Dr. L. SCHMITZ, F.R.S.E. With Questions, by J. ROBSON, B.A. 18mo, Muslin, 75 cents.

A Treatise on Popular Education:

For the Use of Parents and Teachers, and for Young People of both Sexes. Printed and Published in accordance with a Resolution of the Senate and House of Representatives of the State of Michigan. By IRA MAYHEW, late Superintendent of Public Instruction. 12mo, Muslin, $1 00.

The Conquest of Canada.

By the Author of "Hochelaga." 2 vols. 12mo, Muslin, $1 70.

Health, Disease, and Remedy,

Familiarly and practically considered in a few of their Relations to the Blood. By G. MOORE, M.D. 18mo, Muslin, 60 cents.

www.ingramcontent.com/pod-product-compliance
Lightning Source LLC
LaVergne TN
LVHW020217110826
845151LV00003B/747